Cognitive Styles and Learning Strategies

Understanding Style Differences
in Learning and Behaviour

Richard Riding and Stephen Rayner

David Fulton Publishers
London

David Fulton Publishers Ltd
Ormond House, 26–27 Boswell Street, London WC1N 3JZ
www.fultonpublishers.co.uk

First published in Great Britain by David Fulton Publishers 1998
Reprinted 1999, 2000,2001

Note: The right of Richard J. Riding and Stephen G. Rayner to be identified as the authors of this work has been asserted by them in accordance with the Copyright, Designs and Patents Act 1988.

British Library Cataloguing in Publication Data
A catalogue record for this book is available from the British Library

ISBN 1–85346–480–5

Typeset by Sheila Knight, London
Printed in Great Britain by The Cromwell Press Ltd, Trowbridge, Wilts.

Contents

Preface

This book deals with what may well turn out to be the missing element in the study of individual differences – cognitive style. Its intention is to distinguish between, and integrate, the research attempts, particularly over the past half-century, to make sense of style differences.

In several respects this book is unique in that it contains material that is not covered in any other, and draws together the various aspects of psychology relevant to the study of individual differences. It is in this sense both a textbook and a source of reference for many professionals working in a range of contexts.

The content of the book has relevance for a wide audience. It contains a message for teachers and trainers that could improve their effectiveness. It provides insights into personal and professional behaviour for counsellors and personnel professionals. It also gives a framework for future research for psychologists.

While emphasis is on the Cognitive Styles Analysis approach, it initially considers style by being as encompassing as possible in its review of the research into style and strategy. The aim has been to examine research from a range of theoretical traditions which have considered style in different ways, and often for different reasons. The intention has been to sort through the evidence in order to lay a firm foundation on which to build a model for further research and application.

The authors wish to acknowledge the generous help of colleagues from a number of organisations and of research students who have collaborated in work in this area. They wish to thank Clive Leslie, Andy Marjerison and Eugene Sadler-Smith for helpful comments on an earlier draft of this book. They also acknowledge the help and support of John Owens of David Fulton Publishers.

Richard Riding and Stephen Rayner
Birmingham, January 1998

CHAPTER 1

Introduction

Chapter overview

The purpose of this chapter is to provide an introduction to the key concepts of the book and to give an overview of its argument and conclusions.

Individual differences

People differ in many respects. We are probably more aware of physical differences in appearance than we are of different styles of thinking and representing information. Yet such differences in style greatly affect the way people are and the manner in which they behave.

The notion of style

The concept of style is an idea used frequently in everyday language. The concept has been used more technically in the psychological study of individual differences in learning and behaviour. In this respect it is used as a 'construct'. A construct is a psychological idea or notion. Examples of constructs are intelligence, extraversion and neuroticism.

The thesis of the book

This book will review work on cognitive style and learning strategy and concludes that there are two fundamental dimensions of cognitive style – the wholist-analytic and the verbal-imagery. It is argued that currently the most efficient way of assessing an individual's style is by means of a computer-presented assessment – the Cognitive Styles Analysis. The validity of this approach comes from evidence of a physiological basis for style, the independence of style from other constructs such as intelligence, personality and gender, and the relationship of style to a range of behaviours. These behaviours include learning performance, social responses and occupational stress.

Individual differences

Since at the heart of this book is an interest in the differences between people in the ways in which they think, feel, learn and behave, this chapter will begin by considering variation between individuals.

Recognising differences

It is very noticeable that people differ from one another. The physical differences are the most obvious, such as height, facial characteristics and tone of voice. However, there are other differences that are apparent, particularly in other people. For example

- some are organised, while others are untidy
- some are balanced in their views, while others tend to extremes
- some are cautious, while others are impulsive
- some are very fluent, while others are hesitant of speech
- some 'see' what they read in mental pictures, while others do not
- some are quiet, while others are noisy
- some are social, while others are reserved
- some are placid, while others are reactive
- some are tense, while others are relaxed
- some are intelligent, while others seem less able.

Readers may wish to rate themselves on these characteristics as a way of focusing attention on individual attributes.

It is a matter of both personal and practical interest to understand why people differ; personal since it helps them to understand themselves better, and practical because with such understanding individuals can be helped to their full potential and more appropriately guided into particular occupations.

Among possible contributors to individual difference are intelligence and personality. It is the argument of this book that a further significant contributor is what we shall term 'cognitive style'.

Figure 1.1 (adapted from Riding and Rayner 1995) gives brief descriptions of four fictitious people. Readers are invited to consider which of the four is most like themselves or perhaps a friend or colleague.

In terms of the approach of this book cognitive style labels can be applied to the people described above, as shown in Figure 1.2.

Figure 1.1 Descriptions of four individuals

John   Socially he is friendly although restrained and moderately formal. He is organised and can get on with things himself rather than needing help from others. He is consistent, but the negative side of this will be an inclination to rigidity and stubbornness.

He is structured in his approach to learning, and likes to lay ideas out in a structured form, with clear headings and paragraphs. He has a good verbal memory, and is able to retain facts readily, particularly when presented in verbal form. His preferred primary mode of expression is words rather than illustrations although he may like to set information out in tables.

In relationships with strangers he is moderately formal, and prefers to keep some distance between himself and them. In his work situation he tends to be structured, with him in control.

Christine   Socially she is restrained and formal. At times she is socially unaware, and often shows a rather stern exterior, which does not reflect how she really feels. She is organised and self-reliant, and tends to get on with things herself rather than seeking help.

Her approach to learning is structured. She learns best from diagrams and pictures rather than text. She is concise in writing and speech. In speaking, sometimes she can be hesitant, since words do not always come naturally, and she is not always fluent. Her preferred mode of expression is typically in terms of illustrations and diagrams rather than words.

Her relationship with strangers is formal, and she prefers to keep them at a distance. In work she is structured, and prefers to be in control of situations. However, her manner is typically interactive and she likes feedback from colleagues. She prefers to work as one of a pair rather than in larger groups.

Graham   Socially he is informal, extraverted, and lively. He prefers to be with people and enjoys group activity. He is warm and open, and is easy to get on with. He has a lot of go, although he can be changeable and may be unreliable. He can be too dependent on others for help.

He has a good verbal memory and is able to retain facts readily, particularly when presented in verbal form. He does not find diagrams and illustrations particularly helpful. Also he is less good spatially and does not have a strong sense of geographical direction. He is articulate and rarely lost for words, although this is sometimes a little overwhelming. His preferred mode of expression tends to be words rather than illustrations.

In relationships with strangers he is informal. At work he does not tend to be highly structured, and he is happy to be directed in his activities. His manner tends to be outgoing and active.

Debbie   Socially she is fairly informal and appears moderately relaxed. She is fairly easy to get on with in her relationships. She is usually diplomatic, socially aware and polite. She tends to be reasonably outgoing. She is social, spontaneous, and warm in relationships although she is restrained and polite.

She benefits from having learning material structured for her. She learns best from diagrams and pictures, rather than text. In speaking, she can sometimes be hesitant since words do not always come naturally and she is not always fluent. Her preferred mode of expression is when possible in terms of illustrations rather than words.

In relationships with strangers she is moderately formal. Her work style does not tend to be highly structured, and she is generally happy for others to organise her work.

Figure 1.2 Cognitive style labels

John is an **ANALYTIC-VERBALISER**	Christine is an **ANALYTIC-IMAGER**
Graham is a **WHOLIST-VERBALISER**	Debbie is a **WHOLIST-IMAGER**

Although it is not intended that these labels should be meaningful at this stage, if readers did identify themselves or a friend in one particular person then they may like to remember the style description as they read through the book.

Assessing differences

Although differences in behaviour between people are obvious when considered, easy and efficient ways of assessing them are more elusive. If we take John as an example, suppose you are an employer and that John has applied to you for a job. How would you assess what he is like? You would probably ask him to say what he thinks he is like, as in an interview situation, or by filling in a questionnaire. However, this approach is difficult because even if John were honest, and there is the problem that he may say what he thinks you want to hear, rather than what he believes to be the case, he may not actually know what he is like.

At first sight this would appear strange, since in some respects no one knows John better than John. However, people are often not good at seeing themselves as others see them. Further, what they say they think they would do in a particular situation is not necessarily what they would actually do. For instance, the test of whether individuals are racially biased is not what they say about themselves, but how they actually behave in a situation that involves someone of another racial group.

In assessing differences, the *direct method* of observing actual behaviour is preferable to introspective self-report. While this may not be practicable in the case of someone applying for employment, in psychological research it is very important for objective assessment to take place.

Having had a snapshot of the differences, the obvious next step is to enquire into the ways in which style operates. A real challenge for psychology is to identify the dimensions which underlie these behaviours, and to determine their bases.

The notion of style

Several researchers, and the title of this book, have used the word 'style' in describing differences between people. 'Style' is used as a term both in popular usage and in a more restricted technical sense.

A matter of style

The concept

The concept 'style' is used in a variety of contexts: in high street fashion, the sports arena, the arts, the media, and in many academic disciplines including psychology. It has a wide appeal which reflects an enduring versatility, but this same appeal can lead to overuse which unsurprisingly creates a difficulty for definition and understanding. Yet, the notion of style remains an important and popular expression of individuality. It is used, time and again, to describe a set of individual qualities, activities or behaviour sustained over a period of time.

Style awareness

The term style may be used, for example, to describe the grace of a gymnast, or the game of a football team, the manner and cut of a new fashion on the modelling catwalk, the shape and form of a building, the approach used by a commercial company to organise itself, or the way a person may think, learn, teach or even talk! Tannen (1995) observed, for example, that conversational style can be identified as a key feature in human relations. She suggested that conversational style 'makes or breaks your relations with others', since frustration or mis-understanding can be created by a clash of style. She argued that

> Clashing conversational styles can wreak havoc at the conference table as well as at the breakfast table, with consequences as frustrating and even more dangerous, since people's welfare and even lives can be at stake. Everyone's frustration will be reduced, and companies as well as individuals will benefit, if we all begin to understand and accept each other's styles.
>
> (Tannen 1995: 17)

The significance of an awareness of style is its potential for enhancing and improving human performance in a variety of contexts. The fascinating and enduring appeal of style lies in its use as a 'conceptual framework' for individuality. It may be quite possible that the continuing interest in the idea of style in so many different contexts reflects a basic human need to create a sense of identity, which is after all, the essence of individuality. In other words, we all perhaps need to know we matter, that we make a difference in our own life, and making this difference is quite simply, a matter of style!

The 'style' construct and the individual

The style construct

The term 'construct' refers to a psychological idea or notion. Examples of constructs are intelligence, extraversion and neuroticism.

A 'style construct' appears in a number of academic disciplines – in psychology it has been developed in a number of different areas such as: personality, cognition, communication, motivation, perception, learning and behaviour. Its emergence in psychology as a theory entails separate and related developments, reflecting both philosophical and psychological concerns for individuality. Unfortunately, the widespread use of the term 'style' has led to workers in the field often adopting different definitions and terminology. Consequently, those workers interested in reaching agreement, in terms of definition or use of an accepted nomenclature for a theory of style, have faced considerable difficulty.

Style in educational psychology has nevertheless been recognised as a key construct in the area of individual differences in the learning context. Riding (1997), for example, suggested that cognitive style reflected the fundamental make-up of a person. He argued that style has a physical basis and can and does control the way in which individuals respond to the events and ideas they experience. Importantly, he identified the 'temporal stability' of style, suggesting that it is a constant aspect of a person's psychology which does not appear to change. It is therefore impossible, according to Riding, for a person to 'switch off' their style.

Style and the individual

Cognitive style as a subject includes several aspects of 'differential psychology' associated with individual differences in the learner and the learning environment (Jonassen and Grabowski 1993). The key elements in this construct are formed from the basic aspects of an individual's psychology; namely, *affect* or feeling, *behaviour* or doing and *cognition* or knowing. These 'primary elements' in an individual's personal psychology are structured and organised by an individual's cognitive style. This psychological process, in turn, is reflected in the way that the person builds a generalised approach to learning.

It is this dynamic which involves the individual in a life-long process – the building up of a repertoire of learning strategies which combine with cognitive style – to contribute to an individual's *personal learning style*. As part of this process, these 'primary elements' of personal psychology interact with cognitive style to influence the formation of attitudes, skills, understanding and a general level of competence realised in the learning process.

Cognitive style and learning strategy

Personal style describes the way in which a person habitually approaches or responds to the learning task. It comprises two fundamental aspects: first, *cognitive style,* which reflects the way in which the individual person thinks; second, *learning strategy,* which reflects those processes which are used by the learner to respond to the demands of a learning activity.

A person's cognitive style is probably an in-built and automatic way of responding to information and situations. It is probably present at birth or at any rate is fixed early on in life and is thought to be deeply pervasive, affecting a wide range of individual functioning. A person's cognitive style is a relatively fixed aspect of learning performance and influences a person's general attainment or achievement in learning situations.

Style and education – a practical example

The implications of cognitive style for the educator and trainer are far-reaching, but to date conspicuously underdeveloped in working practice. Hamblin (1981) commented that constructive teaching of 'study skills', with the aim of raising the level of achievement, should not be regarded as a search for a single correct 'way to do it'. Nor should 'study skills' or 'learning how to learn' be left to random chance, individual adaptiveness, or a haphazard management of pedagogy. Hamblin advised that teachers' work is about

> encouraging pupils to engage in a long-term process of building a style of learning which is meaningful and productive. Pastoral care embodies the ethic of a profound respect for individuality. To try to impose a learning style is the pedagogic equivalent of imposing a false self upon someone – an act which is inevitably as destructive in the long run.
>
> (Hamblin 1981: 21)

The importance of understanding cognitive style should be self-evident. Yet, it is equally evident that generally, its inclusion in approaches to pedagogy is patchy and inconsistent. There is an obvious need for more research and development in the field of individual differences, styles of learning and pedagogy. The aim of such activity should be to gain a better and more fully developed understanding of individual differences in learning, teaching and training. Such an understanding will, it is hoped, lead to a consistent and appropriate inclusion of cognitive and learning styles in pedagogical practice.

The thesis of the book

This section will lay out an overview of the basic thesis of the book, to provide a structure for the reader. At this stage evidence for the statements will not be provided since this will be given at some length in the chapters that follow.

Individual differences

Individual variation poses a considerable problem for psychology. On the one hand, it is helpful to have general rules about behaviours, such as how people learn, that apply to the whole population. On the other, if there are individual variations then such rules do not really apply. Thus if individual differences are such that each individual is unique and learns in a different way, then the task of describing such variation is so infinite as to be practically useless.

Alternatively, if some intermediate position exists whereby variation can be usefully explained in terms of the combination of a relatively small number of dimensions, then the task of identifying these, and of using them to predict behaviour, is possible and potentially useful. It is the belief of the authors that this is the situation.

The challenge then becomes one of identifying the dimensions of variation. In explaining individual differences, it is argued that in addition to the constructs of intelligence and personality, there is also cognitive style as a distinct construct, and that style is different in nature and in the way it affects behaviours.

The nature and source of the construct of cognitive style

Cognitive style is seen as an individual's preferred and habitual approach to organising and representing information.

Between the early 1940s and the 1980s, various investigators observed what they felt represented style dimensions. Generally the researchers worked in their own contexts, in isolation from one another, developed their own instruments for assessment and gave their own labels to the styles they were studying with little reference to the work of others. Not surprisingly, this led to the development of a large and confusing variety of style labels. A number of workers have suggested that many of these are simply different conceptions of the same dimensions (e.g. Coan 1974; Fowler 1980; Brumby 1982; Miller 1987; Riding and Buckle 1990).

Riding and Cheema (1991) found over 30 labels and, after reviewing the descriptions, correlations between them, methods of assessment, and effect on behaviour, concluded that they could be grouped into two principal cognitive style dimensions; the wholist-analytic and the verbal-imagery style dimensions. A further review by Rayner and Riding (1997) supported this conclusion.

Figure 1.3 The cognitive style dimensions

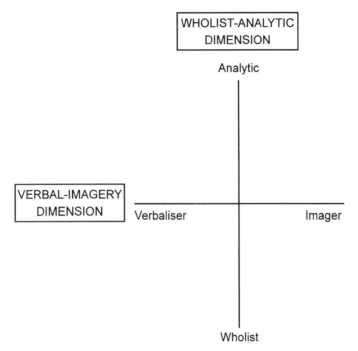

The two basic dimensions of cognitive style are shown in Figure 1.3:

- The wholist-analytic style dimension of whether an individual tends to *organise* information into wholes or parts.
- The verbal-imagery style dimension of whether an individual is inclined to *represent* information during thinking verbally or in mental pictures.

The nature of cognitive style is considered in detail in Chapter 2.

The assessment of cognitive style

The valid and efficient assessment of a construct is obviously required before its usefulness can be established; valid in that it needs actually to measure what it claims to measure, and efficient, in that it can be assessed in a reasonably short time by a simple practical method.

The approach to style assessment developed in this book avoids using introspective self-report measures of style because they have inherent weaknesses.

These include individuals' possible inability to accurately and objectively report their behaviour, unwillingness to make the necessary effort to respond accurately, bias due to the pressure of social desirability in making responses, and inclination to contrive their responses.

The approach used by Riding (1991a) was to assess performance on simple tasks that might then be representative of processing generally, with the intention of measuring an individual's position on both the wholist-analytic and the verbal-imagery dimensions. A simple computer-presented method of assessing an individual's position on these two dimensions, the Cognitive Styles Analysis (Riding 1991a) was developed.

A significant point here is that both dimensions are assessed by simple cognitive processing tasks which are likely to reflect the underlying cognitive processing natural to the individual, and which reflect the way in which the individual habitually organises information and represents it during thinking.

Evidence of a physiological basis for style

A very real problem for psychology is the demonstration that a construct has a reality. For instance, the idea that there is an unconscious has rightly been questioned because its existence cannot be proven since it cannot be directly examined. A significant form of evidence is measurable brain activity which may be related to a notion. One approach to measuring brain activity is by recording the electrical activity at the scalp in different positions on the head – an electro-encephalogram (EEG). A study of EEG activity and performance on verbal tracking tasks has been found to be related to both the style dimensions (see Chapter 5), so cognitive style has been found to be related to physiological measures.

Style as independent of other constructs

Reference has already been made to a problem regarding style research; that of various investigators using different labels for what turned out to be the same style. This problem can also arise between notions that appear to be different. For the construct of cognitive style to be useful, the style dimensions must be shown to be separate from intelligence, different from personality, and unrelated to gender.

Intelligence
Cognitive style affects learning performance, but then so does intelligence. Are they facets of the same variable? When performance on measures of intelligence

is compared with style, the correlation between tests of intelligence and style are very low, in fact approaching zero.

The distinction between style and ability is important. What are the characteristics of style that distinguish it from ability? Both style and ability will affect performance on a given task. The basic distinction between them is that performance on all tasks will improve as ability increases, whereas the effect of style on performance for an individual will be either positive or negative, depending on the nature of the task. It follows from this that, for an individual at one end of a style dimension, a task of a type they find difficult will be found easier by someone at the other end of the dimension, and vice versa. For instance, if the dimension were the verbal-imagery style, then verbalisers would find pictorial tasks more difficult than would imagers, but they would find highly verbal tasks easier than would imagers. In other words, in terms of style, a person is *both* good *and* poor at tasks depending on the nature of the task, while for intelligence, they are *either* good *or* poor.

Personality

While the cognitive style dimensions affect behaviours which are similar to those generally included within personality, each has a very low correlation with tests of the basic personality dimensions, such as introversion-extraversion and stability-neuroticism (see Chapter 5). Given the distinctly different tasks used to assess the wholist-analytic and the verbal-imagery dimensions, and the lack of correlation between them, cognitive style seems to be at least as fundamental as personality, while it appears to be different in its source and action.

Gender

Numerous differences in behaviour and performance have been found between males and females. However, studies have generally shown no style differences related to gender, and this is dealt within Chapter 5.

The conclusion is that cognitive style is distinctly separate from intelligence, personality and gender.

Cognitive style as distinct from learning strategies

It is useful to distinguish between *style* and *strategy*. Style probably has a physiological basis and is fairly fixed for the individual. By contrast, strategies are ways that may be learned and developed to cope with situations and tasks, and particularly methods of utilising styles to make the best of situations for which the styles are not ideally suited. Within the literature, the term 'learning style' is sometimes used to refer to what here is considered to be learning strategies. A useful distinction has been made by Curry (1983). Style is considered in Chapter 2 and strategies in Chapters 3 and 4.

Style should be related to observed behaviours

A very important aspect of the validity of style is that it should be related to observed behaviours. Further, these relationships should be large enough to have practical significance. This is the case, as indicated by the following examples taken from studies described in Chapters 6, 7 and 8.

- *Learning performance.* Imagers almost double their learning performance if they are presented with the same information as text-plus-illustration compared to just text, while verbalisers are not affected.
- *Learning preferences.* Given a choice of learning material, verbalisers will choose the textual version, and imagers will choose a version with illustrations.
- *Subject attainment.* Studies from the UK, Canada and Kuwait have found that between the ages of 11 and 14 years the wholist-verbalisers have the lowest attainment in mathematics.
- *Social behaviour.* Wholists are more assertive and analytics are more shy. Verbalisers are more active while imagers are more modest.

To be useful, a construct must have potential practical applications. This is the case with cognitive style in the areas of education and training, occupational guidance, career development and team building, and counselling and personal development.

This then, in outline, is the thesis of the book. It is for the reader to decide how convincing is the evidence. Although much of the emphasis will be on the Cognitive Styles Analysis approach, because the authors feel that evidence supports the view that it is currently the most satisfactory one, other approaches and models will also be considered.

Layout of the book

The book is in two parts. The first reviews the work on style and strategy in order to identify the basic style families. The second presents the evidence for the Cognitive Styles Analysis approach and the practical implications that come from it. These implications have practical relevance for teachers, trainers, counsellors and personnel staff.

PART 1

COGNITIVE STYLE AND LEARNING STRATEGIES

The concepts of style and strategy

Part 1 will critically review research into cognitive style (Chapter 2). Its purpose is to attempt to make sense of the wide range of labels that have been applied to style, consider the nature of cognitive style, and to argue that style dimensions can be grouped into two basic families.

It will also distinguish between cognitive style and learning strategy, where the former is probably inbuilt and the latter learned as a way of adapting to situations for which the natural cognitive style is not ideal. It will be seen that many labels that claim to be learning styles are in fact a description and measurement of learning strategies. In Chapter 3 these will be categorised in a critical reappraisal of the research in this area.

Chapter 4 will consider more closely learning strategies and their development. The discussion will focus on the nature of learning strategies, and will argue that the task of learning is a strategic activity.

Although this first part is obviously an important part of the authors' argument, Chapters 2 and 3 in particular are of necessity more in the nature of a review of the various approaches to style and strategy. At a first reading some may wish to jump to the start of Part 2 which follows on from the conclusion of this part. This is that there are two basic dimensions of cognitive style – the wholist-analytic and the verbal-imagery dimensions. Furthermore, while cognitive style is relatively fixed, individuals can develop learning strategies to improve their performance in learning situations.

CHAPTER 2

Cognitive style

Chapter overview

This chapter reviews and compares a range of approaches to style.

The origins of cognitive style

Since the mid-1940s, there have been various influences which have contributed to the emergence of several models of cognitive style. A major problem is that a large number of researchers working in relative isolation have generated an extensive list of style labels. However, when this list is examined it is appropriate to group similar labels into two style distinct families – the wholist-analytic dimension and the verbal-imagery dimension.

Models of style featuring the wholist-analytic dimension

The wholist-analytic style family includes style measures which assess whether an individual tends to *organise* information into wholes or parts. Typical members of this group include field-dependence–independence, leveller–sharpener and impulsive–reflective.

Models in the verbal-imagery dimension

The verbal-imagery style family comprises measures whether an individual is inclined to *represent* information during thinking verbally or in mental pictures. Early work on this dimension began with a consideration of individual differences in the vividness of mental imagery. Typical members of this category include verbalisers-visualisers and verbal-imagery.

A model integrating the wholist-analytic and verbal-imagery dimensions

Having identified the two fundamental dimensions the next step was to develop a simple and efficient way of assessing them. This development has resulted in the computer-presented Cognitive Styles Analysis.

The origins of cognitive style

The concept of individual differences and cognitive style

In view of the fact that there are several antecedents of style research, it is helpful to trace the development of a style construct from its various beginnings. An early interest in cognitive style as a construct is associated with the work of several areas of psychology. Some writers, for example, have approached style from an organising perspective of 'differential psychology' (Jonassen and Grabowski 1993; Messick 1996), while others have been cognitive psychologists interested in the processes and abilities in cognition (Furnham 1995; Grigerenko and Sternberg 1995; Riding 1997).

Vernon (1973) claimed that primary antecedents of style can be traced back to a description of personality in classical Greek literature. Messick (1996: 638) also suggested this same origin for style. The idea that 'different individuals have contrasting personalities that differentially influence their modes of cognition and behavioural expression', he explained, could be traced back to ancient classifications of temperament and physique. The typology to which he referred was an early model of human personality created by Hippocrates. This typology consisted of four personality types: the melancholic, the sanguine, the phlegmatic and the choleric.

Over the last one hundred years, various traditions of psychology have contributed to the emerging field of cognitive style. Allport (1937), in work which developed the idea of 'life-styles', was probably the first researcher to deliberately use the 'style' construct in association with cognition. For a working definition in the present context, cognitive style is understood to be an individual's preferred and habitual approach to organising and representing information.

The development of a theory of cognitive style

There have been several streams of work contributing to the development of cognitive style. A contemporary theory of style appears to flow from four areas of psychology:

- perception
- cognitive controls and cognitive process
- mental imagery
- personality constructs.

Each of these areas will be briefly described here, but are considered more fully later as part of a general discussion of style theory.

Perception

The first influence in an emerging theory of cognitive style was in the psychology of perception, exemplified by the work of Witkin and co-workers, which began in the 1940s. Experimental work – reflecting an emphasis on the 'regularities' of information-processing – derived from the gestalt school of perceptual psychology, led to an early development of the 'style construct' of field-dependence–independence (Witkin *et al.* 1962; Witkin 1964; Witkin *et al.* 1971; Witkin and Goodenough 1981).

Cognitive controls and cognitive process

The second was the study of cognitive processes related to individual adaptation to the environment exemplified by the work of Gardner and co-workers (1959). This work was influenced, originally, by theories of psychoanalytic ego psychology – which was typified by studies focused on variables in ego adaptation to the environment. This led to the identification of several cognitive processes including perceptual attitudes, cognitive attitudes and cognitive controls. Further work related to this area led to several stylistic labels and models and supported the general notion of a cognitive style (Messick 1996).

Mental imagery

A third area involved work looking at mental representation. Early in the scientific study of psychology, attention was given to the notion that some people have a predominantly verbal way of representing information in thought, while others are more visual or imaginal (Galton 1883; James 1890). Paivio (1971) further developed this notion with a dual coding approach to the measurement of mental imagery. Riding and Taylor (1976) identified, as fundamental to the construct of cognitive style, the verbal-imagery dimension of cognitive style.

Personality constructs

A fourth area of work involved researchers utilising personality-based constructs to develop a model of learning style (Myers 1978). Much of this approach is attributable to a psychodynamic perspective on the question of individuality. The single most significant contemporary example of this kind of construct is the assessment model presented by Myers-Briggs (Myers 1978). While we will deliberately not give as much attention to this stream of development, it is a style model which has been adopted by several researchers in the field. Its origins lie in Jung's typology of personality constructs and 'psychoanalytic ego psychology' (Jung 1923).

An interest in style among cognitive psychologists was given further impetus, according to Grigerenko and Sternberg (1995: 207), by frustration with research on ability and intelligence which failed to 'elucidate the processes generating individual differences'. Research carried out by various workers focused upon cognitive and perceptual functioning. A range of models emerged, including descriptions of perceptual attitudes, cognitive attitudes and cognitive controls. It is this general movement of cognitive research to which we next turn, beginning with a consideration of research investigating cognitive abilities and processes.

Cognitive style labels

A bewildering number of models and labels was generated by psychologists researching cognitive abilities and processes. Many of them contributed to an emerging notion of cognitive control or style. Others generated additional notions and descriptions of thinking and learning that were related to individual differences. The list below includes early attempts at identifying style dimensions.

- *Tolerant–intolerant* (Klein and Schlesinger 1951; Gardner *et al.* 1959; Klein *et al.* 1962).
- *Flexible control-constricted automatization v restructuring* (Klein 1954; Gardner *et al.* 1959; Santostefano and Paley 1964; Jenson and Rohwer 1966).
- *Broad–narrow categorization* (Pettigrew 1958; Bruner and Tajfel 1961; Messick and Kogan 1963; Kogan and Wallach 1964).
- *Form – articulation versus element articulation* (Messick and Kogan 1963).
- *Cognitive complexity/simplicity* (Bieri 1966; Signell 1966 Schroder *et al.* 1967).
- *Broad versus narrow scanning,* (Gardner and Long 1962; Benfari 1966; Holzman 1966, 1971).
- *Conceptual integration/integrative complexity* (Harvey *et al.* 1961; Schroder *et al.* 1967).
- *Cognitive simplicity versus cognitive complexity* (Harvey *et al.* 1961; Allard and Carlson 1963; Bieri 1966; Messick and Kogan 1966).
- *Risk taking versus cautiousness* (Kogan and Wallach 1964, 1967; Kogan and Morgan 1969).
- *Splitters and lumpers* (Cohen 1967).

Many of these labels reflected single experiments and were not subsequently supported by further empirical work. This, together with a lack of conceptual agreement over basic terminology, created a fragmented understanding of the nature of cognitive style. It is important, however, to retain an awareness of this early work, partly because of its influence upon an emerging construct of cognitive style, and partly because some labels provided useful opportunity for further developing the style construct.

The categorisation of cognitive style

The need to rationalise and synthesise much of this work has been identified by several workers (Curry 1983, 1987, 1991; Riding and Cheema 1991; Rayner and Riding 1997). It is worth noting, too, that the need for an integration of style constructs is well supported in the literature (Curry 1983; Curry 1987; Griggs 1991; Grigerenko and Sternberg 1995). Indeed, Furnham (1995: 410) described such an attempt to introduce a 'higher-order classification of the various constructs' as long overdue, and applauded such an attempt made by Riding and Sadler-Smith (1992). Furthermore, Lewis remarked that the diversity of style theory was unhelpful and misleading, if the theory of style was ever to prove useful in practice. He stated that

> In my opinion, the right thing to do is to focus . . . on the search for individual differences which are basic, in the sense that they underlie (and to that extent, explain), a whole range of more readily observable differences.
>
> (Lewis, 1976: 304–5)

This approach, which is akin to 'boiling down' the plethora of various models and constructs existing in the field, reflects the approach taken by Riding and Cheema (1991). They proposed the organisation of 'style' models into two cognitive style families, a wholist-analytic group and a verbaliser-imager group. The former, they argued, included over 30 different labels and models of style identified by a wide number of workers. Messick (1984) took a similar view, when he stated that contemporary research revealed the existence of 19 different models of cognitive style, but that there existed a need to review these claims, with a particular view to drawing a distinction between cognitive style and cognitive abilities.

Riding and Cheema (1991) also identified a third group of models of style in the field. They argued that this group lay outside the work which had investigated cognitive processes, but had nevertheless attracted the label of cognitive styles or learning styles. They suggested that this third group of 'learning style' models in fact more properly described 'learning strategies' and were therefore consequently deemed outside the cognitive style construct (Riding and Cheema 1991: 196). This group of models will be considered in the next chapter. For the moment, however, the consideration will be restricted to the key models that featured in the cognition-centred approach and are shown in Table 2.1.

The categorisation of the models described in Table 2.1 has been made on the basis of an identification of two fundamental dimensions of cognitive style originally identified by Riding and Cheema (1991). This categorisation of models of cognitive style will assist in the integration of various constructs or labels of cognitive style. In particular, it is helpful to attempt this kind of synthesis on the basis of identifying fundamental dimensions of cognitive style (see Rayner and Riding 1997).

The cognition-centred tradition of style included several models of cognitive functioning which are central to the development of a theory of cognitive style. As argued by Riding and Cheema (1991) and Rayner and Riding (1997), the research and development associated with this tradition can be further organised into three groups of models or labels which

- relate principally to cognitive organisation – the wholist-analytic style dimension
- relate principally to mental representation – the verbal-imagery style dimension
- reflect a deliberate attempt to integrate both the wholist-analytic and verbal-imagery dimensions of cognitive style.

These three groupings are shown in Table 2.1.

The following discussion examines several key models in each of these major aspects of cognitive style. The models are grouped according to the dimension of style to which they relate, which in turn reflects the integration of 'style families' described by Riding and Cheema (1991).

Models of style featuring the wholist-analytic dimension

It is the authors' view that much of the research carried out within the cognition-centred tradition focused upon functioning which reflected the wholist-analytic dimension of style. Indeed, some researchers, noting this fact, referred to evidence suggesting the existence of a superordinate dimension of style (Miller 1987; Allinson and Hayes 1996). While cognitive style may include more than one dimension, it is likely that a number of labels and descriptions of cognitive functioning are related to a single dimension of cognitive style. In this instance, it may be identified as a wholist-analytic dimension of cognitive style (Riding and

Table 2.1 Descriptions of style dimensions

The wholist-analytic dimension		
Field-dependency–independency	Individual dependency on a perceptual field when analysing a structure or form which is part of the field.	Witkin and Asch (1948a, 1948b); Witkin (1964); Witkin et al. (1971, 1977)
Levelling–sharpening	A tendency to assimilate detail rapidly and lose detail or emphasise detail and changes in new information.	Klein (1954); Gardner et al. (1959)
Impulsivity–reflectiveness	Tendency for quick as against a deliberate response.	Kagan et al. (1964); Kagan (1966)
Converging–diverging thinking	Narrow, focused, logical, deductive thinking rather than broad, open-ended, associational thinking to solve problems.	Guilford (1967); Hudson (1966, 1968)
Holist–serialist thinking	The tendency to work through learning tasks or problem solving incrementally or globally and assimilate detail.	Pask and Scott (1972); Pask (1976)
Concrete sequential/ concrete random/ abstract sequential/ abstract random	The learner learns through experience concrete and abstraction either randomly or sequentially.	Gregorc (1982)
Assimilator–explorer	Individual preferences for seeking familiarity or novelty in the process of problem-solving and creativity.	Kaufmann (1989)
Adaptors–innovators	Adaptors prefer conventional, established procedures and innovators restructuring or new perspectives in problem solving.	Kirton (1976, 1987)
Reasoning–intuitive active–contemplative	Preference for developing understanding through reasoning and or by spontaneity or insight and learning activity which allows active participation or passive reflection.	Allinson and Hayes (1996)
The verbal-imagery dimension		
Abstract versus concrete thinker	Preferred level and capacity of abstraction.	Harvey et al. (1961)
Verbaliser–visualiser	The extent to which verbal or visual strategies are used to represent knowledge and in thinking.	Paivio (1971); Riding and Taylor (1976); Richardson (1977); Riding and Calvey (1981)
An integration of the wholist-analytic and verbal-imagery dimensions		
Wholist-analytic, verbal-imagery	Tendency for the individual to process information in parts or as a whole and think in words or pictures.	Riding (1991b, 1994, 1996); Riding and Cheema (1991); Riding and Rayner (1995)

Source: Adapted from Rayner and Riding (1997)

Cheema 1991; Rayner and Riding 1997). It refers to an individual's typical method for organising new information.

Research has produced several versions or labels to describe aspects of this cognitive process, for example, 'serialist and holists', 'splitters and lumpers', 'field-dependent and field-independent'. The following account provides a critical review of key models of cognitive style which feature this wholistic-analytic dimension of cognitive style.

Perceptual-functioning and cognitive style

Workers led by Witkin and Asch (1948a, 1948b) focused initially on perception, as they identified differences in individuals who were deciding whether an object was upright in space. Their work reflected earlier research into perception by the Gestalt School of German psychology. Further experiments led to the discovery of field-independence and field-dependence as a perceptual style. Individuals were found to rely upon the surrounding 'field' or context to a greater or lesser extent, when reorientating an object relative to the vertical. Early work carried out by Witkin and co-workers was with pilots from the Second World War, who had experienced disorientation and problems with reorientation, after flying through thick cloud formation.

Research into this construct took place over a thirty-year period, leading to an awareness that competence at disembedding shapes and objects was strongly associated with competence at disembedding in other non-perceptual, problem-solving tasks. This resulted in the construct being broadened to encompass both perceptual and intellectual activities and was referred to as the 'global-articulated dimension'. Later, with additional evidence on self-consistency, extending to the areas of body concept, sense of self, and controls and defences, the construct became even more comprehensive and was labelled as 'psychological differentiation' (Witkin et al. 1962; Witkin 1964; Witkin et al. 1971; Witkin and Goodenough 1981).

Assessment
In early work, the first Body Adjustment Test was used to measure field-dependency. This attempted to replicate those conditions experienced by pilots in fighter aircraft flying through low cloud formation. The early version of the test involved the person being seated on a tilted chair, in a tilted room, and being asked to adjust the body to the upright. A further version of the test, called the Rod and Frame Test, involved the individual being seated in a completely darkened room. The person was asked to view a tilted luminous rod, within a tilted luminous frame. The individual was then asked to disregard the frame,

and adjust the rod until it was in a totally upright position. Interest was focused on the relationship between a person's visual and kinaesthetic cues, and the levels of dependence on the visual context displayed.

Assessment of field-dependency was further developed to include several variations of the original tests. A pencil and paper assessment, the Embedded Figures Test (EFT), was developed reflecting earlier work on the discrimination of shape carried out by Thurstone (1944). All of these measures involve the disembedding of a shape from its surrounding field. This assessment included the following tests.

- *Embedded Figures Test (EFT):* a 12 item, individually administered test, made up of two sets of cards displaying complex figures and simple figures respectively.
- *Children's Embedded Figures Test (CEFT):* a 25 item, individually administered test which combines a series of simple and complex figures, and incomplete pictures requiring the subject to disembed or recognise embedded shapes. The test was norm-referenced with children from 5 to 12 years of age (Witkin *et al.* 1971).
- *Group Embedded Figures Test (GEFT):* a group-administered 25 item test for adults in which the format is very similar to the EFT (Witkin *et al.* 1971).

Empirical evidence

Numerous experiments exploring this 'style' of perceptual field response are reported in the literature. Indeed, McKenna (1984) reported that, by the year 1980, there were over 3,000 references in the area related to field-dependence.

A typical example of such research is the use of field-dependency as a basis for investigating the effect of matching or mismatching teachers and pupils with specific field-dependent or field-independent cognitive style (Saracho and Dayton 1980; Renninger and Snyder 1983; Saracho 1991). Evidence provided by these researchers has proved inconclusive, with some workers supporting the relevance and validity of perceptual style, while others question its validity and reject its relevance for the teacher interested in improving learning performance in the classroom.

A major criticism of field-independence is that it may well be, at least in part, a measurement of 'fluid ability'. Grigerenko and Sternberg (1993) have argued that fluid ability is best understood as a combination of intellectual skills and strategies. They believed this raised the possibility that the Embedded Figures Test actually measured an individual's intellectual capacity. This meant that the construct may in fact be an indicator of ability rather than style. Grigerenko and Sternberg (1993: 209) concluded that 'field dependence is a deficit rather than a style'.

McKenna (1983, 1984) argued, similarly, for the need to distinguish between cognitive style and ability. After analysing several limitations and contradictions in the design of measures of field-dependence, McKenna (1984: 593) concluded that 'the measures of field-dependence do not meet the criteria for a cognitive style at the conceptual level and at the empirical level there are substantial correlations with standard ability tests'. Jonassen and Grabowski (1993: 87) also reached a similar conclusion, choosing to describe the construct of field-dependence as one of cognitive control.

It is the view of the present authors that the criticism of field-dependence and field-independence is really of its measurement by means of the EFT, rather than the notion itself. The authors feel that Witkin and his co-workers were generally correct in their understanding of field-dependence, but failed in its measurement. The implications that are described in the following sections therefore need to be treated with obvious caution, given that the tests used to assess field-dependence and field-independence were flawed.

Leveller and sharpener

Holzman and Klein (1954) first used the term 'levelling and sharpening' to describe individual differences in memory processing. Gardner *et al.* (1960: 122) described this cognitive process as 'the characteristic degree to which current precepts and relevant memory traces interact or assimilate in the course of registration of the current precepts and memories'.

The distinction between 'levellers' and 'sharpeners' is based on how the visual task is perceived. Holzman and Klein noted that while some individuals oversimplified their perceptions ('levelling'), others had a tendency to perceive the task in a complex and differentiated fashion, showing little assimilation ('sharpening').

While 'levellers' tend to assimilate new events with previously stored ones, 'sharpeners' in contrast tend to accentuate the perceived events and treat them more discretely from those already stored. How well the perceived task was assimilated led to the dimension of assimilation, with 'sharpeners' at one end, showing very little assimilation to 'levellers' at the other end, showing high levels of assimilation. The continuum from levelling through to sharpening was described as a dimension of cognitive style, which altered during maturation, to reflect a movement away from levelling towards sharpening. This involved, more specifically, a movement away from 'fluid' to a 'stable' memory structure, as well as from a 'global' to an 'articulated' differentiation of past and present images and events.

It has been noted that this model of cognitive style has two main forms of manifestation:

- a tendency to 'gloss over' inconsistencies, or
- the condensing of information, involving simplification, on the one hand, and/or generalisation involving caricature on the other.

The differences in approaches to learning which were associated with a leveller–sharpener dimension of cognitive style are listed in Table 2.2.

Table 2.2 Characteristics of levelling–sharpening

Levellers	Sharpeners
present–past confusion	clear perception of time
prefer abstract reasoning	prefer concrete reasoning
images in the memory are unstable	images in the memory are stable over time
blurring of images/memories	key mode of perception – visual
generalised perception	focused perception
integrated view	separated view

Assessment

'Levelling and sharpening' has generally been measured by the Schematising Test (Holzman and Klein 1954). This entails the test subjects first becoming dark-adapted and then judging the sizes of squares of light of increasing size. Overall, there is a tendency to underestimate size as new squares of increasing size are added. Subjects who make greater underestimates are 'levellers' whilst those that make smaller errors are 'sharpeners'. Jonassen and Grabowski (1993: 201–2) commented that reliability data to support this test were not evident. They also remarked that respondents taking the test could easily suffer from fatigue. This was because of difficulty in discriminating difference in size between the squares forming the test, thereby affecting its result. There have been a number of tests developed to measure levelling and sharpening, utilising computer-based equipment to help make the assessment more accurate and user-friendly (see Jonassen and Grabowski 1993).

Empirical evidence

Overall, the leveller–sharpener dimension resulted in relatively few studies, most of them carried out on adults. Consequently, studies examining the relationship between it and other cognitive styles are few. Jonassen and Grabowski (1993) reported several studies investigating the construct, some of which supported the contention that memory functioning takes on an increasing 'bias' to one or other end of the continuum as the individual becomes more stressed. Riding and Dyer (1983) completed a factor analytic study of several dimensions of style and found that leveller–sharpener loaded on the same factor as field-dependence–independence as assessed by the GEFT.

To this extent, at face value, it is easy to hypothesise a relationship between levelling and sharpening, as a label, and the wholist-analytic style dimension.

Impulsivity-reflectivity

This construct was introduced by Kagan *et al.* (1964). The style dimension derived from earlier work investigating conceptual tempo which measured the rate at which an individual makes decisions under conditions of uncertainty. Learners fell into four distinct categories, namely those who

- reached a decision quickly, frequently with more errors, after a brief review of options and were labelled 'cognitively impulsive'
- would deliberate before making a response, committed relatively fewer errors, carefully considered all options and were labelled 'cognitively reflective'
- showed faster reaction times but who made relatively fewer errors and were called 'quick'
- responded far more slowly, while committing more errors, and were labelled 'slow'.

Researchers investigating this dimension have generally tended to focus only on the first two groups, namely the reflective and the impulsive aspects of cognitive style (Grigerenko and Sternberg 1993).

Assessment
The Matching Familiar Figures Test (MFFT) is a booklet comprising twelve standard pictures, each with eight alternatives. Individuals are required to point at the matching picture for each. Patterns of response are observed and the response times measured. Respondents are grouped according to the categories previously described. It should be noted that there have been several additional instruments developed to measure impulsivity and reflectivity, but that the MFFT has remained the most widely used in research.

Empirical evidence
The existence of this dimension has been supported by a series of investigations which have demonstrated stability over both time and tasks. Messer (1976) reported a number of studies which showed meaningful findings after inves-

tigating the application of the dimension to cognitive tasks. These included research which reported that 'reflectives' were found to be significantly more field-independent than 'impulsives' (Campbell and Douglas 1972; Keogh and Donlon 1972; Massari 1975; Neimark 1975).

Further work utilising the label involved researchers focusing on child development and the relationship between impulsivity–reflectivity and behaviour. Of particular interest was the link between this label and hyper-activity or attention-deficit disorder. The relationship between the impulsivity–reflectivity dimension and its effect on cognitive tasks has been investigated by Kagan *et al.* (1966) who studied the relationship between conceptual tempo and children's skill in inductive reasoning tests. With 6-year-olds, their study showed a significant relationship between reflectivity and inferential skills.

Zelniker and Jeffrey (1979) drew attention to a parallel asymmetry in their style research. They found that reflectives consistently performed better than impulsives on tasks requiring detail processing, but that impulsives usually performed only as well as reflectives on tasks thought to require global processing. Banta (1970) reported a highly significant correlation between field-dependence–independence and impulsivity–reflectivity in a sample of lower-class children aged 3–6 years. Massari and Massari (1973), using disadvantaged preschoolers, obtained significant correlations between MFFT and EFT scores. Schleifer and Douglas (1973), using the EFT and impulsivity–reflectivity measures on middle-class and disadvantaged preschoolers, found identical significant correlations for both samples.

Research by Gullo (1988) has shown that differences between impulsive and reflective children appear to flow from a concern or anxiety about error. A part of this concern reflected a sensitivity to judgements made about their personal competence. Impulsive children perceived speed of response as a primary indicator of competence. Reflective children perceived rate of error as a primary indicator of competence. The implications of this research appear to open up issues about the relationship between cognitive style, self-perception as learner, and perceptions of the learning task.

Convergent–divergent thinking

This dimension was proposed by Guilford (1967). The dimension reflects a type of thinking and associated strategies for problem-solving. The learner will typically attack a problem or task by 'thinking' in a way which is either open-ended and exploratory, or close-ended and highly focused. Assessment of convergent thinking was made by using existing tests such as the EFT or alternatively, an intelligence test, and identifying 'open-ended' items which were then used to infer an ability to 'generate' answers.

The theory was further developed by Hudson (1966, 1968) and its implications for the process of teaching and learning more fully explored. Hudson reported that learners who were *convergers* preferred formal problems and structured tasks demanding logical method. In contrast, learners who were *divergers* preferred more open-ended tasks which required creativity. The divergent thinker was far more likely to react negatively to routine, or to the task involving the familiar or expected and requiring a correct answer. It follows from this that convergers are likely to be analytic and divergers wholist in style.

Assessment

There is no specific instrument for assessing convergent–divergent thinking. Assessment of 'convergent thinking ability' has usually been inferred from success on tests which may be based on 'figural' input (such as the EFT or the MFFT) or on verbal or numerical input (such as the items on intelligence tests). However, in assessing 'divergent thinking', the emphasis is not on finding the correct solution (as there is not one) but on the ability to 'generate' answers. Examples of such 'open-ended' test items again can be non-verbal/figural (such as the 'circles' the 'squares' and the barrelled lines tests) or verbal (such as the Uses of Objects test, Consequences test and the S test).

Empirical evidence

Haddon and Lytton (1968) investigated the effects of differing primary school teaching strategies on divergent thinking abilities. Their results showed that pupils from the 'informal' schools were significantly better in divergent thinking, compared with 'formal' schools. Further support for the view that certain approaches foster convergent thinking and others divergent thinking comes from studies such as Crutchfield (1965), Barker-Lunn (1970), Covington *et al.* (1974).

Noppe and Gallagher (1977) reported a correlation of 0.44 between Mednick and Mednick's (1967) Remote Associates Test, a measure of creativity, and the GEFT for college undergraduates. Contrary to expectation, field-independent individuals have sometimes been found to be more creative than the field-dependent individuals. Studies indicate that although all subjects who score highly on field-independence are not necessarily creative, those scoring high on divergent thinking tend to score higher on field-independence (Spotts and Mackler 1967; Bloomberg 1971; Noppe and Gallagher 1977). Furthermore, learners studying 'more creative' disciplines have been found to be more field-independent than learners studying 'less creative' subjects. For example, Bergum (1977) and Morris and Bergum (1978) found that students of architecture regarded themselves as more creative than business students and were also more field-independent than business students. It should however be borne in mind that field-independence as measured by the GEFT correlates with intelligence, and this may explain the apparent reversal compared with Hudson (1966).

In general, Hudson has found that convergers prefer formal problems and tasks that are better structured and demand greater logical ability than the more open-ended problems favoured by divergers. Convergers apparently are more emotionally inhibited than divergers, and appear to keep the different aspects of their lives 'compartmentalised' (Austin 1971). One explanation is that convergers prefer to structure their experience at all levels, more than divergers do and are more capable of utilising any structure present.

Overall, evidence seems to suggest that while divergent thinking is an invaluable cognitive quality, socially it is considered as irritating, disruptive and even threatening by teachers. Indeed, Getzels and Jackson (1962) found that teachers preferred learners who were low in divergent thinking (i.e. conformist and orderly) to those higher in divergent thinking, even though all the learners were of similar intelligence, and even though the divergent thinkers produced more imaginative and original responses. Since many schools are inherently rule-bound and conservative institutions this may come as no surprise. This inevitably means that much of the divergent thinking (creativity) is likely to contrast or even conflict with what is routine, familiar, expected and 'correct'.

Holist–serialist thinking

This label was introduced by Pask and Scott (1972) as two competencies which reflected an individual tendency to respond to a learning task either with a holistic strategy which is 'hypothesis-led' or a focused strategy which is characterised by a step-by-step process and is 'data-led'. The construct reflected the belief that learning a complex subject-matter involves two basic operations:

- building a description of how elements in a topic interrelate, that is, forming an understanding of internal structure
- building operations, that is, manipulating the underlying interrelationship between concepts in a topic.

Holists, Pask (1972) argued, will typically adopt a global, thematic approach to learning, which involves building broad descriptions. They will often focus upon several aspects of the topic at the same time, and work simultaneously at several different levels of thinking. Serialists, on the other hand, will adopt an 'operations' approach to learning. They will concentrate on detail, procedure, and often conceptualise information in a linear structure. A step-by-step method, built upon clearly identified chunks of information which are used to link concepts and parts of the topic, characterised the serialist's approach to learning.

Pask (1984) believed that 'versatile' learners who learned to employ both holist and serialist strategies would realise a deeper and far fuller understanding of the topic. This type of learner would progress to become 'proficient at learning from most or all modes of instruction'. This work led to the development of a 'conversational theory of learning' which emphasised the ability of the learner to 'teach-back' learned material (Pask 1976, 1984).

The differences which characterise the holist–serialist dimension of style, as approaches to learning, are listed in Table 2.3.

Table 2.3 Characteristics of holists–serialists

Holist	Serialist
top-down processor	bottom-up processor
global approach to learning	local approach to learning
simultaneous processing	linear processing
spans various levels at once	works step by step
interconnects theoretical and practical aspects	aspects learned separately
conceptually orientated	detail orientated
comprehension learning bias	operational learning bias
relates concepts to prior experience	relates characteristics within concept
broad description building	narrow procedure building
low discrimination skills	high discrimination skills

Assessment

Pask and Scott administered a problem-solving task (i.e. the keyboard task) in a 'free-learning situation'. Overall, this resulted in two broad types of individual competence – holist and serialist. In order to establish that these individual differences might be generalised, Pask and Scott devised a series of experiments *requiring* a deep level of understanding. The respondents, in this case, had to establish for themselves the principles of classification underlying the division of two imaginary species of Martian animals – the Clobbits and the Gandlemullers – into a series of sub-species. Information about Clobbits was provided in the form of 50 cards. These were placed face down in ten columns (each column representing a separate sub-species). The five rows contained separate categories of information about the ten sub-species (e.g. habitat, physical characteristics, drawings of animals, etc.). Students could also write their own information cards if they found it helpful.

Students were instructed to turn over the cards to obtain the information they required. However, they were to turn the cards over one at a time and to give a reason for 'choosing' that card. Each reason amounted to a hypothesis about the nature of the classification system which the information on the card was expected to test. A record was kept of the order in which the cards were used and also of the hypothesis given at each step. Finally, students were to 'teach-back' to the experimenter what they had learned about the Martian animals.

Pask noted that some students concentrated on a step-by-step strategy in which they used simple hypotheses to assess one property (of the animals) at a time, e.g. 'Do Gandlemullers have sprongs?', while others used more complex hypotheses which combined several properties simultaneously, e.g. 'Are there more kinds of Gandlers with mounds (dorsal or cranial) than Plongers?'

Students who used the step-by-step approach indicated a logical linear progression from one hypothesis to the next; they were designated serialists. Their focus was narrow, concentrating on each step of the argument, cautiously and critically. In contrast, students adopting the holist approach, had a tendency to use global strategies. Holists who, in addition to having broad perspectives, personalise their learning to the extent that they almost 'create' information, have been labelled by Pask as 'redundant holists'. He argued that while the redundant holists succeed in attaining the same level of understanding as both the holist and the serialist, unlike these, they had to rely on personal (redundant) elaboration to aid that understanding. Indeed, in certain cases, there was even incorrect information being reinterpreted from the presented information.

Pask (1988) argued that the holist and serialist strategies are manifestations of important underlying stable differences in the way individuals perceive problems. He claimed that whereas some learners are disposed to act 'like holists' whenever they are given the opportunity, others behave 'like serialists'.

In observing students adopting extreme styles, Pask noted that there appear to be two main types of 'pathologies' from which such learners suffer: first, those that rely more on a serialist-like style of cognition and are unable to take a global view are likely to suffer from 'improvidence' pathology; second, those adopting the holist-like style have a tendency towards 'globe-trotting', that is making hasty decisions from insufficient evidence.

Empirical evidence

Pask (1976) assessed students on standardised tests for cognitive traits such as logical reasoning, embedded figures, analogy completion, perceptual discrimination and a test for divergence; he found that the only differences in the mean score between holist and serialists were on the analogies test and the divergence test, in both of which holists scored higher than serialists.

Criticism of this construct, reported by Riding and Cheema (1991), observed that Pask's research was based upon relatively small samples of students, and that they were all aged 15 or more years old.

It is unfortunate that, as far as we are aware, the dimension has not been empirically correlated with other styles of learning. That is, no empirical evidence exists linking the holist–serialist dimension with other styles of the wholist-analytic family.

The style delineator

Gregorc's learning style construct (style delineator) maintains that an individual learns through concrete experience and abstraction either randomly or sequentially (Gregorc 1982). He identified four 'styles' of learning: concrete sequential learners who prefer direct, step-by-step, orderly and sensory-based learning; concrete random learners who rely upon trial and error, intuitive and independent approaches to learning; abstract sequential learners who adopt an analytic, logical approach to learning and prefer verbal instruction; and abstract random learners who approach learning holistically, visually and prefer to learn information in an unstructured experiential way. These may be represented as shown in Figure 2.1.

Figure 2.1 Style delineator dimensions

abstract sequential	concrete sequential
abstract random	concrete random

Assessment

The Style Delineator is a self-report measure made up of 40 words; the respondent is asked to rank the extent to which each word best describes their self-perception as a thinker and learner. The measure indicates the position an individual occupies in the 'bi-dimensional channels' of 'learning preferences for making sense of the world through the perception and ordering of incoming information' (Jonassen and Grabowski 1993: 289).

Empirical evidence

Jonassen and Grabowski (1993) reported little independent research to support this model of learning style. Generally, they found that the literature supporting the style delineator was descriptive rather than empirical. Grigerenko and Sternberg (1995) similarly criticised this model for lack of an empirical base, and argued that Gregorc's notion of 'channels' of stylistic perception brings the nature of styles to a point where their 'fluidity' as a concept makes them irrelevant in any development and management of pedagogy.

The assimilator–explorer (A–E) cognitive style

Kaufmann's (1989) work flowed from an interest in problem solving and creativity. He identified two groups of problem solvers, *assimilators* and *explorers*, and extrapolated an A–E theory of cognitive style to apply to problem-solving behaviour. Martinsen (1994) has continued work in this area, specifically with respect to the relationship between cognitive style, insight and motivation in the process of problem solving. The construct was defined as two relatively stable individual differences in cognitive strategy use (Martinsen 1994: 14). Martinsen further noted that while the A–E theory was developed independently, it revealed marked similarities to earlier work carried out by researchers into cognitive controls and stylistic disposition (Gardner, 1953; Klein 1954).

Assessment

Kaufmann developed an A–E Inventory, a 32 item forced choice self-report questionnaire, in which items described dispositions towards cognitive 'novelty-seeking against familiarity-seeking'. Explorers reflected a higher score on the bi-polar continuum. Assimilators reflected a lower score along the continuum. The instrument was organised to measure three factors: 'novelty against structure seeking', 'high against low ideational productivity', and 'opposition against preference for structure'. Kaufmann (1989) reported that these three factors were defined as reflecting a 'second order' assimilation–exploration factor, which Kaufmann (1989) subsequently interpreted as a stylistic disposition towards assimilation or exploration.

Empirical evidence

The development of this construct is relatively recent, and there is limited empirical evidence to support it. Martinsen (1994) reported that a pilot study by Kaufmann was successfully replicated by Goldsmith and Matherly (1985), but that the same workers failed to find any correlation between the A–E measure and the construct of adaptor–innovator (Kirton 1987). Martinsen also reported on his own work, in which he used the construct of A–E as a measure in investigating the relationship between cognitive style and experience, creativity, motivation and insight.

Martinsen argued that the key implications for the A–E theory lay in exploring the relationship between intelligence and styles. He described how explorers presented as more efficient in information-seeking strategies. Assimilators, on the other hand, presented as more efficient in utilising relevant experience in implementing a strategy. Crucially, he found that intelligence did not influence these results. He concluded that certain conditions would lead to a better performance for each of the styles respectively. Furthermore, Martinsen (1994: 35) argued that the A–E styles were found to show a significant 'interactive role in the mediation of experience and problem-solving'.

This raises questions about whether the A–E style is or can be learnt or at least 'changed'. Martinsen also asked if style awareness can and should lead to better learning performance. He cited a single experimental study (Martinsen and Kaufmann 1991) which investigated the effect of a structured approach to the learning task, and which found particular modes of delivery profited the A–E styles. Martinsen reported that assimilators learn 'optimally' through a highly structured approach, while explorers learn 'optimally' from an independent approach. He concluded that further work should be aimed at exploring the way in which direct intervention might facilitate A–E strategy learning. It appears likely that explorers reflect the wholist and assimilators the analytic approaches to learning.

The adaptor–innovator cognitive style

Kirton (1994) argued that style relates to the preferred cognitive strategies involved in personal response to change, and the strategies associated with creativity, problem-solving and decision-making. A second key assumption made by Kirton was that these strategies were related to numerous aspects (traits) of personality that appear early in life are particularly stable, and may be recognised as a cognitive style. The dimension adaptation–innovation (A–I) was understood to exist early in an individual's cognitive development, and be 'stable over both time and incident'.

The adaptor, therefore, generally has a preference for 'doing things better', while the innovator will tend to like 'doing things differently'. Kirton's A–I theory, in summary, advanced a style construct which is bi-polar, and consists of the adaptor–innovator continuum. A list of characteristics associated with the A–I dimension is in Table 2.4, which suggests that wholists may be innovators and analytics, adaptors.

Table 2.4 Characteristics of adaptors and innovators

Adaptor	Innovator
precise, methodical approach to the task	random, non-sequential approach to the task
convergent thinker – works within the task remit	divergent thinker – works by challenging the task remit
consensus seeker who relies upon established method	independent and group 'shaker'
emphasises solving problems by increasing efficiency, continuity and stability	unpredictable and idealistic
seeks to follow established structures	leads in unstructured situations
conformist and challenges rules cautiously	non-conformist
prefers repetitive, detailed work which can be sustained over time	unable to sustain maintenance work/ activity
compliant, low self-confidence, and reverts to conformity when challenged	high self-esteem linked to activities involving the generation of ideas
good at administrative management but stays systems-bound	good at crisis management
liable to make goals of process and method	liable to justify the end with no regard for the means

Kirton's theory of style, and construct, reflected several key principles, which defined style and distinguished it from other constructs of cognitive functioning. He listed these principles as indicating how style is conceptually independent and 'lying orthogonally to'

- cognitive capacity, that is, style is bipolar and non-pejorative
- success, that is, style is basically non-evaluative
- cognitive techniques, that is, style is not readily changed
- coping behaviour, that is, a limited repertoire of non-style-based behaviour which cannot be sustained by the individual.

Kirton, in summary, regarded the A–I construct to be a cognitive style which reflected an individual's preferred mode for problem-solving. The A–I construct is described as unrelated to level, or capacity (for example, to intelligence), or cognitive complexity or management competency. Finally, Kirton stated that the construct is assumed to be a dimension of cognitive process and is therefore not context specific. He also added that it should be regarded as a basic dimension of human personality possessing 'meaningful relationships with other personality characteristics'.

Assessment

The assessment instrument developed by Kirton to measure the adaptor–innovator continuum was the Kirton Adaptor–Innovator Inventory (KAI), a self-reporting inventory originally designed for adults with experience in the workplace and life. The instrument consists of 32 items each scored on a scale from 1 to 5. The KAI produces a score which is used to identify, along a continuum, an individual's preferred cognitive style, that is, as an adaptor or an innovator.

Empirical evidence

Kirton (1994: 14–24) reported various studies supporting the measure with statistical analysis. He provided a summary of studies utilising factor analysis to support the reliability and validity of the instrument (1994: 14–19). This has in turn been corroborated by other writers (Clapp 1993; Taylor 1994; Van der Molen 1994). Grigerenko and Sternberg (1995) referred to a single correlational study between the A–I Inventory and the Style Delineator (Gregorc 1982), which showed a limited relationship between the dimensions. The KAI inventory was originally designed to be used with adults in the workplace, and Kirton warns that reliability can be expected to diminish when it is used with other groups.

Work looking at the implications of this construct has been generally restricted to three areas: the field of management, leadership and organisational development. Kirton argued that if cognitive style was to be regarded as stable, then it carried implications for 'cognitive fit', that is, the match between person and environment. More precisely, he referred to the 'correspondence' between person (style) and task or event (problem-solving). Kirton speculated that further effects would be likely with respect to approaches to team-work and management practice, as well as dealing with personal stress. Implications for education and learning, while not immediately apparent, reflect similar effects for a person's response to the learning task. There are larger possible effects, in respect to the structure and process of workplace training and life-long education.

Cognitive style index (CSI)

According to Allinson and Hayes (1996: 119), the CSI was developed to measure the 'generic intuition-analysis dimension of cognitive style'. They argued that practical utility of a measure is essential if the operationalisation of cognitive style is to be achieved (in this instance within a business management context). They stated that the CSI was designed, principally, to further research and development of style in management practice.

While the CSI does not purport to produce a 'full' measure of cognitive style, it is focused on a single 'superordinate' dimension which, Allinson and Hayes have argued, reflects the duality of 'human consciousness' and problem-solving responses which are either intuitive or analytic.

Assessment

The CSI is a 38 item self-report questionnaire, scored on a trichotomous scale. It is relatively short and produces a score that reflects an individual's position on an analytic–intuitive continuum, which its authors argue, reflects the superordinate dimension of cognitive style. The construction of the questionnaire is described in some detail by Allinson and Hayes, as part of an attempt to identify a unitary construct of cognitive style and operationalise the same construct in the professional context of business management.

Empirical evidence

As this instrument has only recently been developed, as yet there is little empirical evidence to support it. Allinson and Hayes provided an account of the development of the measure, based on a sample of 1,000 adults. They utilised item analysis, factor analysis, descriptive statistics, construct validity and concurrent validity. While they acknowledged the need to have these findings replicated and extended, they concluded that the measure possessed robust psychometric properties, including good reliability, in terms of internal consistency and temporal stability, as well as good initial evidence of construct and concurrent validity. They therefore argued that their aim, which was to produce a psychometrically sound instrument for application in a large-scale organisational setting, was realised.

From the description of the measure as being of the 'intuitive–analysis dimension' it might be expected that this is similar to models in the wholist-analytic family of styles. However, a small-scale preliminary study by Sadler-Smith using 99 business studies university students who did the CSI and the Cognitive Styles Analysis (Riding 1991a) suggested that the CSI does not assess the wholist-analytic dimension of style.[1]

---

1 An analysis of variance of gender by wholist-analytic style by verbal-imagery style with intuition-analysis as the dependent variable did not show a significant effect of wholist-analytic style ($P > 0.10$). Further, there was a marginally significant interaction ($P = 0.05$) between gender, wholist-analytic style and verbal-imagery style in their effect on intuition-analysis such that while analysis increased from wholist to analytic for the male imagers and the female verbalisers, there was no effect for the male verbalisers and the female imagers.

The wholist-analytic dimension of cognitive style: an evaluation

Riding and Cheema (1991) argued that research suggests the existence of a wholist-analytic dimension of cognitive style. The various stylistic labels and models of cognitive style which are discussed in this section in many respects complement each other and lend support for Riding and Cheema's assertion. However, these same models and labels, together with others, are also responsible for a legacy of continuing confusion in terminology and understanding of cognitive style and learning. The case for rationalisation and synthesis is compelling. To this end, it is perhaps helpful to attempt an evaluation of these models and identify those which are most relevant. Table 2.5 describes some limitations of the models related to the wholist-analytic dimension. In so far as they appear to reflect the wholist-analytic dimension of style, the labels have been put in the order of wholist first and analytic second.

The attempt to recategorise the various labels and models which make up the various approaches to cognitive and learning styles should, as has already been argued, attempt to synthesise the theory. It should also have an eye to those models with potential impact on practice and which might be a foundation upon which to build new developments. The early work on cognitive process and controls, previously identified as cognitive styles, are now better regarded as aspects of cognitive functioning which refer to abilities and regulatory controls. Other models which indicate a style dimension or family should be evaluated using the key criteria of construct validity, empirical research which links the construct to observed behaviour and learning performance, and utility within the professional context.

The various models which purport to describe and measure cognitive style all carry limitations and weaknesses, principally to do with construct validity, reliability or utility. The 'credibility gap' between levels of conceptual and empirical validity is a serious issue, the more so because extremely high levels of reliability in a measure does not equate to validity. More recently developed self-report measures of style require empirical data to demonstrate their construct validity and reliability.

In reviewing studies of style labels, one is left with the impression that most workers were subjectively correct in sensing many of the attributes of the wholist-analytic dimension of style, but that they were unable to effectively find a valid method of assessing the dimension. Some, as in the case of Witkin and his co-workers, measured ability rather than, or as well as, style. Others had a general notion of some aspects of the dimension which they then sought to determine by means of the introspective self-report. This latter method is fraught with difficulty, partly because people are not always good at knowing what they think about themselves, but more particularly because what the

Table 2.5 An evaluation of models of cognitive style

Model	Evaluation	References
Field-dependency–independency	Criticised for not meeting the criteria for cognitive style either at a conceptual or an empirical level, since it correlates with ability.	McKenna (1983, 1984); Grigerenko and Sternberg (1995)
Levelling–sharpening	More research is needed to support this model; tests are criticised in terms of demands made of the subject and little reliability data are available.	Jonassen and Grabowski (1993); Tiedemann (1989)
Impulsivity–reflectivity	May include cognitive processes as well as style; developmental rather than a stable characteristic; supported by a strong research base; carries strong levels of face validity.	Grigerenko and Sternberg (1995); Gullo (1988)
Divergent–convergent thinking	Conceptual validity is established, supported by a moderate research base; no specific measure is available.	Grigerenko and Sternberg (1995)
Holist–serialist thinking	A construct which appears to describe an individual's information-processing strategy rather than a cognitive style dimension; assessments are complex and time consuming.	Jonassen and Grabowski (1993); Riding and Cheema (1991)
Concrete random–concrete sequential	Criticised for a narrow research base; construct validity is supported by phenomenological research but little psychometric data is available.	Jonassen and Grabowski (1993)
Explorers–assimilators	Needs a larger empirical base; may not be a unidimensional construct.	Kaufmann (1989)
Innovators–adaptors	Moderately sized empirical research base; however, uncertainties include its unidimensional structure, relationship to cognitive ability, and the uniqueness of the A–I dimension.	Furnham (1995)
Intuitive–analytic	While the face validity of the construct is moderately high, clear evidence is required to link the aspects of style measured by the CSI to the wholist-analytic dimension.	See note 1

investigator thinks makes a clear item to assess an aspect of style, is often in fact interpreted quite differently by the individual.

The challenge is to break out of this situation and to find a more objective method of assessing the wholist-analytic dimension that avoids measuring ability by positively assessing both ends of the continuum, is direct, and is relatively objective.

The theory of cognitive style is still developing. An important movement toward defining and measuring a single style construct, comprising one or more fundamental dimensions, helps to make sense of the many models considered in this review. The inescapable conclusion of this section is the recognition of one such dimension, the wholist-analytic continuum, which can be reconciled with other research in the area of individual differences and learning.

Models in the verbal-imagery dimension

A second fundamental dimension of cognitive style identified by Riding and Cheema (1991) was the verbal-imagery continuum, which comprises the principal modes for representing information. Furthermore, they argued that while individuals obviously have the capability to use either mode of representation, and will do so from time to time, there exists a marked tendency to consistently use one rather than the other, and this signifies in the individual a particular orientation or 'style'.

An interest in the mode or manner of thinking and knowing has involved a concern for imagery since early work by Galton (1883) and subsequent work of Bartlett (1932). Paivio's (1971) 'dual-coding theory' has provided the basis for further work investigating the nature of a verbaliser-imagery dimension in the cognitive process. Riding and Taylor (1976) argued that learning performance was affected by two basic sets of differences in the way knowledge was represented during thinking either using imagery, or verbally, using words.

Richardson (1994) described two measures of 'imaging differences', general and specific measures of vividness and control. Riding and Cheema (1991) identified several imagery questionnaires of imaginal abilities, all comprising self-reporting formats, which involved rating images with regard to quality. Some of the better known included:

- Betts Inventory (Betts 1909)
- Betts Inventory (Shortened Scale) (Sheehan 1967)
- Marks Vividness of Imagery Questionnaire (Marks 1973)
- Gordon Scale of Imagery Control (Gordon 1949)

Both Richardson (1994) and Riding and Cheema (1991) commented on the difficulty of measurement in this area. Indeed Richardson referred to Cattell's (1936) original list of variables likely to affect any attempt to measure individual differences, in a useful discussion of the subject (Richardson 1994: 13–14). Ernest (1977) reported that first, general difficulties with these measures included the lack of internal controls for response sets such as acquiescence and social desirability; second, they were difficult to validate, failing to show correlations with objective performance on tasks where good images would be helpful.

Riding and Cheema (1991) found only three key measures for assessing the verbaliser–imagery cognitive dimension:

- Individual Differences Questionnaire (Paivio 1971)
- Verbaliser-Visualiser Questionnaire (Richardson 1977)
- Verbal-Imagery Code Test (Riding and Calvey 1981)

These measures will be discussed in more detail as they relate to the construct of a verbal-imagery dimension of cognitive style.

Individual Differences Questionnaire (IDQ)

The work of Paivio (1971) was a significant development in this area of verbal-imagery and measurement, drawing upon the dual-coding theory to tap verbal abilities, habits and preferences, on the one hand, as well as imaginal habits, preferences and abilities, on the other.

Assessment

The IDQ is an 86 item test which purports to measure ways of thinking, using a true-false response format. In its original form it consisted of 47 items for assessing the strength of preference for processing information in the verbal mode, and 39 items for assessing the strength of preference for processing information in the imaginal mode. It is scored on a single dimension which reflect visual tendencies on a high score and verbal tendencies on a low score. Those respondents who scored in the middle range were deemed to own a mixed 'cognitive style' but were also perhaps capable of switching from one mode to the other, given the nature of the task required.

Empirical evidence

Riding and Cheema (1991) commented that the IDQ had not been widely used in research and evidence to support its validity was not available. Several studies looked at its reliability, and generally reported that the measure carried a moderate level of reliability (Richardson 1977; Irwin 1979; Paivio and Harshman 1983; Cohen and Saslona 1990).

Verbal-Visualiser Questionnaire (VVQ)

Richardson's (1977) work developed from an interest in brain hemisphericity and its relationship to lateral eye movement. Richardson (1994) explained how research into hemispheric specialisation had suggested that verbal or visual loaded questions triggered two separate sets of eye movement. The development of the VVQ was an attempt to combine the two research traditions and utilise the direction of gaze break as an indicator of brain hemispheric specialisation.

Assessment
The VVQ comprises a 15 item true-false self-reporting test, derived from Paivio's IDQ, and scored on a single dimension. Respondents who score highly indicate visual tendencies, those with low scores indicate verbal preferences in representing information.

Empirical evidence
As with the IDQ, Riding and Cheema (1991) reported that the VVQ had not been widely used in research and evidence to support its validity was not available. They explained, however, that while several studies looked at its reliability, the evidence for such is generally inconclusive. Richardson (1994: 35–7) provided further discussion of this model, and while citing additional studies using the measure, offered little evidence to support reliability. Indeed, he concluded that factor analysis showed that the test was not measuring only one dimension, and that stability of the VVQ 'is no more reassuring'. What emerges from Richardson's work is a well-presented case for the construct validity of the verbaliser-visualiser dimension and a stability associated with individual differences, in spite of a continuing difficulty in the measurement of these differences.

Verbal-imagery dimension of cognitive style

Riding and Cheema (1991) argued that most individuals are capable of using either a visual or verbal mode of representation, but that individuals will prefer to use one rather than the other. Riding and his co-workers developed two verbal-imagery tests: the Verbal-Imagery Code Test (VICT) (Riding and Calvey 1981) and the Verbal-Imagery Learning Style Test (VILST) (Riding et al. 1989).

Assessments
The VICT was in fact a development of an earlier test devised by Riding and Taylor (1976), which aimed at assessing the degree to which an individual relied upon the imagery mode of representation when completing a task. This test

required 7-year-old pupils to listen to ten short prose paragraphs, each of which was followed by a question. The questions required answers that were not provided in the paragraphs but, which could be 'read off' by the learner if an image had been generated by the information that had been read. For example, for the statements, 'Finally, Giacco saw a little house under a mulberry tree. He knocked at the door', the question was: 'What colour was the door?' The response time from the end of the question to the beginning of the answer was noted.

Riding and Taylor (1976) made the assumption that children who formed an image of the information during reception would answer quickly by supplying the answer to the question from the image, whereas those who did not form a clear image, or any image, would take longer to respond as they would have to search their lexical memory for suitable door colours. On their mean response times, Riding and Taylor divided the children into three groups – fast, moderate and slow responders. All three groups next listened to a concrete and an abstract prose passage, each followed by an immediate test of questioned recall. A significant interaction was found between response speed and passage type such that fast responders performed best on concrete passage whilst the slow responders excelled on the abstract passage, thus suggesting that fast responders are imagers and slow responders verbalisers. However, this approach did not directly assess verbal coding but only inferred it from slow imagery responses.

Riding and Calvey (1981) extended the Riding and Taylor test by including questions to assess verbal coding as well as imaginal coding. Furthermore, by obtaining the ratio of the response times to questions assessing the verbal and imagery performance, it was considered that an individuals verbal or imaginal coding preference could be detected. However, while the verbal-imagery code test was effective in demonstrating the existence of the verbal-imagery style (see Riding and Ashmore 1980; Riding and Dyer 1980; Riding and Calvey 1981), it was difficult to administer and time consuming to score.

To overcome difficulties in administration Riding *et al.* (1989) devised a computer-presented test of verbaliser-imager cognitive style. Basically, the test consists of the computer presentation of pairs of words. The individual has to decide whether the relationship between the first word presented and the second word belongs to the same category. The two categories are Same Group and Same Colour. There are 24 pairs of words in each category, and half of the items in each category are true, whilst the others are false. It is anticipated that imagers respond more quickly to the same colour category since they can readily generate images for the objects in question; while verbalisers will have a shorter response time for the Same Group category because of its verbal associations and which would be difficult to visualise. A ratio of response times gives an indication of an individual's position on the verbaliser-imager style continuum.

Further refinement of this work led to the development of the Cognitive Styles Analysis as an integrated measure of cognitive style (Riding 1991a).

Empirical evidence

A number of studies have been reported investigating the relationship between cognitive tasks and preference for representational mode (see Riding and Ashmore 1980; Riding and Dyer 1980; Riding and Calvey 1981). However, there is little evidence available to support the reliability of these tests over time.

The verbal-imagery dimension of cognitive style: an evaluation

The existence of a verbal-imagery dimension of cognitive style is supported by a number of studies which point to an interrelationship between individual preferences for modes of representation and other psychological structures and processes. The prevailing problem within the field of individual differences remains one of measurement. But this should not be allowed to lead to a confusion between construct validity and reliability. In the case of Riding's work, there exists a growing number of studies which report significant relationships between recorded behaviour and the visual-imagery dimension of style. In Richardson's work, a similar case is made for acknowledging the strong construct validity of the verbal-imagery continuum. Richardson stated that thought imagery 'is not an epiphenomenon but a genuine phenomenon that has psychologically significant consequences. These consequences define its adaptive functions' (Richardson 1991: 11).

In a similar light, the interrelationship between verbal and visual modes of representation and the construct of a cognitive style dimension infer considerable implications. What is required is

- the integration of the verbal-imagery continuum into a more fully developed construct of cognitive style
- the development of an objective measure of the verbal-imagery dimension.

Further work developing this measure is discussed in the next section, but a final word is left to Richardson (1994) who stated that support for the existence and significance of the visual mode of representation lay with noting its relationship to subsequent experiential, behavioural and physiological changes in the individual. He concluded that such evidence exists, and suggests that relatively stable differences in preference for representing knowledge in visual or other form also occur in the individual.

A model integrating the wholist-analytic and verbal-imagery dimensions

Cognitive Styles Analysis (CSA)

The identification of distinct families of cognitive style, the wholist-analytic and verbal-imagery, leads naturally to the need for a satisfactory and efficient means of assessing both dimensions of style. This section will describe the development of an instrument designed to do this – the Cognitive Styles Analysis (CSA).

The aim in this work was to overcome assessment problems associated with the GEFT, as well as the traditional self-report rating scales used to assess imagery performance. Riding and Cheema (1991) pointed out that a fundamental weakness of most measures of style was that they assessed positively only one end of a dimension. For example, on the GEFT, a high score indicated field-independence. An individual obtaining a low score was assumed to be the reverse, that is, field-dependent. However, the score could be attributable to several factors, such as low motivation, inability to follow the instructions or even a visual defect. This deficiency may have been responsible for causing field-dependence–independence to be related to intelligence, and may certainly explain why field-independents usually do best on many types of tasks.

The tests assessing mental representation typically used introspective self-report formats, carrying limitations in design. For example, individuals completing the task might not have really known what they think as they responded to a question, or alternatively may have given the researcher what they thought was the desired response.

Assessment

The development of the CSA marked an attempt to integrate a theory of cognitive style into a single construct (Riding 1991a). The instrument reflected previous research in cognitive functioning related to learning performance in a variety of learning tasks (Riding and Taylor 1976; Riding and Ashmore 1980; Riding and Dyer 1980; Riding and Calvey 1981; Riding et al. 1989; Riding and Buckle 1990). The CSA was devised as a computer-presented assessment to measure the two dimensions of cognitive style. Riding and Cheema (1991) explained that these two dimensions of style were independent, and consisted of

- the wholist-analytic dimension – which reflected the way in which an individual would organise information, either in parts or as a whole;
- the verbal-imagery style dimension – which reflected the way in which an individual would represent knowledge, in mental pictures or in words.

The CSA directly assesses both ends of the wholist-analytic and verbal-imagery dimensions, and comprises three sub-tests. The first assesses the verbal-imagery dimension by presenting statements one at a time to be judged true or false. Half of the statements contain information about conceptual categories, while the rest describe the appearance of items. Half of the statements of each type are true. It was assumed that imagers would respond more quickly to the appearance statements, because the objects could be readily represented as mental pictures and the information for the comparison could be obtained directly and rapidly from these images.

In the case of the conceptual category items, it was assumed that verbalisers would have a shorter response time because the semantic conceptual category membership is verbally abstract in nature and cannot be represented in visual form. The computer records the response time to each statement and calculates the verbal-imagery ratio. A low ratio corresponds to a verbaliser and a high ratio to an imager, with the intermediate position being described as bimodal. It may be noted that in this approach individuals have to read both the verbal and the imagery items so that reading ability and reading speed are controlled for.

The second two sub-tests assess the wholist-analytic dimension. The first of these presents items containing pairs of complex geometrical figures which the individual is required to judge either the same or different. Since this task involves judgements about the overall similarity of the two figures, it was assumed that a relatively fast response to this task would be possible by wholists. The second presents items each comprising a simple geometrical shape (e.g. a square or a triangle) and a complex geometrical figure, and the individual is asked to indicate whether or not the simple shape is contained in the complex one by pressing one of the two marked response keys.

This task requires a degree of disembedding of the simple shape within the complex geometrical figure in order to establish that it is the same as the stimulus simple shape displayed, and it was assumed that analytics would be relatively quicker at this. Again the computer records the response times, and calculates the wholist-analytic ratio. A low ratio corresponds to a wholist and a high ratio to an analytic. Ratios between these positions are labelled 'Intermediate'.

In doing the sub-tests the testees are not made aware that the assessment uses response time, because the intention is that they undertake the tasks in a relaxed way that reflects their usual manner of processing information. Since ratios are used overall response speed does not influence the style result. The background to the development of the CSA is given in Riding and Cheema (1991).

Each of the cognitive style dimensions is a continuum, and labels are attached to ranges on a dimension only for descriptive convenience. The dimensions are independent of one another, in so much as position on one dimension does not influence position on the other. Cognitive style has been found to affect a wide range of behaviours, and this evidence for its construct validity has been considered by Riding (1997).

The CSA provides a simple, quick and convenient means of assessing an individual's position on the two fundamental cognitive style dimensions (see Riding, 1991b). The instrument has several advantages:

- It is an objective test, as defined by Cattell and Warburton (1967), since it is objectively scored and its method of assessment is not obviously apparent to those being assessed. It is consequently difficult for those taking the test to contrive their results.
- It positively assesses both ends of the style dimension. This is important, since otherwise it could be objected that the assessment is simply of ability and not of style.
- Since it does not contain questionnaire-type items, or difficult language, it can be used with a wide age range from children to adults.
- It is context free, and can be used in a wide range of situations, such as, for instance, schools, industry, and the health service.
- It is probably culture free in nature, and it has been used in a number of countries.[2]

Empirical evidence

A number of studies have been reported utilising the CSA in a variety of investigations exploring the educational effects of the construct upon aspects of individual differences in the learning context. Riding (1997) has provided a summary of these studies as they related to the general construct of cognitive style, and this summary is amplified in Part 2. The CSA, in summary, is a computerised measure which reveals an individual's tendency to think visually or verbally, and to process information wholistically or analytically (Riding 1991a, 1994).

Implications of the model

An important implication of this construct is reflected in its deliberate intention to integrate fundamental elements of style theory. This, more recently, has been extended to include the aim of developing a learning style model which would have application in the field of education, whether it be school and teaching or workplace and training (see Riding and Rayner 1995).

---

2 The Cognitive Styles Analysis is available in various languages: English versions for the UK, North American and Australasian contexts, and also in Arabic, Dutch, French, German, Malay, and Spanish. Other language versions are in preparation.

The wider implications of the model for education reflect the several principles and processes enunciated by various workers in the field of cognitive style and learning style. There is likely to be a similar implication for the workplace, not only in terms of education, but also for management practice and organisational psychology.

A final evaluation

Vernon (1963) provided an early critique of cognitive style, tracing its development from work carried out by German Gestalt psychologists. She explained that subsequent work on style flowed from a 'considerable number of experiments . . . devoted to studying individual differences in perception' (Vernon 1963: 221). Vernon, generally, was critical of style development in the psychology of perception, pointing to a serious problem with the style construct, which many writers subsequently have repeated. She commented that cognitive style had largely evolved from theories generalised on single experiments and little empirical evidence. The result was one of problematic validity, reliability and generalisation for the style construct. Indeed, the difficulty has led some writers to reject the style construct in cognitive psychology as a 'chimera' or illusion or, at best, a construct which is impossible to operationalise and therefore undeserving of further research (Freedman and Stumpf 1980; Tiedemann 1989). Further, there has been a reliance upon subjective data, usually elicited using self-report formats. Tiedemann (1989: 272–3) understandably criticised this practice, and declared that most style models merely reflect 'behaviour correlates of different performance dimensions'. He commented that 'my personal opinion of the state of research into cognitive styles has to be: there is no point in chasing a chimera!'. The most critical educationalists suggest style is, at best, irrelevant, but at worst dangerously misguided, in any application to the learning context. Those educationalists with an interest in style regard it as an underdeveloped aspect of teaching and learning which may be the key to greatly enhancing levels of individual performance.

This gives a picture of style similar to vaguely discerned objects in a fog, where the individual stumbling though the mist thinks that there are features ahead but cannot make them out. There are, however, signs that the fog is lifting, driven away by three systematic developments.

The first of these has been more recent work on cognitive style in the attempt to clarify a coherent theory of cognitive style (Curry 1987, 1991; Miller 1987; Riding and Cheema 1991; Grigerenko and Sternberg 1995). A second important step forward has been the gathering of evidence to support the construct of cognitive style by means of empirical research which shows a relationship between these models, cognitive style and individual learning behaviour. In conjunction with this has been the important step in the collection of objective data which moves beyond emphasis on subjective self-report.

A third movement has been evidence of a growing desire to apply the theory in a variety of professional contexts. Such a development has involved the search for style constructs tied to a specific test, forming the basis for an application of cognitive style in the workplace. Indeed, it is perhaps the latter trend which has contributed to the emergence of the learning-centred tradition of style theory.

CHAPTER 3

Learning styles

Chapter overview

This chapter presents a critical review of selected models of learning style associated with a learning-centred tradition.

The learning-centred approach

It is possible to distinguish between models from the cognitive-centred approach described in Chapter 2 and those which emphasise the learning process – the learning-centred approach – which will be considered in this chapter. A recategorisation of these models is proposed.

Learning style models

The models are arranged in four groups, and for each model there is a consideration of the rationale for the construct, the instrument associated with the model, and the evidence to support it. The model groupings are:

- Style models based on the learning process
- Style models grounded in orientation to study
- Style models based on instructional-preference
- Style models based on cognitive skills

An evaluation of the models

The chapter concludes with a summary evaluation identifying which models may help in developing a better understanding of the relationship between cognitive style and learning strategies.

The learning-centred approach

An activity-centred approach to style

A survey of 'theories of style' conducted by Grigerenko and Sternberg (1995: 218) identified an 'activity-centred approach' as a distinct tradition of 'style-based work in psychology'. This approach was described as a separate development from earlier work carried out by researchers looking at cognitive style. The 'activity-centred' tradition is reported as dating back to the 1970s and was associated with educationists addressing the environment in which the learning takes place, and process-based issues related to meeting individual differences in the classroom. Grigerenko and Sternberg explained that

> At that time, educators and school psychologists found themselves caught between a theoretical understanding of individual differences and the practical problem of dealing with such differences in their schools and classroom.
>
> (Grigerenko and Sternberg 1995: 218)

This difficulty led to frustration and disappointment with constructs of intelligence and ability, and an increasing interest in the learner's interaction with the learning context. The focus, then, moved more emphatically towards a categorisation of style according to an individual's 'active' response to the learning task. It is, at this point, perhaps more helpful to call this tradition a 'learning-centred approach', to emphasise the educational and training perspective shared by researchers contributing to the field. Their first concern has always remained the development of learning style as a basis for improving pedagogical practice.

The learning-centred tradition of 'style' is arguably distinguished by five major features:

- a focus on the learning process – specifically, aspects of this process which relate to individual differences as the person interacts with their environment
- a primary interest in the impact of individual differences upon pedagogy
- the aim of developing new constructs and concepts of learning style
- the enhancement of learning achievement
- the construction of an assessment instrument as a foundation for the exposition of theory.

The learning context remains the first and prime concern for educationists working within the learning-centred tradition. However, it is important to think, more carefully, about learning strategy and what is meant by the term 'learning style'. It is also worth reflecting upon how the notion of an individual's personal psychology can help in the development of successful teaching or training and learning. After all, such an evaluation should arguably be the ultimate 'test' for a theory of learning. The learning-centred approach, quite obviously concerned with this question, reflected an ongoing attempt to provide an activity-centred understanding of the processes of pedagogy.

Learning style constructs and their recategorisation

As is the case with of the cognitive style tradition, there is a need to rationalise the contemporary theory of learning styles (Rayner and Riding 1997). Key models which may be regarded as commanding a significant place in the learning-centred tradition are listed in Table 3.1. The selection of models has been made after a lengthy review of the literature and a consideration of the justification underpinning each style construct. The table is organised into three style groups on the basis of similarities in the following: psychometric design; concept-ualisation of learning; and a relationship to the formation of learning strategy.

To avoid further confusion, the descriptor 'learning style' is retained. It should be remembered that, when used more exactly or precisely, the term 'learning style' should be understood to refer to an individual set of differences that include not only a stated personal preference for instruction or an association with a particular form of learning activity but also individual differences found in intellectual or personal psychology.

The classification that follows is divided into the following groups of style models based upon

- the learning process – based on experiential learning
- the learning process – based on orientation to study
- instructional-preference
- cognitive skills and learning strategy development.

The first three groups of style construct are generally concerned with the process of learning and its context. They are characterised by a specific focus on individual differences in the process of learning rather than within the individual learner. This movement towards concern for the learning process reflects a definition of individual differences in learning suggested by Bloom (1976). The style of the learner is distinguished by relating an 'ability' or 'tendency' to learn in a particular way. In Kolb's (1984) construct, for example, there is a framework drawn from a theory of experiential learning, or again, in Entwistle and Ramsden's (1983) case, with a framework drawn from information-processing theory and an orientation to the task of academic study (see Pask 1972). The fourth group of learning style constructs is more concerned with an individual's developing cognitive ability and repertoire of cognitive skills and ability to learn, together with related behavioural characteristics which are understood to form an individual's learning profile.

The learning process models have several limitations if each is to be regarded as a measure of learning style. First, they reflect a construct that is by definition not stable because it is grounded in process and is therefore susceptible to rapid change. Second, they do not describe a developmental rationale for the concept of learning style nor easily correspond to other models of assessment, thereby suggesting a problem for conceptual validity. Third, they have attracted a good deal of criticism for lacking psychometric rigour and a systematically developed theory supported by empirical evidence (Grigerenko and Sternberg 1995). However, the tradition reflects a continuing need for a theory of individual differences which can be used in the learning context.

The purpose of a recategorisation of these models of learning style has been in the first instance to attempt a rationalisation of learning style. A plethora of learning style models has had the effect of inhibiting the development or application of learning style in the field of education. A synthesis of theory, while highly desirable, is not easily achieved. Yet it remains imperative, as Curry has rightly emphasised when she stated that 'it would be unwise to utilise an instrument that is measuring constructs at one level if the purpose is to predict behaviour governed by another level.' (Curry, 1990: 17).

To sum up – there is an urgent need to move forward with the conceptualisation and utilisation of learning style theory. The basis for such a development must be a consideration of the construct validity of individual models of learning style. This should form part of a broader attempt to develop an integrated approach to individual differences in learning. For such an approach to succeed, a recategorisation of contemporary models of learning style should lead to a clearer definition and assessment of learning style.

Learning style models

Style models based on the learning process

There are several learning style models included in this section, all of which are regarded by the authors as 'process-based' constructs, but it should be acknowledged that the selection is by no means comprehensive. The authors have made the selection on the basis that the model has

- made a significant contribution to the historical development of learning style

Table 3.1 Models and key features of learning styles

Dimension	Description	References
Style models based on the learning process		
Concrete experience/ reflective observation/ abstract conceptualisation/ active experimentation	A two-dimensional model comprising perception (concrete/abstract thinking) and processing (active/reflective information processing).	Kolb (1976)
Activist/ theorist/ pragmatist/ reflector learners	Preferred modes of learning which shape an individual approach to learning.	Honey and Mumford (1986, 1992)
Style models grounded in orientation to study		
Meaning orientation/ reproducing orientation/ achieving orientation/holistic orientation; later developed to include deep, strategic, surface, lack of direction, academic self-confidence	An integration of instructional preference to information processing in the learner's approach to study.	Entwistle (1979); Entwistle and Tait (1994)
Surface-deep-achieving orientation/ intrinsic-extrinsic-achievement orientation	An integration of approaches to study with motivational orientation.	Biggs (1978, 1985)
Synthesis-analysis/ elaborative processing/ fact retention/study methods	The quality of thinking which occurs during learning relates to the distinctiveness, transferability, and durability of memory and fact retention.	Schmeck *et al.* (1977)
Style models based on instructional preference		
Environmental/ sociological/ emotional/ physical/ psychological elements	The learner's response to key stimuli: environmental (light, heat); sociological (peers pairs, adults, self); emotional (structure, persistence, motivation); physical (auditory, visual, tactile); psychological (global-analytic, impulsive-reflective).	Price *et al* (1976, 1977); Dunn *et al* (1989)
Participant-avoidant/ collaborative-competitive/ independent-dependent	A social interaction measure which has been used to develop three bipolar dimensions in a construct which describes a learner's typical approach to the learning situation.	Grasha and Riechmann (1975)
Style models based on cognitive skills development		
Visualisation/ verbal symbols/ sounds/emotional feelings	Learning style defined in terms of perceptual modality.	Reinert (1976)
Field-dependency/ scanning-focusing/breadth of categorisation/cognitive complexity/ reflective–impulsivity/ levelling–sharpening/ tolerant–intolerant	A cognitive profile of three types of learners reflecting their position in a bi-polar analytic-global continuum which reflects an individual's cognitive skills development.	Letteri (1980)
Cognitive skills/ perceptual responses/ study and instructional preferences	Identifies 24 elements in a learning style construct grouped together into 3 dimensions. The model presupposes that cognitive skills development is a prerequisite for effective learning.	Keefe and Monk (1986); Keefe (1989a, 1989b, 1990)

- been supported by empirical studies and psychometric evaluation
- been or is considered relevant to a further development of the learning style construct.

Learning Style Inventory (LSI)

Learning style is described by Kolb (1976) as the individual's preferred method for assimilating information, principally as an integral part of an active learning cycle. This is grounded in a more elaborate theory of experiential learning. The experiential learning cycle involves several key propositions that learning

- is best conceived as a process and ideas are formed and re-formed through experience
- is a process grounded in experience
- as a process requires the resolution of conflicts between dialectically opposed modes of adaptation to the world
- is a holistic process of adaptation to the world
- involves transactions between the individual and the environment
- is the process of creating knowledge.

Kolb remarked that 'Learning is the process whereby knowledge is created through the transformation of experience.' (Kolb 1984: 38)

He identified four adaptive learning modes, extrapolated from his model of experiential learning: concrete experience (CE); reflective observation (RO); abstract conceptualisation (AC); and active experimentation (AE). Each of these learning modes was seen to possess unique learning characteristics – for example, abstract learners comprehended information conceptually and symbolically, whereas concrete learners responded primarily to kinaesthetic qualities of the immediate experience. Active learners learned primarily by manipulating the environment, while reflective individuals typically learned by introspection and internal reflection on the external world.

Kolb's learning style construct consists of two dimensions – perceiving and processing; the first describes concrete and abstract thinking; the second an active or reflective information-processing activity. This construct mirrors the continua described in Kolb's model of experiential learning. The two dimensions are integrated to form a structure describing the following four types of learning style where learners typically perceive information:

- *diverger* – concretely and process it reflectively and they need to be personally engaged in the learning activity;
- *converger* – abstractly and process it reflectively and they need to follow detailed, sequential steps in thinking in a learning activity;
- *assimilator* – abstractly and process it actively and they need to be involved in pragmatic problem-solving in a learning activity;

• *accommodator* – concretely and process it actively and they need to be involved in risk-taking, making changes experimentation and flexibility in a learning activity.

The rationale for this approach to style was that an individual possesses a number of strengths and weaknesses which will vary according to the nature of the learning task and the knowledge they hope to acquire. Given the fact that experiential learning forms the conceptual context for Kolb's theory, it is not surprising that he attaches great importance to identifying individual differences in the learning process and uses this as a basis for extrapolating individual learning style.

Kolb's theory of learning embraces the notion of an individual progressing through several life stages in 'human growth', during which an improving balance or synthesis of style-based learning is deliberately refined. This schema resembles other models of humanistic psychology in which a motive for self-actualisation is presumed (Maslow 1970). Kolb argued that

> Individuals shaped by social, educational and organisational forces develop increased competence in a specialised mode of adaptation that enables them to master the particular life tasks they encounter in their chosen career path.
>
> (Kolb 1977: 7)

It is inferred, generally, that individuals will naturally seek to 'grow' as they 'learn', which will involve a process of developing and maturing their 'learning style'.

A profile of each style, listing respective strengths and weaknesses, mostly involves reference to abilities or tendencies to 'learn' in a specific manner is shown in Table 3.2. It is important to remember that Kolb believed that, while an individual will have a tendency to learn in a particular way – for example, 'divergently' – this will occur as part of a larger process of personal growth. The developmental nature of this personal growth means that the individual is continuously moving through the experience of learning, enabling a more flexible interchange of learning style. It is therefore crucial to an understanding of Kolb's construct that we accept his theoretical description of the learning process. This means accepting the notion of an individual ultimately learning to use each learning style, or a combination of each learning style, to cope with the learning task.

Learning styles, as described by Kolb, appear to be construed as an individual's preferred method of 'learning'. Interestingly, Kolb's model appears to presuppose a mix of 'hard-wiring' and 'soft-wiring' in an individual's learning approach, but lends greatest emphasis to a developmental view of learning ability and styles. The model therefore reflects a set of less stable individual differences which can change over time. As previously stated, this is

Table 3.2 Learning style characteristics and the LSI

Diverger	Assimilator	Converger	Accommodator
summarises well	abstract thinker	good problem-solver	action-orientated
synthesises well	reasons inductively	decisive, pragmatic	inquisitive, intuitive
empathetic	synthesises well	rational, analytic	target-seeker
imaginative	enjoys theorising	systematic, organised	opportunity-seeker
intuitive	values understanding	leads well, focused	adaptive, flexible
flexible	generates multiple perspectives	reasons inductively	pragmatic, risk-taker
sociable	analytic, logical, systematic	discriminates well	spontaneous, committed
values understanding	good organiser	task-orientated	open-minded
enjoys discovery	enjoys numbers	enjoys technical issues	leads well, sociable
generates ideas	enjoys design	thinks laterally	good organiser
non-systematic	enjoys concrete tasks	enjoys experimentation	'concrete' thinker
indecisive	not action-orientated	narrow focus/ closed mind	impulsive, experimenter
irrational, emotional	less sociable	less empathy/ intuition	a-theoretical
illogical, spontaneous	indecisive	unimaginative	person-dependent
non-mechanical	non-mechanical	a-theoretical	little analytical ability
non-theoretical	passive learner	imprecise thinker	non-systematic

perhaps not surprising, given Kolb's primary interest in experiential learning and process-bound theory of learning.

Assessment

The original LSI is a nine item self-reporting questionnaire which forces the respondent to rank four words in each item, thereby revealing a specific preference for the identified modes of learning. Two scores are calculated, reflecting positions along each of the learning style dimensions: the first is the abstract conceptualisation–concrete experience continuum, which shows the degree to which the individual's style is biased toward abstraction or concreteness; the second continuum, reflective observation–active experimentation, shows the degree to which the individual's style is biased toward reflection or activity. A revised edition of the inventory has been produced, containing twelve items, aimed at improving reliability and construct validity (Kolb 1985).

Empirical evidence for the LSI

Several studies have criticised the psychometric properties of the LSI, alleging low levels of reliability and little correlation with other indicators or models of learning style. Freedman and Stumpf (1980, 1981) were particularly pessimistic about the value of 'learning style' for educators, and reported that the LSI loaded only on two of the bipolar dimensions, and only with extremely low factor loadings. Sims *et al.* (1986) rejected the LSI as an assessment tool, criticising its lack of reliability or validity. Cornwell *et al.* (1991) reported a study of over 300 subjects which found support for only two of the individual ability dimensions in Kolb's theory and little support for the two bipolar dimensions measured by the LSI.

Newstead (1992) in a comparative study of the LSI with Entwistle's *Approaches to Studying Inventory* also criticised the LSI as relatively unreliable, with an underlying factor structure which did not correspond as predicted.

Further doubt about the psychometric soundness of the LSI was raised by Atkinson (1988) who reported the failure of attempts to strengthen psychometric properties of the LSI, which also resulted in a weakening of its test/re-test reliability. Veres *et al.* (1991), on the other hand, found an increased stability in the modified version of the LSI and argued for the utility of the instrument in the study of learning style. Finally, Tennant (1988) questioned the validity of the experiential learning cycle while acknowledging its usefulness as a pedagogical framework. Tennant warned against a wholesale acceptance of Kolb's learning style, which he described as misleading, because of its focus upon the learning process and not 'individual differences' in the learner. De Ciantis and Kirton (1996) also criticised the model for 'conflating style evaluation and learning process' and argued for the need to maintain a separation of level, style and process.

Learning Styles Questionnaire (LSQ)

Kolb's model has attracted considerable interest since the mid-1970s and has influenced the development of several 'new' models of learning style. Honey and Mumford's (1992) model was representative of work replicating Kolb's theory while attempting to develop learning style theory in a commercial context. The pencil and paper LSQ (Honey and Mumford 1986) was an attempt at a practical application of learning style theory in the management of the workplace. The questionnaire was used to explore the implications for management of a four-fold style model consisting of the following types of learner who would as

- activists – enjoy new experiences, engaging in activity, intuitive decision-making and group-work, but who disliked administration or the implementation of procedure
- theorists – focus on ideas, logic, generalisations and systematic planning, but who mistrusted intuitive insight or social/emotional involvement
- pragmatists – enjoy group-work, discussion, debate, risk-taking and practical applications which got results, but who avoided reflection, observation and levels of deeper understanding
- reflectors – focus on understanding meaning, observing and describing process or predicting outcome, and who were concerned with the 'what is' rather than the 'how' in any directed activity.

Honey and Mumford (1992) argued that an individual naturally relied upon one of these learning modes in their approach to learning and task activity. They stated that learning design and individual performance in the decision-making process should attempt to maximise the benefit gained from style awareness. This could be achieved by creating both a mix and match of style to learning activity. While matching styles to learning task was presumed to enhance learning, controlled style mismatching was expected to stimulate style growth. Mismatching learning styles and activity was also seen as a way to 'energise' team-work. This was important for both improving an individual's performance and group productivity.

The optimum learning or training programme enabled workers to adopt appropriate learning styles for specific tasks or situations (Honey and Mumford 1992). As with Kolb, styles are regarded as types of activities reflecting individual differences in the learning process. Learners are subsequently 'associated' with preferring one or more kinds of activities. Honey and Mumford (1986, 1992) described several applications of the LSQ in management situations, involving the organisation of workshops, project teams and improving work-related performance.

Assessment

The LSQ originally consisted of a 63 item questionnaire which was later extended to 80 items, using a single forced response pattern, aimed at eliciting a respondent's preferred learning style. Learning style is defined as a set of learning habits which the measure will reveal, thereby enabling individuals to determine positive and appropriate learning experiences. The LSQ results are interpreted using a set of norm-referenced tables, and identify the preferred learning style of the respondent, who will be seen as an *activist, reflector, theorist* or *pragmatist*.

Empirical evidence for the LSQ

Allinson and Hayes (1988) and Hayes and Allinson (1988) reported a factor analysis of the LSQ which identified two factors accounting for over 70 per cent of the variance: the first was analysis; the second was action. However, Allinson and Hayes (1988) urged caution in accepting the general utility and predictive validity of the LSQ. A similar criticism was made by Presland (1994) who argued that more evidence was required to support the predictive validity of the instrument. Sadler-Smith and Riding (a) reported a factor analysis of the LSQ and stated that its factor structure remained unconfirmed.

Allinson and Hayes (1990), however, have argued that the LSQ is preferable to the LSI as a style construct, because it has accurately distinguished two related dimensions of cognitive style – that is, the dimensions of 'analysis' and 'action' or 'doing'. They suggested that the instrument has some diagnostic capabilities in terms of these specific style dimensions. However, their concluding commentary suggested that the LSQ construct should not be uncritically accepted as a model of learning style. Furnham (1995: 407) related Eysenck's personality traits to this measure of learning style and reported many predicted correlations, particularly between extraversion and the activist (r = 0.52), converger (r = 0.33) and accommodator (r = 0.33) learning styles). Furnham (1995: 407) remains unconvinced, however, about what he described as the 'all important question of face and predictive validity of the LSQ'.

Style models grounded in orientation to study

Curry (1987) and Grigerenko and Sternberg (1995) have commented on the close relationship between a group of psychologists, including Entwistle (1979), Schmeck *et al.* (1977) and Ramsden (1979) who were interested in learning processes and learning style. The group was initially influenced by work which looked at information-processing undertaken by the learner in a learning situation (Craik and Lockhart 1972; Marton 1976; Marton and Saljo 1976).

Approaches to Study Inventory (ASI)

Entwistle (1979, 1981), who was initially interested in the duality of levels of processing in an approach to learning, found that this reflected either a surface or deep engagement with the study task. The approach was supported by the thinking of Ausubel and Robinson (1966), who identified two principal types of learning, passive versus active and rote versus meaningful.

Entwistle's work can be seen as an attempt to link instructional preference to information processing. He developed a model of learning 'style' which consisted of four aspects: meaning orientation, reproducing orientation, achieving orientation and holistic orientation (Entwistle 1981). As part of this model of learning style, Entwistle developed an integrated conception of the learning process, which described a series of learner actions linked to specific learning strategies identified in his original model.

Thus, a student engaged in 'reproductive learning', characterised by 'extrinsic motivation', would adopt a style called 'surface approach'. The learner would be expected to realise a learning outcome consisting of 'surface level understanding' (Entwistle 1979, 1981). Each of these stages or approaches reflects a range of cognitive controls running from deep to surface 'thinking' in the individual student's response to the learning task. Further refinement of this approach attempted to identify specific style features which characterised the 'learning interface'. The aim in this work was to provide formative assessment which teachers might use to enhance the pattern of study required of students in their class (Ramsden 1979, 1988). Entwistle and Ramsden collaborated to produce a revised version of their approach to student learning (Entwistle and Ramsden 1983).

The primary focus in Entwistle's account of 'learning style' was the development of an empirical model of the processes underlying individual orientation in a general approach to learning. He explained that an approach had both a referential and a relational component: the referential component referred to the student's intention when tackling a learning task. Entwistle was interested in whether the student was focused upon meaning or upon the structure of the task. The relational component referred to both the student's 'cognitive approach' and the learning 'process'. Entwistle was interested in whether the student was attempting either a deep, holistic approach or a surface, atomistic approach.

Entwistle stated that 'This definition of approach makes it clear that approaches, as originally defined by Marton (1976) are both context dependent and student dependent' (Entwistle 1988: 212).

The notion of a person-situational basis to learning strategy formation is fundamental in Entwistle's explanation of learning orientation. Schmeck (1988b) presented a clear case for learning strategies both reflecting this axiom and representing a structure for the dynamic created during the learning process. This point is important for an understanding of how cognitive style interacts with the learning demand to produce the formation of learning strategies. The nature of this process is a pattern of learning behaviour which we can identify as an individual's learning style.

Assessment

Entwistle (1979) further refined work carried out by Pask (1976), Marton (1976) and Biggs (1979). His model of an approach to learning comprised the aspects shown in Table 3.3.

Table 3.3 Aspects of an approach to studying

• achieving	• reproducing	• meaning
• comprehension learning	• operations learning	• versatile approach
• learning pathologies	• prediction of success	

The ASI was developed by Entwistle and colleagues over a period of years and is available in several forms. One version is a 30 item inventory designed to tap into a number of dimensions of study attitudes and behaviour (Entwistle 1979), yielding scores representing the eight dimensions previously described. Entwistle (1981) subsequently published a shortened version that measured 'deep and surface approaches' to learning as well as comprehension learning, operation learning and learning pathologies. A further version of the ASI was published by Entwistle and Ramsden (1983) and comprised 64 items and extended to include a measurement of a deep versatile approach to learning.

Subsequently, Entwistle and Tait (1994) developed this approach to produce the 'revised' Approaches to Studying Inventory. This 38 item instrument included a number of aspects to the student's orientation to study which were: deep, surface, strategic, lack of direction and academic self-confidence.

Empirical evidence for the ASI

The ASI has a considerable number of studies giving supporting evidence for its validity and reliability as a construct and a measurement. It is perhaps fair to say that Entwistle's work has involved a depth of empirical support not so immediately obvious for many models of learning style found in the literature. Curry (1987) reported detailed evidence including high levels of internal and temporal reliability and good levels of validity. Newstead (1992) in a comparative analysis of the ASI and Kolb's LSI, used the shorter version of the ASI in his study, which he claimed carried several advantages as a research tool. He also discovered moderate levels of reliability and found that predicted factors within the measure emerged during data analysis confirming the measure's predictive validity.

Other significant studies offering support for the ASI include Harper and Kember (1989), Richardson (1990) and Sadler-Smith (1996). Sadler-Smith (1996: 377) reported that the ASI had 'demonstrated clearly and consistently a robust factor structure both at item and scale level'. Further support for the validity of this construct can be found in Jonnassen and Grabowski's (1993) account of its development as an empirical model of the processes underlying serialist/holist/versatile learning.

Study Process Questionnaire (SPQ)

Biggs (1978, 1979, 1985, 1987), building upon research interests in the same field of study, further extended Entwistle's work by discovering three second-order motivational factors to develop a new measure of learning strategy. He was primarily interested in the interaction between motivation and cognitive processes underlying an approach to learning. Curry (1987) described these features as motive-strategy dimensions involving a 'surface', 'deep' and 'achieving orientation'. Jonassen and Grabowski (1993) described Biggs' work as an extension to Entwistle's operationalisation of the holist-serialist theory of cognitive style. Biggs took previously identified surface and deep processing activities and widened them to include motivational factors, which were labelled: *intrinsic, extrinsic and achievement orientation*. Entwistle subsequently developed an empirical model of these processes identified as underlying serialist-holist-versatile learning (Entwistle 1981).

Biggs continued his work investigating the relationships between learning outcomes, the formation of learning strategy and the cognitive structures apparent in the learning context. The interaction taking place between person and context was viewed as involving a specific process called 'meta-learning', which Biggs (1985: 185) explained was a 'sophisticated kind of metacognition'. Biggs used this term to refer to a person's awareness of his or her own learning method and approach. Biggs went on to claim that,

> Ability patterns, locus of control, variety and quality of certain non-school experiences, and extent and kind of motivation all seem to be involved in the development of meta-learning capability.
>
> (Biggs 1985: 185)

Interest in the learning context, and the way in which the teacher might influence the nature of the person-context interaction, was also applied to a subject-specific context (Biggs 1988). He suggested the existence of two domains of cognitive processes – cognitive skills and cognitive strategies (style) – and explored the way in which both contribute to the learning task of writing an assignment essay, described as the 'most typical of academic tasks'. Again, much emphasis was given to the basic process of meta-cognition and Biggs' own conceptualisation, 'meta-learning'. The latter was identified as a key element in the development of a successful approach to learning.

Assessment

The SPQ (Biggs 1987) is a 42 item, self-report questionnaire that purports to measure the extent to which students endorse different approaches to learning by identifying the motives and strategies which comprise these approaches. Items are rated on a five-point Likert scale, in response to statements about the student's usual approaches to studying. Three scores on an 'approach to studying' scale are produced, surface, deep and achieving, and an additional 'deep-surface' score is compiled from the sum of deep and achieving scale scores. There are in total ten scores, and the results can be used to create six student profiles: deep, achieving, deep-achieving, surface-achieving, surface and low-achieving. The basic rationale for this instrument rests with the conception of a student's approach to study being seen as a function both of a motive and a strategy.

A student's motive was perceived to be extrinsic or instrumental (surface), intrinsic (deep), or achievement (achieving) orientated. A student's motive, Biggs argued, would influence the choice of strategy used to complete the learning task. Surface strategies will usually involve the reproduction of information through rote-learning; deep strategies would entail understanding concepts and the meaning of content; achieving strategies would determine the student's use of time management and related study method.

Empirical evidence for the SPQ

Christensen *et al.* (1991) criticised the SPQ for inconsistent factor loadings and low internal reliability of the Surface Approach Scale, while they found that the Deep and Achieving Scales demonstrated an acceptable level of internal consistency. Curry (1987) reported that the SPQ was supported by evidence of good reliability and fair validity, although no data was given to support the predictive validity of the instrument. Correlations with self-related performance and school performance formed the basis for Curry's conclusion.

Murray-Harvey (1994) leant support to this instrument while noting some criticism of inconsistent factor loadings and low internal reliability. She pointed to Biggs' own dismissal of the appropriateness of test-retest reliability as an index of reliability for the construct, while adding that, ironically, over time and situation, the measure had proven relatively stable. She concluded that the SPQ supported Biggs' general contention that while students might change their motives and strategies for learning, they do remain fairly stable indicators of a general approach to learning.

Inventory of Learning Processes (ILP)

Schmeck *et al.* (1977) elaborated a theory of learning which focused on the notion of quality in thinking. The quality of thinking, they argued, affected the distinctiveness, transferability and durability of memories that resulted from the learning event (Schmeck 1988b). A key factor impinging upon the quality of learning, was the way in which an individual actually tackled the task of learning. Schmeck suggested that learning style represented a predisposition on the part of the learner to adopt a particular strategy regardless of the specific demands of the learning task. Learning strategies were subsequently perceived as a generalised pattern of information-processing activities that the individual used in preparation for utilising the memory. The range of strategies was conceived as forming a continuum – on the one hand, consisting of shallow, repetitive and reiterative processes; on the other, extreme, deep and elaborative processing.

As the depth of the processing increased, Schmeck argued, so too did the number of conceptual associations and therefore levels of meaning processed by the learner. De Bello (1985b) explained that accepting this idea of a processing continuum presumed a range of processes used by the elaborative learner. An individual, for example, might switch from strategy to strategy, to classify, compare, contrast, analyse, and synthesise information. This process would also lead progressively to an improving performance as learner adaptability also increased.

Schmeck *et al.* (1977) originally developed the ILP which consisted of four dimension sub-scales comprising synthesis-analysis, elaborative processing, fact retention and study methods. Schmeck was later to qualify his use of the term 'style', arguing that his focus was primarily on 'strategy' or 'orientation', and that learning style should be regarded as a more stable set of individual differences in the learner, perhaps more properly referred to as cognitive style.

Further development of this approach to the study of learning processes was reported by Schmeck *et al.* (1991). They provided a historical account of the development of the ILS, the instrument forming the foundation of Schmeck's theory of learning style. As with Entwistle (1981) and Biggs (1978), Schmeck *et al.* (1977) were originally influenced by Craik and Lockhart's (1972) work on depth of information processing. Schmeck *et al.* (1981) described the development of their theory, based on the use of the original ILP. They identified two main forms of learning strategy, 'reflective processing' and 'agentic processing'.

Reflective processing was described as 'somewhat free-associative and ultimately dialectical, deriving personal meaning by contrasting opposing perspectives on one's experience'. Reflective processing, Schmeck and co-workers stated, involved 'deep and elaborative processing together with a desire to express a personal perspective'. Agentic processing, on the other hand, was described as 'highly directed, purposive and responsive to external contingencies' (Schmeck *et al.* 1991: 343). It included conventional serial processing and fact retention. Both concepts of learning strategy clearly showed a continuing interest in the work of Marton (1988) and Pask (1988), which reflected research into serial and holist cognitive processing. The authors subsequently presented a revised version of the ILP, supported with reliability and validity data (Schmeck *et al.* 1991).

Assessment

The original ILP was a self-report questionnaire comprising 62 items aimed at assessing students' behavioural and conceptual processes engaged in the learning task. The measure comprises four scales: synthesis analysis, study methods, fact retention and elaborative processing. The later version of the instrument comprises a 160 item questionnaire consisting of statements regarding school-related behaviours, attitudes, opinions and motivations. The format is changed from a true-false response to a six-point Likert scale, and gives four main scales: academic self-concept; reflective processing; agentic processing; and methodical study.

Schmeck and his co-workers claimed that the refinement of this instrument has led to the development of a new theory regarding school learning. They argued that a 'smooth flow of cognitive processing during studying' required emotional investment in self-as-student and confidence in one's cognitive skills (Schmeck *et al.* 1991: 358). The ILS provided data, they suggested, which could be used to help in the guidance of students in their approach to study.

Empirical evidence for the ILP

A useful account of the work carried out to confirm the validity and reliability of the ILP was presented by Schmeck *et al.* (1991). Curry (1987) provided an independent report on the psychometric features of the original ILP, describing it as being supported by evidence of strong reliability and validity. She commented upon the strong overlap between this model and that developed by Entwistle (1979). The measure was found to correlate with scores on trait tests and was successfully used to predict success on the various evaluation components of undergraduate programmes of study.

Style models based on instructional preference

The two preference-based models of learning style in this review focus more or less exclusively upon the learning environment. They both attempt to measure individual preference for a range of environmental or instructional factors affecting an individual's learning behaviour. These models represent a construct of learning style which is markedly less stable than cognitive style constructs, and therefore susceptible to fluctuation. However, it should be noted that the Learning Styles Inventory (Dunn *et al.* 1977) is predicated on a notion of learning style remaining a relatively fixed characteristic of the learning event (Dunn and Dunn 1974).

While teachers might initially see an immediate relevance in these models, as they appear to deal directly with the learning process, it should be noted that they seem to lack a firm psychological foundation for construct validity. However, these models remain important, as further work is merited in exploring the nature and effect of instructional preference as an aspect of learning strategy and an individual's learning style.

Learning Style Inventory (LSI)

Dunn and Dunn (1974) defined learning style as the way in which biological and developmental personal characteristics make different methods of teaching appropriate for some students but not for others. This approach presumed a wide array of individual learning styles in any group of learners. Their learning styles would reflect the manner in which five basic stimuli affected their ability to perceive, interact with, and respond to the learning environment (Dunn *et al.* 1989). These workers argued that it was personal response which determined an individual's preferred mode of learning, particularly for concentration and processing difficult information. This style was not, therefore, regarded as a constant feature, but was expected to change as factors altered in the learning environment or instructional process.

The learning style elements identified in the LSI are: environmental stimulus (light, sound, temperature, design); emotional stimulus (structure, persistence, motivation, responsibility); sociological stimulus (pairs, peers, adults, self, group, varied); physical stimulus (perceptual strengths, including auditory, visual, tactile, kinaesthetic, mobility, intake, time of day – morning versus afternoon); and psychological stimulus (global/analytic, impulsive/reflective, and cerebral dominance). The focus remains the individual response pattern to these stimuli, and the assumption is made that matching a personal preference with a learning context will result in improved learning behaviour and performance.

The LSI provides information about an individual's preference for learning conditions rather than psychological processes and factors involving intellectual functioning. This led to Dunn *et al.* (1989) advocating a teaching method which aimed to capitalise on individual students' modes of learning by matching environmental factors to learning style. Utilising the LSI naturally leads to an assessment-based programme aimed at influencing pedagogy and teaching arrangement such as those outlined in Table 3.4.

Griggs (1991) took this approach further by applying the learning styles model to counselling in the North American secondary school context. She provided a well-presented case for including style-based assessment in teaching programmes and, more significantly, in guidance/counselling programmes aimed at enhancing or supporting academic achievement. She proposed an approach which involved student needs analysis. She described the development of a comprehensive, developmental counselling programme including: a

Table 3.4 Matching learning styles to learning conditions

The environmental element	The emotional element
Noise level – quiet areas or background noise.	**Motivation** – use a range of positive conversational areas as strategies to reinforce a continuum of high-low learning and motivation.
Light – seat students according to preference for brightness of light.	**Persistence** – use a range of positive strategies to reinforce a continuum of high-low rate of persistence.
Temperature – control and regulate areas to suit personal preference and group accordingly.	**Responsibility** – increase levels of responsibility or opportunity for independent learning according to evidence of self- responsibility.
Design – furniture and seating to meet student preference for informal/formal/ soft/hard.	**Structure** – adapt structured learning tasks/activity involving learning sequences, contracts, timelines, to fit levels of preferred freedom of action.
Sociological element	**Physical element**
Learning groups – organisation of learning in a variety of groupings: large, small, paired and individual according to learner preference.	**Perceptual** – organise and structure learning materials or activities to cater for learning strengths/dispositions in the four perceptual modes: auditory; visual; tactile; and kinaesthetic.
Presence of authority figures – locating learners in proximity to adult figures reinforcing this with matching levels of supervision.	**Intake** – provide opportunity for eating/ drinking as intake on demand.
Learning in varied ways – structure programmes and completion schedules to match activities with the individual learner.	**Time** – organise personal task – to contain a menu ranging from options and variety correspond in to tightly sequenced routine to meet student disposition preference.
	Mobility – enable opportunity for movement in or around the learning environment and support with appropriately designed learning activities.
Psychological element	
Global vs analytic – structure teaching activities/method/materials to suit learner disposition.	**Hemispheric dominance** – structure/ design activity to engage left/right side brain processing and deploy according to learner bias.
Impulsive vs reflective – offer opportunity for either mode of learning, that is, experimental/discovery learning; structured/programmed learning; and opportunity to model improved reflection.	

programme of assessment of individual learning styles for both students and staff; the planning of teaching and counselling interventions designed to be compatible with the learning needs of students; and an evaluation of teaching and counselling outcomes to determine the extent to which programme objectives had been achieved. She confidently stated that 'If counselling approaches are compatible with the individual learning style preferences of the counselee, the goals of counselling will be achieved.' (Griggs 1991: 34).

She suggested developing arrangements for support for learning and presented case-study evidence for the relevance and success of a style-based approach to guidance and counselling within the school system.

The 'learning style' that Dunn *et al.* (1989) developed is a good example of a construct which more properly describes a repertoire of learning preferences, rather than a learning style. A second characteristic of this 'style' construct is its multidimensional nature, which is comparable to a second learning style model subsequently developed in the USA, the Learning Styles Profile (Keefe and Monk 1986). A third and crucial characteristic of this style construct is its requirement for an awareness and exercise of preference for modes of learning on the part of the individual. Empowerment of the learner and exercise in choice must be built into the pedagogy based upon the Dunn and Dunn conception of learning styles, if it is be used in a worthwhile way, a requirement that fits perfectly well with the cultural values and school systems prevailing in the USA. This might well explain the continuing great interest in the USA for an operationalisation of learning style in the national educational system.

Assessment

The original instrument devised by Dunn and Dunn was the Learning Styles Questionnaire (Dunn and Dunn 1978), comprising 228 items and aimed at eliciting factors in learning for children in grades 3–12 in the USA. However, this was quickly revised to form the Learning Styles Inventory (LSI), which comprised a 104 item self-reporting questionnaire employing a three-choice Likert scale, true, false and unsure. The authors produced several versions of this instrument, one aimed at the primary level and another at students in the secondary age range. A third version, developed for use with adults, the Productivity Environmental Preference Survey (PEPS) reflected the same elements of learning style. Each version used self-report methods to measure factors which reflected key variables identified by the authors as forming an individual's typical response to the learning environment.

Each preference factor in the LSI represents an independent continuum and is not necessarily related to other factors. Examples of factors for the environmental variable include response to noise level, to light and temperature; for the sociological variable, preference for group learning, response to authority and typical response to adults; for the emotional factor, motivation, responsibility and persistence; for the physical factor, modality preferences which include auditory, visual, tactile and kinaesthetic, as well as food/fluids intake and time of day. Individual and group profiles are produced from the assessment data, and the authors provided guidance for planning style-led instructional methods.

Empirical evidence for the LSI

A considerable number of research studies have been carried out using the LSI to investigate and explore the application of this learning style construct to the school context (Griggs 1991; Jonassen and Grabowski 1993). The research has mostly taken the form of doctoral theses – the following are included as a representative sample: studies investigating the effectiveness of matching versus mismatching learning preferences on learning outcomes (DeBello 1985a; Gianitti 1988); studies seeking to identify developmental patterns (Price *et al.* 1976, 1977), studies seeking to establish relationships between learning style and the learning environment (Brennan 1984; Clark-Thayer 1987; Bruno 1988); and studies devoted to discriminating preferences between specific sub-populations (Bauer 1987; Brunner and Majewski 1990).

An extensive annotated bibliography giving further details of dissertations and papers on the Dunn and Dunn model of learning style, as well as other related collections of articles on learning style, is published by the Learning Styles Network, based at St John's University, New York. Dunn, Dunn and co-workers have published a considerable number of articles and papers relating to the development of the LSI, together with its 'adult' version, the PEPS, describing their application to the learning context.

Grabowski and Jonassen (1993) reported a large number of studies supporting the reliability and validity of the LSI, as well as studies presented by the authors themselves. However, there appears to be no 'independent' verification of the instrument, with little research aimed at investigating the psychometric properties of the measure. Grigerenko and Sternberg also note that this theory of learning style ignores the learning process in favour of a focus upon environmental elements affecting the learner's ability to learn. They criticised the approach for 'raising more questions than it answers' (Grigerenko and Sternberg 1995: 219), pointing out that there is little information on the construction of the instrument, and no explanation for the interaction of the elements.

Curry (1987) reported a limited amount of data with which to assess the reliability of the LSI, and cited no evidence for the support of the instrument's construct validity. Her summary psychometric rating of the LSI stated that it was supported by levels of good reliability evidence and good validity evidence. However, the paucity of data analysis relating to the measure is also commented upon by Murray-Harvey (1994). Furthermore, she reported on her work in analysing the Productivity Environmental Preference Survey (PEPS), the adult version of the LSI, and concluded that learning style as measured by the PEPS is not as stable a construct as the authors had claimed.

Style of Learning Interaction Questionnaire

The style of learning described by Riechmann and Grasha (1974) is very similar in appearance to the construct devised by Dunn *et al.* (1989), in that it focuses upon an individual's learning preference. Riechmann and Grasha presented a social and affective perspective on patterns of preferred behaviour and attitude which underpin learning in an academic context. They identified three bipolar dimensions in a construct which described an individual's typical approach to the learning situation. These dimensions of 'learning style' included the following:

- participant–avoidant
- collaborative–competitive
- independent–dependent.

Riechmann and Grasha concluded that each style of learner will exhibit a set of characteristics which are relatively stable and are described in Table 3.5.

Jonassen and Grabowski (1983: 281) described this style construct as a 'social interaction scale because it deals with patterns of preferred styles for interacting with teachers and fellow student'. A comparison is made with Kolb's learning style model, which described preferred learning methods such as concrete experiential activity which correlate with students who would prefer to avoid interaction in the classroom.

The theoretical background to this construct involved an interest in individual differences in learning behaviour which was initially linked to personality. The authors developed a theoretical construct on the basis of identifying five key categories of learning behaviour. These included cognitive, sensory, interpersonal, intrapersonal and environmental. The construct was deemed to be useful as a means of accessing and understanding the individual differences in students' learning behaviour in the classroom (Jonassen and Grabowski 1983).

Assessment

The construct is measured by completing the Student Learning Styles Scale (SLSS) (Riechmann and Grasha 1974), which is a 90 item self-report inventory consisting of six sub-scales reflecting dimensions of the learning 'style'. The respondent is asked to rate their agreement or disagreement to questions aimed at general learning behaviour in the classroom. A composite score is totalled and

Table 3.5 Differences of learning interaction

Participant	Avoidant
wants to know about course content	no desire to know about course content
enjoys classes	dislikes classes
wants to learn	disinterested in learning
is compliant and follows direction	non-compliant and resists direction
Collaborative	**Competitive**
prefers sharing activity	competitive and self-centred
cooperative	self-interested and motivated by winning
enjoys collaboration	enjoys games or tournaments
likes to interact	likes to engage in win-lose activities
enjoys group-work	enjoys group games
Independent	**Dependent**
works on his or her own	relies upon the teacher for guidance
completes tasks	requires support and extrinsic motivation
responsive	non-responsive and little curiosity
free-thinker	does the minimum and follows the lead

the respondent's position is plotted on the six aspects of 'style'. It is worth noting that there are two forms of this measure, one to assess a general class, the second to assess individual style on a specific course. Grasha and Riechmann (1974) expect style to change in different classes and for a different subject.

Empirical evidence for the SLSS

Grabowski and Jonassen (1993) pointed to several weaknesses with this instrument, aligned to the way in which it focused only on student behaviour. Indeed the authors themselves alluded to two key problems: first, the frames of reference in the questionnaire, which involve ambiguity in the individual rating response to experience in class, reflected a lack of control over various factors which might affect a response; and second, respondents might not respond 'honestly', and 'social desirability' or various self-perceptions might well 'corrupt' the response to the learning style instrument.

Ferrell (1983) reported good levels of test-retest reliability but commented that inconsistent sub-scale relationships were problematic, producing varying level of internal and external validity. Curry (1987) has referred to a limited number of studies addressing the psychometric properties of this measure. There appears to be more data supporting construct and predictive validity, but much of this is far from conclusive. Curry's summary psychometric rating described the SLSS as supported by a fair level of reliability and validity evidence (Curry 1987).

Style models based on cognitive skills development

The cognitive-skills-based models of learning style are predicated on an approach to learning which presumes success only when a progressive development in skills and method is realised by the individual. Learning style is typically perceived as a multi-modal construct which is understood to describe a range of intellectual functioning relating to the learning activity. Each has had significant influence on the development of the learning-centred tradition.

Edmonds Learning Style Identification Exercise (ELSIE)

Reinert's (1976) model reflected an attempt to identify an individual's natural 'perceptual modality' as they respond to the learning environment. The ELSIE yielded information about four categories of learning modality:

- visual modality
- verbal modality
- auditory modality
- activity-based modality.

The individual learner was identified as displaying strong or weak disposition for the use of each modality in the learning process. Reinert's work influenced both the development of the Dunn, Dunn and Price learning style model, as well as the work of Keefe in developing the NASSP *Learning Style Profile* (Keefe 1987; De Bello 1990).

Assessment

The ELSIE is composed of 50 one word items which are used to characterise the respondent's reaction on four possible levels: visualisation or creation of a mental picture; alphabetical letters in writing form; sound; and an emotional or physical feeling about the stimulus word. The purpose of this assessment is to provide the teacher with information which will be used to work to the student's strengths or preferred mode of responding to learning stimuli.

Empirical evidence for the ELSIE

There appears to be little information on the reliability or validity of this instrument (Jonassen and Grabowski 1993). Curry (1987) has reported a study assessing its temporal reliability, but has concluded that the measure is supported by poor levels of reliability evidence and no validity evidence. This clearly imposes severe limitations on this model for the teacher or researcher seeking a way forward in the application of learning style. However, the significance of the model lies primarily in its 'conceptual content', which has influenced the development of other models of cognitive-skills-based learning style (Letteri 1980; Keefe and Monk 1986).

Cognitive Style Delineators (CSD)

Letteri (1980) described learning as an exercise in information-processing involving the storage and retrieval of information. The process of learning was categorised into six stages ranging from initial perception to long-term memory. A failure to process information in any one of these stages was interpreted as a deficit in cognitive skills acquisition. The teaching of cognitive skills or 'augmentation' as Reinert (1976) described the process of cognitive skills training, formed the basis for assessing and developing learning style and intellectual development. Letteri's style construct is important for its presumption that assessment and style awareness should be used to change a student's cognitive profile and learning style. The question of whether a development of style can be 'forced' is relevant to our own notion of strategy formation and a strategic approach to the learning process. The idea has also played a continuing part in discussions about operationalising learning style in the learning context.

Assessment

Letteri integrated the work of several models of cognitive style to create a combined assessment of individual skills on a bipolar continuum. The assessment identified three types of learners: Type 1 was characterised by reflective, analytical dimensions of learning style; Type 3 was characterised by impulsive, global dimensions of style and were typically non-focused in their learning; Type 2 learners were identified as reflecting a central position in the continuum. These learner types corresponded with student groupings characterised by levels of academic achievement in school. Type 1 learners were associated with school success, Type 2 learners met with moderate levels of success in school; Type 3 learners were students who met with little or no success in school.

Letteri's research led him to advocate an active and aggressive approach to utilising style assessment in the school context. He devised the term 'augmentation' to describe an intervention aimed at teaching cognitive skills in order to facilitate a process of change in learning style. Training in information-processing operations and 'cognitive structure construction principles' was expected to result in improved ability, performance and a change in learning style. As DeBello (1985b) has observed, there is some controversy over whether 'style' can be changed, but there is also a pressing need to consider the concepts and terms being used. Is Letteri truly referring to learning style? Or is the attempt to integrate several models and dimensions of cognitive style confusing a fundamental distinction between strategy and style, on the one hand, and ability and style on the other hand? This issue, not easy to resolve, lies at the heart of the debate about the nature of learning strategies and their relationship with cognitive and learning style.

Empirical evidence for the CSD

There appears to be no published evidence to support either the reliability or validity of this instrument. Its inclusion in this review has largely been to provide an example of a model of learning style which attempted to develop a construct based upon information-processing theory. However, its influence on the LSI (Dunn *et al.* 1989) and the Learning Style Profile (Keefe and Monk 1986) also points to its conceptual significance. Letteri's work raised key issues about the development of learning style and skills development, such as directly attempting to change style. These ideas influenced the development of the NASSP Learning Style Profile (Keefe and Monk 1986), and will figure significantly in any attempt to develop the theory and application of style.

Learning Style Profile (LSP)

Griggs offered as her definitive description of 'learning style' the following statement:

> A comprehensive definition of learning style was adopted by a national task force, comprised of leading theorists in the field and sponsored by the National Association of Secondary School Principals. This group defined 'learning style' as the composite characteristic cognitive, affective, and physiological factors that serve as relatively stable indicators of how a learner perceives, interacts with, and responds to the learning environment.
>
> (Griggs 1991: 7)

Keefe led this national task-force, and attempted to develop a learning styles profile for use in the secondary school (Keefe and Monk 1986). The aim was to produce an integrated model of style. The approach was multidimensional addressing individual differences among learners within the context of the learning process.

Keefe's definition of style centred on the notion of learning being dependent on basic routines of information-processing, cognitive skills and the use of memory. Learning outcomes were recognised as the products of interaction between cognition (intellect) and context (task). He acknowledged the influence of Letteri's model of learning style, stating that it provided a useful synthesis of information-processing theory and cognitive/learning style theory. Keefe believed that cognitive styles acted as control mechanisms 'intrinsic' to the basic information-processing system used in learning (Keefe 1989b: 2–5). His style construct described 24 key elements in learning style, grouped into three areas:

- *cognitive skills* – relating to aspects of information processing activity such as analysis, spatial, discrimination, categorisation, sequential processing, simultaneous processing and memory
- *perceptual responses* – encompassing perceptual responses to data, including visual, auditory and emotive processing
- *study and instructional preference* – referring to motivational and environmental elements of style including persistence orientation, verbal risk orientation, manipulative preference, time (early morning-late morning, afternoon, evening), verbal-spatial grouping, posture, mobility, sound, lighting and temperature preferences.

The construct, and the rationale for its operationalisation, was based on the premise that cognitive skills development is a prerequisite for effective learning. It sought to establish a learning-to-learn dimension in mainstream secondary schooling in the United States. Keefe (1987) argued that if an individual cannot process information effectively, ineffective learning will take place, minimising the effect of a positive learning environment. He has produced several monographs providing guidelines for teachers interested in developing programmes of work based on the model (Keefe 1989a, 1989b, 1990).

Assessment

The LSP is a 42 page, 126 item assessment intended for use with secondary school students. The questionnaire works in a similar way to the LSI (Dunn *et al.* 1989) with tick-box responses to statements being scored and an individual profile of learning style being generated from the results. Keefe (1989b: 33) gave a detailed explanation of how the development of cognitive skills and capability to operate information-processing are central to the concept of learning and the learning style profile. He stated emphatically that 'cognitive skills (and their training) are prerequisites for successful student achievement' and claimed that:

> The NASSP Learning Style Profile and its referent science of information-processing are the latest advances in the field of education. The instrument profiles the levels of students' cognitive skills and provides a basis for the development of relevant intervention and training programmes.
>
> (Keefe 1989b: 34)

The research base testing the LSP remains restricted, and DeBello remarked that this was probably because it is a relatively recent development. Keefe reported on some correlational analysis with other models of style, namely Reinert's ELSIE, but Curry (1987) commented that the LSP failed to offer reassuring levels of reliability or validity.

The LSP marked an important attempt to operationalise an assessment-based approach to utilising learning style as a concept in pedagogy. Nevertheless, the instrument, and related suggestions for application of the profile, fall far short of providing a user-friendly method for interested professionals wishing to include learning style in their practice. A successful 'operationalisation' of the theory of learning style still remains to be achieved.

Empirical evidence for the LSP

Though there is a considerable amount of literature published by the authors detailing the construction and development of the LSP, there is little evidence produced by researchers to support the reliability or validity of the measure. DeBello (1990) pointed to the importance of this model in that he stated that it marked an 'advancement' in the field of learning style, representing the first attempt to build a model from the 'diverse and occasionally opposite philosophies of current theorists'.

DeBello has reported that reliability varies greatly between sub-scales in the measure, the stronger being those drawn from the Dunn and Dunn model, while the weakest are those relating to Witkin's Group Embedded Figures Test (Witkin *et al.* 1971). Curry (1987) reported similar findings rating the instrument as 'average' for results utilising Cronbach's alpha range. Concurrent validities with 'parent' measures, that is, the ELSIE (Reinert 1976), the LSI (Dunn *et al.* 1989) and the GEFT (Witkin *et al.* 1971), are identified the strongest for correlation with the LSI and the ELSIE. It has been noted, however, that the ELSIE has poor levels of reliability and no evidence of validity.

An evaluation of the models

Ultimately, in a critical review of learning style models, the evaluation criteria referred to in Chapter 2 must again be applied. To do this we must attempt

- to consider a construct validity of the model
- to review the psychometric properties of the measurement, particularly their face and predictive validity as well as reliability
- synthesise theory and incorporate a model or models into our developing theory of learning style or
- extract aspects of a model or models which we think reflect a coherent and valid dimension of learning style.

It is important at this point to reflect upon the validity and reliability of each of these models if they are to be integrated into a model of personal learning style. Table 3.6 provides a summary evaluation of key models of learning styles.

Table 3.6 Evaluation of learning styles models

Style model	Evaluation	References
Style models based on the learning process		
Learning Style Inventory (Kolb 1985)	The LSI is criticised for lack of psychometric rigour; empirical studies also report a lack of verifiability using the measure in pilot studies; is the model a description of a specific cycle of active learning rather than individual differences in the learner?	Freedman and Stumpf (1981); Allinson and Hayes (1988); Cornwell *et al.* (1991); Veres *et al. (1991)*; De Ciantis and Kirton (1996)
The Learning Styles Questionnaire (Honey and Mumford 1986).	The LSQ received a mixed review from researchers indicating variable levels of psychometric rigour, especially predictive validity; its construct validity relies upon Kolb's model of learning style and therefore subject to its limitations.	Allinson and Hayes (1990); Furnham (1995)
Style models grounded in orientation to study		
Approaches to Study Inventory (Entwhistle 1979, 1981)	The ASI has a good level of empirical data; researchers reported a robust factor structure with high levels of predictive validity; it provides a useful tool for researching learning strategies.	Harper and Kember (1989); Richardson (1990); Newstead (1992), Sadler-Smith (1996)
Study Process Questionnaire (Biggs 1978, 1985)	More empirical research is required to support the SPQ; it provides a useful reference for researching learning strategies.	Jonassen and Grabowski (1993); Murray-Harvey (1994)
Inventory of Learning Processes (Schmeck *et al.* 1977)	There is little independent empirical support for the ILP; it appears to carry good levels of reliability and validity; it provides a useful reference for researching learning strategies.	Curry (1987)
Style models based on instructional preference		
Learning Style Inventory (Price *et al.* 1976, 1977; Dunn *et al.* 1989).	The LSI targets the learning environment and criticised for not providing data on differences within the learner; several researchers criticised lack of independent data to support this construct; provides a useful reference for developing a construct of learning strategies.	Curry (1987); Jonassen and Grabowski (1993); Murray-Harvey (1994); Grigerenko and Sternberg (1995)
Style of Learning Interaction Questionnaire (Grasha and Riechmann 1974)	Few empirical data are available to support this measure; it is criticised for lacking internal controls; the construct also suffers from ambiguity and underdevelopment.	Ferrell (1983); Curry (1987); Jonassen and Grabowski (1993).
Style models based on cognitive skills development		
Edmonds Learning Style Identification Exercise (Reinart 1976)	Few empirical data are available to support this model; ELSIE is conceptually significant as a model which is based upon the idea of field-dependence.	DeBello (1990); Jonassen and Grabowski (1993)
Cognitive Style Delineators (Letteri 1980)	There is a lack of empirical data available to support this model; the CSD is conceptually significant and an influence on the development of the LSP (Keefe 1989).	DeBello (1990)
Learning Style Profile (Keefe and Monk 1986; Keefe 1989, 1990)	A recently developed model with few empirical data available; the LSP provides a good reference for developing a learning styles profile.	DeBello (1990); Jonassen and Grabowski (1993)

The learning-centred tradition is by definition concerned with the learning process. This has led to models of style being developed which are 'fluid', environmentally orientated and very susceptible to change. Criticism of the approach reflects a concern for construct validity, poor verifiability, over-reliance on self-report in measurement, and an uncertainty about the relationship between learning style, learning strategy and cognition. The research continues to be dominated by assessment-based constructs. This, in turn, may well explain, in part, a prevailing psychometric paradigm in style theory, as well as a continuing focus upon measurement, rather than a concern for predictive validity with respect to observed behaviours and the achievement of a coherent and agreed theory.

The classification of learning style models into four groups – learning processes, orientation to study, instructional preferences, and cognitive skills – moves us forward in attempting a more precise definition of 'learning style'. It becomes clear that rather than producing information about learning style as an aspect of individual difference in the learner, the models of 'learning style' associated with the learning-centred tradition of style theory actually yield information about a range of dimensions, strategies and behaviours that have to do with individual differences interfacing with the learning process. It is also important to realise that this information relates more properly to the formation of learning strategies than it does to cognitive style or to what we might ultimately be persuaded to accept as a definition of 'learning style'.

Part of the problem with the learning-centred approach may be that it was ahead of its time. It has the worthy intention to individualise pedagogy, but this was attempted in advance of the necessary understanding of the psychology of learning and of the nature of individual differences in cognitive style. Consequently it was not possible for the intention to be properly applied. Chapter 2 identified two fundamental dimensions of cognitive style, the wholist-analytic and the verbal-imagery. These are seen as relatively fixed for an individual, and represent the individual's preferred and habitual approach to organising and representing information. It is likely that the student develops *learning strategies* for dealing with the learning environment and the learning task. These strategies are intended to make most effective use of the person's cognitive style. Learning strategies will be considered in Chapter 4.

CHAPTER 4

Learning strategies

Chapter overview

This chapter will consider the nature of learning strategies as distinct from cognitive style.

Style and strategy

Individuals develop learning strategies to deal with learning material which is not initially compatible with their cognitive style. Strategies can be learned and modified while style is a relatively fixed core characteristic of an individual. Models of learning style belonging to the learning-centred tradition appear to describe individual differences in the learning process and are therefore related to learning strategies.

Learning strategies

Learning strategies are formed as part of a response within the individual to meet the demands of the environment. Learning strategies may thus be seen as cognitive tools which for the individual are particularly helpful for successfully completing a specific task. This approach leads to the concept of the strategic learner.

The development of strategic learning

Individuals will sense that there are situations for which their cognitive style is not ideally suited. This will lead to their preferring, for example, one mode of presentation over another. This in turn will lead to the development of a strategy of translating learning material into the preferred mode where this is possible. In the longer term this will produce a repertoire of learning strategies – a cognitive tool-kit.

It may be argued that many of the learning-centred approaches described in Chapter 3 are really to do with learned strategies. A fairly common feature in this tradition is an emphasis on the possibility of an individual 'style' being learned and developed. For instance, in the Learning Process Models both Kolb (1976) and Honey and Mumford (1986) stressed the developmental nature of learning style. Workers in the Orientation to Study tradition emphasised the need for the individual to develop ways of processing information from a surface level to deep approach. With the Cognitive Skills Models, while they tend to be all embracing, they usually include within them the need for the individual student to acquire and develop learning strategies to improve their performance.

By contrast, the Instructional Preference models have to do with adapting the learning environment to suit the individual learner, rather than the development of learning strategies, partly because they are multidimensional and have more to do with cognitive style.

This chapter will review work on learning strategies, first, as part of a consideration of the cognitive style construct, second, in order to consider how learning strategies are formed, and third, in relation to the individual's development of a strategic approach to learning.

Style and strategy

The distinction between style and strategy

Cognitive style and learning strategy

The cognitive-centred approach (Chapter 2) emphasises the consistent and habitual nature of cognitive style in affecting the organisation and representation of information during learning and thinking. Clearly, this has implications for learning. Where a particular style matches the content and presentation of material to be learned, then the individual is likely to find the task easier than when there is a mismatch between style and learning design (see Chapter 7). In the case of a mismatch, individuals may be helped by developing learning strategies for dealing with the material which is not initially compatible with their style.

A learning strategy is a set of one or more procedures that an individual acquires to facilitate the performance on a learning task. Strategies will vary depending on the nature of the task. They may be thought of as tools, and just as one job may need a spanner and a screwdriver, another may require a hammer, so different strategies will be developed for different types of tasks. To continue the analogy, just as the tools can be stored on a tool rack and selected as appropriate for future jobs, so a repertoire of strategies can be stored and be used in future learning situations.

In considering cognitive style and learning strategy it is useful to discuss the way in which different researchers have used the terms 'learning style' and 'learning strategy'.

Learning styles and strategy

Bloom (1976) drew a distinction between individual differences in the learner and individual differences in the learning process. The Learning Styles movement described in Chapter 3 has been characterised by a primary concern for the learning process. This approach reflected a concern for 'pedagogy' which has often characterised the thinking of educationists interested in effective learning (Doyle 1990; Biggs and Moore 1993; Watkins *et al.* 1996). It is not surprising that this interest has led to an increasing focus upon the learning environment.

The learning-centred approach to style presupposed that 'learner characteristics' and 'learning style' were relatively unstable. They were perceived as factors relating to a dynamic process of learning which was 'activity-based'. It was also felt that effective learning involved a continuous development of learning style over time. It was this process of change and interaction with the learning context which was associated with learning outcomes. Furthermore, learning activity provided the basis for identifying types of learning approach and this was used to formulate models of learning method that were subsequently labelled 'learning styles'.

Differences in the understanding of style

It is not surprising, then, to discover that researchers in the learning-centred tradition often use the term 'learning style' but mean something entirely different from one another.

The learning-centred tradition use of the term 'style' is in a strict sense different to the definition adopted by workers in the cognition-centred approach (Riding and Cheema 1991; Kirton 1994; Rayner and Riding 1997). Support for a distinction between cognitive style and learning style is found in work which attempted to integrate previous development of cognitive style and information-processing into a theory of learning and instruction (Entwistle 1981; Biggs 1988; Ramsden 1988). Indeed, Schmeck (1988b: 4) quite carefully argued this distinction, while apologetically retaining the use of the term, 'learning styles', to describe particular aspects of individual difference in the learner's approach to learning. He argued, for example, that such differences were better understood as learning skills, strategies and study orientation displayed by the individual learner.

The need to reconsider what it is that is actually meant by the term 'learning style' is well documented in the literature (Curry 1983, 1987; Riding and Cheema 1991; Furnham 1995; Rayner and Riding 1997). The intention of such an attempt to synthesise theory should be to lay the foundation for the application of style in educational practice. In the first instance, however, it is important to establish a clear understanding of learning style and of the nature of the relationship between cognitive style and learning strategy.

The Onion Model

Curry (1983, 1987) suggested an analogy between the ways in which models of style may be categorised and the layers of an onion as a way of clarifying the differences between the various approaches to style. This offers a method of dealing with what many writers have described as a confusing, confused and disparate body of knowledge (Lewis 1976; Messick *et al.* 1976; Curry 1983; Miller 1987; Riding and Cheema 1991; Murray-Harvey 1994; Rayner and Riding 1997). Indeed, Curry herself stated that learning style theory is characterised by:

1. confusion in definitions;
2. weaknesses in reliability and validity of measurement;

[and failure in the]

3. identification of the most style relevant characteristics in learners and instructional settings.

(Curry 1991: 248)

Curry (1983) suggested that the onion should represent the models of learning style organised into three levels. The style onion proposed by Curry (1987) was described as having, starting from the centre:

- a central core made up of personality-centred models
- a second stratum of information-processing models
- an outer layer of instructional-preference models of learning style.

The core of the onion, the 'cognitive-personality level', was understood to be fundamental to and interactive with the operation of other levels in the model.

Curry (1987) cited contemporary work which tested the concept of separate but interactive 'toponymies' of style in her model, which she felt supported the validity of the 'style onion' (Marshall and Merritt 1985). She also claimed that the model of an 'onion thematic organisation' carried a high level of heuristic value. It is this aspect to the model which is both well established and has been increasingly acknowledged by workers in the field (Curry 1987: 19).

The distinction between inner and outer levels of the onion model is useful, but there is still a need to re-examine the learning-centred approach to style. Educationists need to know more, for example, about how cognitive style interacts with an individual's approach to learning. It is the interaction of cognitive style and learning strategy which combines to influence an individual's approach to learning.

Learning strategies

The nature of learning strategies

Orientations to learning

Schmeck and co-workers (1988a, 1991), Entwistle and Ramsden (1983) and Biggs (1978) have considered orientation to learning. Schmeck's interest in an individual's orientation toward learning, shared by several workers who have investigated orientation to academic study (Biggs 1978; Entwistle 1979; Entwistle and Ramsden 1983), has provided an insight into the relationship between learning style and the process of strategy formation. Schmeck argued that the relationship between skills, tactics and strategies should be regarded as very close, and stated:

> Skills are things we can do; strategies and tactics involve the conscious decisions to implement those skills. [He went on to explain that] Learning strategies are combinations of cognitive (thinking) skills implemented when a situation is perceived as one demanding learning.
>
> (Schmeck 1988b: 6)

However, the basic orientations to study to which Schmeck referred represent only one aspect of a more general formation of learning strategy.

A further distinction drawn by Schmeck (1988b) referred to Entwistle's original distinction between learning 'style' and 'orientation'.

> I agree with Entwistle (1981 [and Entwistle 1988]) that it is important to continue to distinguish between orientation and style. Orientation to studying involves more than cognitive style, it also involves motives and intentions.
>
> (Schmeck 1988b: 344)

Entwistle's work reflected a continuing interest in the learner's approach to study and individual orientation to learning. In developing an understanding of learning method he identified attitudes, motivation and learning behaviours.

Learning activities versus learning strategies

It is useful to distinguish between learning activities and learning strategies. An activity becomes strategic when it is particularly appropriate for the individual learner. This is in contrast to general learning activities which an individual may find less helpful. In this respect, the strategies, as they are called by Nisbet and Shucksmith (1986), represent a very general level of operation which may more properly be called learning activities.

Nisbet and Shucksmith listed several commonly mentioned learning activities/strategies, including those set out in Table 4.1.

Table 4.1 Common learning activities/strategies

Type	Description
Asking questions	defining hypotheses, establishing aims and the parameters of a task, discovering audience, relating a task to a previous piece of work
Planning	deciding on tactics and timetables, reduction of task or problem into components, identification of skills or competencies required
Monitoring	a continuous attempt to match efforts, answers and discoveries to initial questions or purposes
Checking	carrying out a preliminary assessment of performance and results at a particular stage of an activity
Revising	a review response to assessment involving redrafting or recalculating or the revision of set goals
Self-testing	final assessment both of results and performance on task

The existence of 'learning activities', as distinguished from 'learning strategies' raises questions about the structure of strategy formation. How, for example, does the individual generate a learning strategy? How many kinds of strategies exist and are they different? A consideration of these issues leads to discussion about the structure of learning strategy formation.

The structure of learning strategies

Learning strategy hierarchy

Several writers have argued for the existence of a hierarchy in learning strategy operations in the individual. Baron (1978), for example, identified three types of strategies according to a level of generalisation:

- *relatedness search strategies* – actions aimed at defining a new problem in reference to previous knowledge

- *stimulus analysis strategies* – actions aimed at analysing a task and breaking it down into its constituent parts
- *checking strategies* – actions aimed at controlling and evaluating responses to the learning task in order to arrive at an appropriate response.

Kirby (1984) made a distinction between two levels of specificity of learning strategy:

- *micro-strategies* – were task specific, related to particular knowledge and abilities, closer to performance and amenable to direct instruction
- *macro-strategies* – were generic and tended to be more pervasive in nature, closely related to emotional and motivational factors, more easily influenced by individual differences such as style, or intelligence and therefore were regarded as less amenable to direct instruction.

An individual's approach to learning: a strategies schema

Nisbett and Shucksmith (1986) argued that most conceptualisations of strategies could be related to a central 'strategy' for learning which they have called 'planfulness'. They added, however, that this 'planfulness' is not easily changed, in that it represents a level of processing close to the 'grain of an individual's psychology'. It was understood to form the basis of an individual's intellectual functioning. In this respect, it inferred a process of learning strategy formation akin to the authors' construct of cognitive style, learning strategy and an integration of the two influencing an individual's approach to learning.

Nisbett and Shucksmith also pointed out that not all strategies are equal, either in their generalisation or their 'instructability', and presumably, it might be added, their role in the process of learning. Again – this corresponds with our own developing notion of learning strategy – there will always exist a variety of specific strategies, all of them reflecting factors such as style, ability, and other individual differences, yet at the same time, being formed as part of a unique pattern of strategy formation embedded in the individual's method of learning.

Learning strategies and learning performance

In his work with pupils experiencing learning failure, Weber (1978, 1982) developed a pedagogy and curriculum model which was constructed around the idea of teaching 'efficient learning' strategies. The strategies Weber identified included the following types of thinking and learning activities:

- attending to detail
- identifying starting points

- establishing and testing hypotheses
- forward planning
- systematic exploratory behaviour
- reasoning and deducing
- divergent thinking.

Weber did not claim that this list represented a general or comprehensive list of learning strategies. The authors would repeat at this point the need to distinguish between learning activities and learning strategies. However, Weber argued much the same, stating that learner needs and individual differences would determine the range and nature of what learning strategies should be taught. He explained that

> It was in the classroom that the seven strategies on this chart were first isolated for teaching purposes, and it is in the classroom that a teacher may choose to add to them, alter them, ignore some, expand upon others.
>
> (Weber 1982: 109)

What is important in Weber's argument is the belief that effective learning, enhanced learning and efficient instruction will reflect an emphasis upon students becoming aware of learning how to learn, developing a sense of control, improving levels of self-confidence and developing a sense of purpose through this self-awareness. The building of a strategic approach to learning reflects a further extension of an awareness of learning strategy development. What is conspicuous by its absence in this thinking, although it is clearly inferred in the rest of Weber's work, is the notion of an individual student's learning style.

Developing a learning strategy

The nature of strategy development

The development of learning strategies will involve the interaction of relatively fixed individual characteristics with the learning activity. Riding and Sadler-Smith (1997: 204) argue that 'individuals may not be able to change their styles but they can develop strategies to make themselves as effective as possible in a given learning situation'.

Performance in a learning task is linked to the development of learning strategy, the learning process and individual difference. The learning outcome will reflect the success or failure in strategy formation. Achieving levels of understanding, acquisition of knowledge, and skills development will similarly reflect this process of strategy formation.

The development of a learning strategy is an extended process, carried out repeatedly, and often spontaneously by the individual. There are, in the individual, several levels of personal awareness or response to a problem or task. For instance, some basic routines will be quickly 'automated' or 'internalised' and require little conscious thinking. Other routines will initially require thought and rehearsal before reaching a level of automation. Other extended routines will require more elaborate planning, continuous monitoring and consistently high levels of self-awareness as a learner.

It is this same generalised process of strategy formation which comprises sets to be used in the learning situation. Individual differences reflected in learning style and the formation of learning strategy, are key variables in this inter-action. It is likely too, that it is these individual differences which play a significant role in shaping performance and contributing to the learning outcome.

Meta-cognition – self-awareness

Weinstein and Van Mater Stone (1996) argued that awareness of one's own thinking (meta-cognition) is a critical step in the acquisition and improvement of a learning strategies repertoire, as well as the immediate implementation of any particular set of strategies.

Meta-cognition and the cognitive process

Flavell and Wellman (1977) set out a model of cognition which described four stages of cognitive processing:

- basic operations, described as the 'memory hard-ware' of the brain
- cognition consisting of a 'knowledge' component representing the effects of attainment, which were thought to be accumulative and expand with experience
- potentially 'conscious' behaviours called 'strategies', which enabled the individual 'to know how to know'
- processing, which was called 'meta-cognition' or 'knowing about knowing'.

Nisbet and Shucksmith (1986) made the point that while the relationship between cognition and meta-cognition is not entirely clear, the important question is can meta-cognition be used to foster superior strategy development?

Meta-cognition concerns knowledge of one's own mental processes. This self-awareness forms a major part of personal development and utilisation of style. A similar statement might also be made about the benefits of building a more specific self-awareness of cognitive style and the development of learning strategy into the enhancement of learning (Riding and Rayner 1995). Arguably introducing this consideration into pedagogical practice will contribute directly to the enhancement of learning.

In one way or another, it seems as if a variety of learning to learn approaches utilise self-awareness and the concept of learning style as an important part of their programme (Hamblin 1981; Blagg 1991). Unfortunately, many educationists are not very clear about what they actually mean by learning styles, nor how they should be incorporated into pedagogical practice.

Formation of learning strategies

Nisbet and Shucksmith (1986) used a footballing analogy to explain the relationship between cognitive resources, strategies and the development of learning strategy. The same analogy also offers a useful way of linking performance and effectiveness to the development of learning strategy.

An approach to learning: the game plan

A football team is made up of individual players who possess an innate ability and a personal flair – their footballing potential or 'resource'. They also possess specific skills, a number of rehearsed techniques, and some personal as well as shared strategies or tactics for playing the game. The latter include basic, individual actions and reactions when playing the game, for example, tackling or heading the ball in a certain way when defending the goal-box. There are also, at a higher level, strategies, tactics or techniques which involve other team members and the game-plan. This involves the coach coordinating a series of extended strategies, for example, holding a defensive line to play to the off-side rule and playing a sweeper role within a team formation.

Nisbet and Shucksmith (1986) used the analogy of football to point out the desirability for developing adaptability and review in strategy formation to achieve learning goals – if a football team sticks to the same tactics when they are not working, they lose, no matter how skilful the individual players.

An approach to learning: key elements.

It is possible to emphasise, by using the same analogy, the interaction of a number of 'key concepts' or 'cognitive processes' which combine to produce a learner's (player's) performance. Basic skills and 'talents' reflecting a level of ability are channelled into four levels of strategy formation:

- intuitive actions
- low-level automated actions
- deliberate and consciously extended actions
- high-level automated actions.

There are different levels of operation which move from the specific to the general, reflecting Kirby's (1984) description of micro-strategies and macro-strategies. However, strategy formation is a process of reaction and action during the learning event. Indeed, the four levels of functioning could be represented as a cycle of learning strategy formation. This process involves the generation of various learning tactics, for example, learning behaviour more usually described as passive, active, experiential or independent learning. The same process can be further related to study orientations identified by Entwistle (1981). These included surface to deep processing and comprehension. They may be extended to include other examples of learning orientation such as individual and collective, simple and single to complex and multiple learning activity (Watkins *et al.* 1996).

The strategic learner

The strategic learner: a personal performance

The transition from lower order, 'primary' cognitive functioning to higher order, 'executive' processing has been described by several writers (Nickerson 1985; Perkins 1985; Sternberg 1985, 1987; Ennis 1987; Ashman and Conway, 1989). Weinstein and Van Mater Stone (1996) presented a similar account of 'learning to learn' when they identified 'executive control processes' as the means by which 'strategic learners' ultimately manage the learning task.

Further, they stated that once students develop a repertoire of routines associated with being a strategic learner, they will achieve far higher levels of effective and efficient learning. Such a structure reflects a similar conception of learning and thinking to the one we have presented. The idea of the formation of learning strategy corresponds with conceptions of intelligence, thinking and learning which describe a dynamic process of information-processing, representation of knowledge and decision-making. It is probable that these operations form essential elements in the general development of a strategic approach to learning.

The notion of the strategic learner must obviously work hand in hand with the utilisation of approaches that promote learning to learn as part of a general approach to instruction.

The strategic learner: key characteristics

Weinstein and Van Mater Stone (1996) have provided a useful description of the strategic learner. They argued that strategic learners can be identified by the way in which they use the following types of knowledge:

- about themselves as learners
- about different types of academic tasks
- about strategies and tactics for acquiring, integrating, and applying new learning

- prior content
- of both present and future contexts in which their knowledge could be useful.

They add that a strategic learner will be characterised by an ability to use this knowledge in order to realise learning goals, and importantly, to be able to monitor and evaluate their own performance. Furthermore, effective learning is linked to factors associated with motivation and the desire to learn. It is also associated with levels of 'metacognitive awareness and control strategies' (Weinstein and Van Mater Stone 1996: 416), which enable the student to manage their own studying and learning.

The strategic learner: key behaviours

In order to manage such an approach to learning, the student will be involved in a number of activities which include:

- creating a plan to reach a goal
- selecting the specific strategies or methods to use to achieve a goal
- implementing the methods selected to carry out the plan
- monitoring progress on both a formative and a summative basis
- modifying the plan, the methods, or even the original goal, if appropriate
- evaluating the outcome in order to make a decision about further learning.

This process is identified by Weinstein and Van Mater Stone (1996: 419) as one which 'helps students to build up a repertoire of strategies that can be called upon in the future when a similar situation arises'. As a general approach to effective learning, it is important to include a consideration of the individual as a strategic learner.

It is self-evident that awareness of learning style and the development of a range of learning strategies will contribute to this process. Indeed, the first and third type of knowledge identified by Weinstein and Van Mater Stone correspond with an awareness of cognitive style and learning strategy development. It is also refreshing to reflect upon how this approach to instruction embodies principles which reflect a desire to empower the learner. It is, after all, important that individual differences are used to promote independent learning rather than stereotype, constrain or reduce the learner's potential of growth.

The development of strategic learning

As has been previously suggested, cognitive style cannot be easily changed, however, strategies are by definition, dynamic and mutable. The development of a strategic approach to learning follows a set of coherent principles.

It is an approach which consists of the following four stages:

- sensing and preferring
- selecting
- extending the learning strategy
- developing a repertoire of learning strategies.

Each of these stages will now be described in further detail in an attempt to explain exactly how the individual learner responds, psychologically, to a learning demand. The interaction, within the learner, between cognitive abilities, style, and the structure of cognitive processing combines with a series of steps or strategies that form the learner's response to the learning activity.

Sensing and preferring

When faced with a learning situation, individuals will sense inwardly the extent to which they feel comfortable with the situation. They may not be very aware of this in a conscious sense of saying to themselves that they feel unhappy, but with respect to certain aspects of learning they will have a sense of the extent to which the learning task is easy or more difficult. This awareness by the student will be with respect to at least three aspects of the learning situation: the mode of presentation of the learning task, the structuring of the task, and the social context of the learning.

Ease of use of the mode of presentation

Riding and Staley (1998) gave a questionnaire to university business studies students which assessed their preferences about the content and presentation of their courses, and this was compared with the actual performance by students on the course modules. Basically, where the mode of presentation and course content matched the verbal-imagery style of the student, then the students underestimated their performance. In cases where the verbal-imagery style did not match, they overestimated their performance. This was interpreted as suggesting that while the performance of students is affected by the extent to which the mode of presentation matches their verbal-imagery style, they are not very consciously aware of the match or mismatch, during actual learning.

However, where students are given an actual choice of mode of presentation, they will choose the one that suits their style. Riding and Watts (1997) told secondary school students that three versions of a sheet giving information on study skills had been prepared for them, and that each sheet contained the same information but that the formats were different. They were then invited to come one at a time to take one of the versions which were laid out on a table. The versions were unstructured-verbal (paragraphs, without headings), structured-verbal (paragraphs, each with a clear heading), and structured-pictorial (paragraphs, each with a clear heading, and a pictorial icon depicting the activity placed in the left margin). No students chose the unstructured-verbal version. With the two structured versions the majority of the verbalisers selected the verbal version and most of the imagers the pictorial. Students were obviously attracted to, and preferred to select, materials that appeared to them to suit their own style.

It appears, then, that students are likely to sense which format of learning material or presentation they prefer, even if they do not actually feel less comfortable when learning from some inappropriate presentations.

Appropriateness of the structure
In the study by Riding and Staley (1998) where there was a match between the structural requirements of the subject matter and the wholist-analytic style of the students, then the students did less well than they expected, but better than they expected when there was a mismatch. This was interpreted as indicating that the students were sensitive to how easy it was to understand a subject, and were consciously aware of the style of structure preferred, and expectation was commensurately higher or lower.

Students will be aware of the extent to which they are understanding the learning they are receiving.

Suitability of the social situation
Riding and Read (1996) individually questioned secondary school pupils on their preferences about learning and working in social contexts. The preferences for group and individual working were that work in groups was particularly liked by wholists, while individual work was least disliked by analytics. Sadler-Smith and Riding (b) in a study of the effect of cognitive style on the learning preferences of undergraduates found further support for this.

The first step to strategy attainment is the awareness that particular formats or situations are more helpful to, and more comfortable for, the individual. This then forms the basis for the next stage.

Selecting

As individuals become increasingly aware of what suits them in learning they begin to select the most appropriate mode or structure, where possible or when a choice is provided. For example, an imager may prefer to focus on a picture in a book than on the text. Riding and Read (1996) asked secondary school pupils about their preferences as to mode of working. Imagers reported that they used less writing and more pictures than verbalisers, especially where the subject allowed, as in science. The tendency by imagers to use pictures, and verbalisers writing, increased with ability. There was evidence that lower ability pupils were more constrained by the usual format of the subject than were those of higher ability.

This development of a strategy of selecting the mode or structure which, for the individual, suits his or her style can then lead on to more effective and conscious strategy development. An important feature here is that there is no 'right' way to learn that applies equally to all individuals, that is, cognitive styles represent *qualitatively* different types of thinking. Teachers need, therefore, to avoid the notion of 'this is the way' to learn. After all, individual teachers' natural teaching styles will be a reflection of their own cognitive style. The students need to be encouraged to use whatever means seems to be right for them as individuals. This can be quite a liberating experience for students!

Extending the learning strategy

Extending the strategy is the third phase of a strategic approach to learning which can involve a range of cognitive and learning strategies. There are at least three key types of strategies which contribute to the enhancement of learning by utilising an awareness of style. These specific strategies can be identified by the function they serve and consist of three types: translation strategies, adaptation strategies, and strategies which aim at a reduction of the processing load. Each has been previously identified in our discussion on the nature of strategies, but in this context are presented as part of a style-based approach to learning.

Translation

Translation involves recasting the information which as presented may be in a form that does not suit an individual's style, into a mode that makes it easier to process and understand. Examples of such translations include the following:

- An imager may 'translate' a page of text into a diagram which represents the same information in visual form.

- A verbaliser may describe a picture with words.
- An analytic may map out the elements of a topic on a sheet of paper to obtain a 'whole' view.
- A wholist may go through a chapter of a book and list the headings to give an indication of its structure.

All of these are attempts to represent the information in a form that is more appropriate to the style of the learner.

Adaptation

This is where a style dimension is pressed into service because a feature is not available on the other dimension of an individual's style. For instance, an analytic-imager obviously does not have the same facility as a wholist to obtain an overall view of situations or information. However, it is often possible to obtain a whole view by generating an image of the whole. Similarly, a wholist-verbaliser lacks an analysing facility, but the analytic nature of verbal representation may to some extent be used as a substitute. Some possible adaptations are shown in Table 4.2.

Table 4.2 Available styles for the four groups

Cognitive style	Styles available
Wholist verbalisers	Wholist and analytic
Analytic imagers	Analytic and wholist
Analytic verbalisers	Analytic only
Wholist imagers	Wholist only

Source: adapted from Riding and Sadler-Smith (1997)

Reduction of processing load

Here the approach is to minimise the information processing load by using a strategy that economises on processing. Although we are not usually consciously aware of it, any information we see or hear we have to analyse and process in order to give it meaning. This analysis takes processing capacity within the brain. If the information is in the preferred mode then the information processing load is less than if it is not. For an individual, additional processing load will, at the least, result in a longer time being required to learn the information. At worst, the load may exceed capacity, and the information may not be learned at all (see, for instance, Baddeley 1996 on working memory). Some examples of strategies to reduce the load are as follows.

- An imager who finds that verbal processing imposes a high load can selectively scan text and extract only the most important sections to save reading the whole.

- A wholist could underline words in text to produce 'headings' to clarify the structure.

Developing a repertoire of learning strategies

This is a combination of the variety of learning strategies employed by the individual. Over time and with experience individuals will develop a range of strategies which contribute to their learning style. However, there is no guarantee that without an awareness of style, or the self-conscious elaboration of a learning style profile, individuals will fully realise their potential with a consistently effective or efficient approach to learning. Serendipity will play its part, as individuals adopt a preferred approach to learning which may or may not allow them to work to their strengths in the learning situation. In this way, the individual will intuitively develop style-based strategies which will not always represent the most appropriate or successful approach to the learning task.

Building a better repertoire of learning strategies
Developing a repertoire of learning strategy over time can be encouraged by teachers or trainers interested in facilitating effective learning. Encouragement of personal style awareness is an important first step towards the development of a repertoire of learning strategies as well as 'instructional design'. Personal assessment using the Cognitive Styles Analysis (Riding 1991a) provides the basis for programmes like the Personal Styles Awareness package (Riding 1994) or the Personal Style and Effective Teaching package (Riding and Rayner 1995). The programmes offer a platform for developing a personal repertoire of learning strategy. Such an approach builds upon an awareness and understanding of individual style in learning, teaching or training.

Extending a personal learning repertoire
An alternative approach aimed at further developing a repertoire of learning strategy is the provision of style-based 'intervention' aimed at learning enhancement. The purpose of this strategy is the introduction of features into a pedagogy intended to support and reinforce individual learning style. For example, style-led principles are incorporated into forms of differentiation such as grouping, pacing, structuring, levelling and presenting material in a programme of study. Similarly, a specific scheme of work aimed at the teaching of learning strategies could form part of the personal and social education of students or a training programme in the workplace. In terms of 'personal development', this approach would align itself with ideas underpinning

professional and institutional development, and life-long learning. Indeed, there is scope within this wider perspective to consider the place of assessment in education. The absence of a learning style profile in a system which is still dominated by an intelligence test, or the subjective measure of academic ability, is very questionable. It is interesting to reflect upon the possibility of developing the style construct as part of a set of criteria for structuring learning and pedagogy in the school context. A similar comment is equally relevant to the workplace and issues surrounding continuing professional development.

Learning and teaching: style, strategies and solutions

The challenge for workers interested in the operationalisation of the style construct in teaching, training and learning is unchanged. This is in spite of a considerable amount of work spent researching the field of learning style. The fundamental question remains one which faced workers in the activity-centred tradition of style research. How do we identify and synthesise the valid constructs of learning style theory into an approach which is relevant, useful and pertinent to the practice of pedagogy in school and workplace?

The answer to this question involves the development of an approach which would incorporate most of the features discussed in this chapter. At the same time, such an approach would need to be user-friendly. It should have as its aim, the intention to encourage take-up in schools, colleges and the workplace. An assessment battery, made up of instruments with high levels of construct reliability and validity, would usefully provide a foundation for accommodating individual differences in the curriculum or training programme. Then assessment could be centred on the learner and organised so that it may be introduced into existing pedagogy. There remains a great deal to do if this development is ever to be fully realised. But at this point, it seems appropriate to end by paraphrasing an adage, 'You never do really stop learning'!

PART 2

STYLE AND BEHAVIOUR

Cognitive style and behaviours

The first part concluded that there are two fundamental dimensions of cognitive style – the wholist-analytic and the verbal-imagery. It was argued that a convenient means of assessing these is the Cognitive Styles Analysis.

In this part the main focus will be on studies using the Cognitive Styles Analysis approach with a view to examining evidence for this construct of cognitive style and its relationship to other constructs.

CHAPTER 5

Cognitive style and other individual difference dimensions

Chapter overview

This chapter will consider two related groups of questions concerning the basis of cognitive style, and style in the context of other individual difference dimensions such as intelligence and personality.

The basis of style

- Are the cognitive style dimensions independent of one another?
- Is there evidence of a physiological basis of style?
- What are the origins of style?

Style in the context of other individual difference dimensions

- Is style different from intelligence?
- What is the difference between style and ability?
- Is style the same as personality?
- Are there gender differences in style?
- How do style and the other sources of behaviour interact?

In Part 1 the notions of cognitive style and learning strategy have been examined, distinction has been made between the style families, and it has been argued that there are two fundamental dimensions of cognitive style.

In this chapter the main focus will be on studies using the Cognitive Styles Analysis approach with a view to examining evidence for this construct of cognitive style, and also its relationship to other constructs. A first consideration is whether these two style dimensions are truly independent of one another, and also whether they have any physiological basis. A further basic question is whether they are distinctly different from other individual difference dimensions such as personality, intelligence and gender. Just as various labels can be given to the same style dimension, it is also possible that style is merely another term for an ability or for an aspect of personality. The purpose of this chapter is to see style in the context of the other individual difference constructs.

The independence of the style dimensions and their physiological bases

Independence of the style dimensions

In Chapter 2 the point was argued that the various style labels might be grouped into two style families – the wholist-analytic and the verbal-imagery, as shown in Figure 5.1.

Figure 5.1 The two cognitive style dimensions

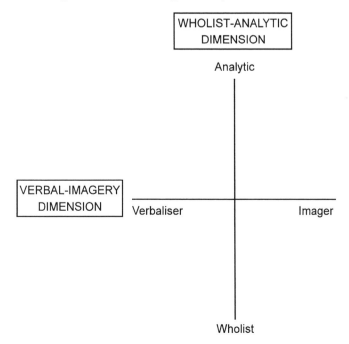

A first concern is whether these two style families represent two fundamental style dimensions that are distinct from one another, or whether they overlap one another. The findings of a large number of studies using the Cognitive Styles Analysis suggest that the two cognitive style dimensions are independent of one another, in that the position of an individual on one dimension does not affect their position on the other.

The correlation between the two dimensions has been found to be consistently low and typically $r = \pm 0.1$ (e.g. Riding and Douglas 1993; Riding *et al.* 1995; Riding and Wigley 1997). Obviously, correlation implies only a linear relationship between the variables. However, inspection of the scatter plots of these data also fails to indicate any curvilinear relationships.

Style and physiological mechanisms

In trying to establish whether a construct validly exists, various types of evidence may be considered, some of which may be psychological while others may be physiological. The evidence will be psychological where it can be shown that a measure is related to other observed behaviours, and physiological where a construct is shown to be related to a physiological measure. The psychological evidence for the validity of the construct of cognitive style, in terms of the relationships between style and observable behaviours, will be examined in Chapters 6, 7 and 8. This section will focus on the physiological evidence.

Brain activity

An important physiological index is brain activity. Obviously there are problems in trying to assess brain activity since the brain is very complex and extensive in terms of processing capacity. A crude view of the brain may be obtained by imagining a concert hall packed full, from floor to ceiling, with electronic circuits and these then being compressed into a space the size of a human brain. Further, the living human brain is rarely open to intrusive research that requires that parts are removed to see what happens.

Put overly simply, the brain may be viewed as follows. The spinal chord extends upwards into the base of the brain as the *medulla, pons* and *hypothalamus*. Behind these lies the *cerebellum*. This whole arrangement is crowned by the two *cerebral cortex* hemispheres of the *cerebrum* which are joined at the surface where they rest on the others by the *corpus callosum*.

Since the brain generates electrical activity, one of the methods of assessing whether and where processing is taking place at the surface of the cerebral cortex is to place sensitive detectors (electrodes) at various positions on the surface of a person's head while the individual performs specific tasks. This approach produces an electroencephalogram (EEG) amplifying and recording the electrical activity of the brain.

The electrical activity is in a frequency range from 1Hz to 60Hz. The frequency band 8–13 Hz is known as the Alpha band and electrical activity here is high when the person is resting and decreases when they are processing information (see e.g. Glass 1984; Fernandez *et al.* 1995). This decrease is termed 'alpha suppression'.

Hemispheric specialisation

The two hemispheres of the *cerebrum* are the left and right upper halves of the brain. Cohen (1982: 89) proposed that individual differences in left–right electrical activity may be due to cognitive style differences. Such hemispheric specialisation has long been associated with the left hemisphere being the location of the verbal function and the right with imagery processing, although evidence for this has not always been clear (see e.g. Bisiach and Berti 1990: 81; Langhinrichsen and Tucker 1990: 171). It is important to note the form of processing undertaken in a given task. For instance, an apparently spatial task will not necessarily be processed by means of images by all individuals. Where studies have paid no attention to individual differences in cognitive style, it is not surprising that results regarding localisation have often been unclear.

Levy (1990) proposed that relative verbal and spatial performance can be predicted by measurement of the balance of hemispheric activation in the resting state, the so-called tonic hemispheric activation. Therefore, alpha asymmetry in the resting EEG could theoretically correspond to the verbal-imagery dimension of cognitive style. It may be noted, however, that just because a person is not asked to perform a task, the brain may not be resting. The person may be very actively thinking about something else – the pattern on the wall, the nearness of lunch time, or plans for that evening.

By contrast, an active EEG alpha asymmetry measured during the performance of a particular task would correspond to a strategy deriving from a cognitive style. If, for example, a person solves a verbal task using a visuo-spatial strategy, then the electrophysiological asymmetries would indicate a relatively greater right hemisphere suppression. That is, the right hemisphere would be used to solve the task, rather than the left. Therefore the individual would not show a reversal of lateralisation on an absolute basis, but there would be a dynamic shift, manifested by a corresponding change in EEG asymmetry.

Style and EEG

Riding *et al.* (1993) reviewed work on EEG and verbal and imagery processing, and they suggested that for the verbal-imagery dimension, EEG alpha suppression (indicating mental activity) during information processing would occur over the left hemisphere for verbalisers and over the right for imagers. With respect to the wholist-analytic dimension, no clear prediction was made other than that it would not be in terms of left–right hemispheric specialisation.

Riding *et al.* (1997) reported a study of EEG and style which recorded EEG alpha in 15 subjects (9 male and 6 female) ranging in age from 18 to 36 years. The sample did 40 computer-presented word targeting trials in which words appeared on a computer screen. Five presentation conditions which represented different information processing loads were used. The tasks were: one word at a time at rates of two words/second, five words/second and ten words/second, and two words at a time, one above the other, at rates of five word-pairs/second and ten word-pairs/second. There were eight trials at each rate. The blocks of trials were pseudo-randomly presented. The words were selected at random from a large dictionary and the task required subjects to monitor the displayed words and respond with a button press whenever a noun from the superordinate categories 'fruit' or 'vegetable' was displayed (e.g. *apple* or *carrot*). Within each trial there were always three target words.

Each trial had a duration of 30 seconds and the EEG over that period was recorded for each of the 15 electrodes located at FP1, FP2, F7, Fz, F8, T3, C3, Cz, C4, T4, T5, Pz, T6, O1 and O2, with respect to mastoid electrodes (these are shown schematically in Figure 5.2). The EEG was digitised and the power for the alpha band (8–13 Hz) computed over the trial epoch.

Figure 5.2 Electrode locations on surface of scalp viewed from above

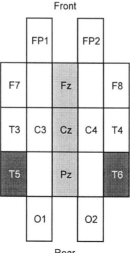

This study showed a significant effect along the Midline (locations Fz, Cz and Pz). There was an interaction between the wholist-analytic dimension and electrode location, with alpha suppression being greater for the analytics and fairly uniform along the line, while for the wholists suppression decreased from anterior to posterior, and this is shown in Figure 5.3 (adapted from Riding *et al.* 1997).

Figure 5.3 Location (Fz, Cz and Pz), wholist-analytic style

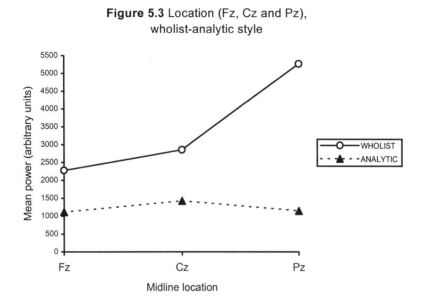

Inspection of Figure 5.3 suggests that the analytics were actively processing at a high level in all three positions, since there is alpha suppression, while the wholists processed less than analytics at Fz and Cz and much less at Pz. Since the task was analytic in nature it is not clear from this study whether this pattern would apply to a more wholist task, but it does show a big difference between wholists and analytics on this particular task especially at Pz. No gender interaction was found with the wholist-analytic dimension.

For the verbal-imagery dimension, differences might be expected particularly between the left hemisphere location T5, and the corresponding right hemisphere location at T6 (see Figure 5.2). The ratio of the power output at T5 (left) to that at T6 (right) correlated with the verbal-imagery ratio r = 0.50 in the expected direction. A further examination of the data reported by Riding *et al.* (1997) also showed some evidence of a gender effect here, with the pattern being that the male imagers showed more processing at T6 (higher suppression) than at T5, with the reverse for the females, as shown in Figure 5.4. This possibility must be viewed with some caution since the numbers of males and females is small, but if it were supported by a further study with a larger sample it could suggest a fundamental difference between males and females in information processing.

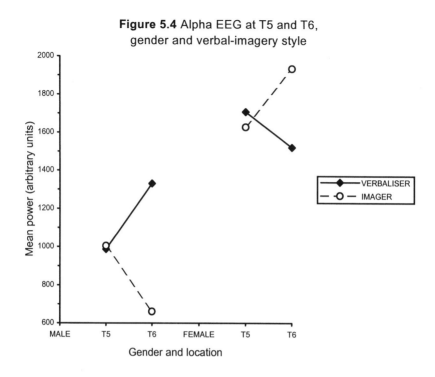

Figure 5.4 Alpha EEG at T5 and T6, gender and verbal-imagery style

Further considerations

In conclusion, the finding of significant style effects on EEG is important as providing physiological evidence for the existence of style. It should be noted that in this study the tasks were likely to favour analytics and verbalisers. Further studies are required using a range of information processing tasks that are in the natural mode for each style.

The results described above show a clear link between both of the style dimensions and brain cortical activity. However, while this study shows that style has a physiological basis, it does not completely clarify the locus of the style dimensions. It may be that these are not cortically based, but located more deeply in the brain. Studies using other brain mapping methods need to be completed to see the activity in the embedded parts of the brain.

Gender may interact with the verbal-imagery dimension but not with the wholist-analytic dimension. For the verbal-imagery style it may be that the males put most processing into their preferred style mode, while females also process in the non-habitual mode as well. However, it may be that female brain processing is different from the male. The section on gender interactions with style, later in this chapter, will consider this further.

The source of style – nature or nurture?

The fundamental question arises as to whether style is inbuilt or develops in response to experiences. This is a question which is difficult to answer, particularly since the assessment of style in infants and young children presents difficulties. Casual observation of young children of one year upwards suggests that they show consistent behaviour from an early age which does not change; a quiet child stays quiet and a talkative child continues to be verbally fluent.

No longitudinal studies of the effect of age by assessing subjects at different ages have been undertaken. However, where samples were from a wide age range no significant correlation between age and style was observed. For example, with a sample of nurses aged 21–61 years the correlations between age and wholist-analytic style, and verbal-imager style, were, respectively, r = 0.00 and r = 0.01, (from the data collected by Riding and Wheeler 1995)

Further, the small amount of available evidence on development stages and style suggests that they are unrelated. Data collected by Gatt[1] on the intellectual development of 14-year-old Maltese pupils in terms of formal operational thought did not show any developmental relationship with either the wholist-analytic or the verbal-imagery style dimensions.

It may be that style is genetically determined, but this needs further study.

Style in the context of other individual difference dimensions

The preceding sections of this chapter have established that the two fundamental style dimensions are independent of one another, and that there is some EEG evidence for the physiological reality of both style dimensions. However, the origins of style are not yet clear.

An obvious next question is how style relates to other established notions, or constructs, such as intelligence, personality and gender. A final area of consideration will be how the style dimensions and the other basic constructs may act together to influence behaviour.

Style and intelligence

Definition
In considering intelligence, one is faced with the situation that, while in practical terms the construct is widely accepted, there is considerable difficulty with its definition and scope (see e.g. Jonassen and Grabowski 1993: 43). The range of

---

1 Suzanne Gatt, University of Malta, personal communication, July 1997.

opinion is very broad, from, on the one hand, a position that views intelligence as encompassing multiple abilities (Gardner 1983), through a wide range of behaviour (e.g. Sternberg 1985), to a much more narrow conceptualisation, with an emphasis on reaction time or inspection time (see, Kline 1991: 97–106). In addition, there are even those who question whether it even exists at all (e.g. Howe 1990).

In the present context, where it is intended to compare intelligence with cognitive styles in order to identify similarities and differences, the all embracing approach is inappropriate, since it assumes that intelligence subsumes all abilities. In any empirical research the approach to intelligence is determined by the measures chosen to assess it, since in practical terms, intelligence is what intelligence tests measure (Boring 1923).

Types of intelligence

Kline (1991: 26–30) among others distinguished between two types of intelligence – *fluid* and *crystallised*. The former is related to processing speed and capacity of the brain, while the latter is affected by learning and experience. By analogy with a computer, fluid is analogous to the characteristics of the hardware such as the processor speed, disk storage, memory, etc., and crystallised to the hardware plus the available software programs. The better the software for a given hardware specification, the better the computer works.

No tests assess only fluid intelligence, and crystallised intelligence will be influenced by the quality of the *strategies* that are learned to make the most of the available ability and styles (Figure 5.5).

Figure 5.5 Intelligence and experience

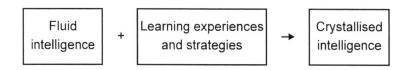

Kline (1991: 49–62; 1995: 506–11) has suggested that, in general terms, fluid intelligence is more likely to be assessed by test items such as matrices, non-verbal analogies, digit span and block design; and crystallised intelligence may normally be assessed by items involving information, comprehension, the similarity of verbally labelled objects, and vocabulary. Basically, items making the least use of prior learning and practice are most likely to assess fluid intelligence.

The relationship between style and intelligence

The items used in the following studies comparing style and intelligence were probably more fluid than crystallised.

Riding and Pearson (1994), with a sample of 119 12–13-year-old pupils, found that intelligence as measured by sub-tests of the British Abilities Scale Short Form (Elliot 1983) was not related to cognitive style. The sub-tests were as follows.

- *Speed of Information Processing*. The first ten items require that rows of circles with small squares in them are scanned and the circle in each row with the largest number of squares in is marked. The second 10 involve scanning lines of digits and marking the largest in each row.
- *Matrices (Test F)*. The matrices are square consisting of four or nine cells with the requirement to draw the correct design in a blank cell in each matrix.
- *Similarities*. There is the requirement to name the superordinate class to which a group of verbally labelled items belong.
- *Recall of Digits (Test B)*. For this scale the digit sequences are read out one at a time by the test administrator and the persons being assessed write them down on the provided pro-forma.

The correlations between the four sub-tests used and the wholist-analytic and verbal-imagery ratios were all very low and non-significant and were, respectively, Speed of Information Processing 0.07, 0.02; Matrices –0.10, 0.04; Similarities –0.03, 0.01; Recall of Digits –0.01, 0.12.

Similar findings came from a Canadian study (Riding and Agrell 1997) of the relationship between style and the Canadian Test of Cognitive Skills (CTCS) with 205 14–16-year-old students. The items were very similar in style to those commonly found in intelligence tests, for example the British Abilities Scales (Elliot 1983) and the Wechsler Intelligence Scale for Children (Wechsler 1974), and the test could be thought of as a test of intelligence. This English-language intelligence-type test comprised the following four 20 item sub-tests (see Canadian Test Centre 1992a, 1992b).

- *Sequences*. Choosing from four items one to continue a given pattern or sequence.
- *Analogies*. Given a pair of conceptually related pictures, choose one of four pictures to go with another given picture to make a second related pair.
- *Memory*. Having before the start of the test learned a nonsense name for an existing word, select from five nonsense words the one that means the given existing word.
- *Verbal Reasoning*. For a given word, or words, indicate the one from four listed that is related to the given word(s).

The respective correlations with the wholist-analytic and verbal-imagery ratios were: Sequences 0.01, –0.10; Analogies –0.01, –0.05; Memory –0.03, –0.03; Verbal Reasoning –0.02 –0.10. Again all the correlations were very low and non-significant.

Cognitive style appears to be independent of intelligence – particularly of the fluid type.

Further considerations

Style and intelligence in interaction

The evidence points to the independence of style and fluid intelligence in performing tasks. It may be that style is more critical for individuals of lower intelligence, since they will be more dependent on the material and the presentation matching their style. They may also have been capable of developing fewer strategies for dealing with situations which do not match their style.

The Riding and Agrell (1997) study also indicated an interaction between style and intelligence in their effect on school achievement, such that style was more critical where pupils were of lower ability and the subject matter did not ideally suit their style. For instance, the difference in performance between high and low ability pupils was greater for the analytic-imagers than the analytic-verbalisers, where in the latter case their style was more naturally suited to learning academic subjects.

Crystallised intelligence, style and variation in performance

In studies which include measures of both intelligence and style, intelligence usually accounts for more variance than style. With respect to crystallised intelligence measures, these are likely to include more than just processing capacity and facility, since the items commonly used in such 'intelligence' tests also assess learned knowledge and the application of acquired skills. They therefore include within the measure, the ability to learn and perform and hence explain more of the variance than style alone, but then they are not pure measures of fluid intelligence.

Style versus ability

An important area related to style and intelligence is the distinction between style and ability, and the requirement that style and ability be unrelated. Carroll (1993: 554–60) considered a number of style measures and concluded that many of them were in reality aspects of ability. It will follow from this that for any measure of style to be valid, it must not also be a measure of ability. These two points will be considered.

The distinction between style and ability

What are the characteristics of style that distinguish it from ability? McKenna (1984: 593–4) in considering the nature of cognitive style as distinct from ability, highlighted four distinguishing characteristics.

- Ability is more concerned with level of performance, while style focuses on the manner of performance.
- Ability is unipolar while style is bipolar.
- Ability has values attached to it such that one end of an ability dimension is valued and the other is not, while for a style dimension neither end is considered better overall.
- Ability has a narrower range of application than style.

Both style and ability may affect performance on a given task. The basic distinction between them is that performance on all tasks will improve as ability increases, whereas the effect of style on performance for an individual will either be positive or negative depending on the nature of the task. It follows from this that for an individual at one end of a style dimension, a task of a type they find difficult will be found easier by someone at the other end of the dimension, and vice versa. For instance, if the dimension were the verbal-imagery style, then verbalisers would find pictorial tasks more difficult than would imagers, but they would find highly verbal tasks easier than would imagers. In other words, in terms of style a person is *both* good *and* poor at tasks depending on the nature of the task, while for intelligence, they are *either* good *or* poor.

It is in the nature of a style, as distinct from an ability, that it should interact with a variable such that the relative performance of an individual at one extreme of a dimension should be higher than that of a person at the other end in one condition, but that the situation should be reversed when the condition is changed. This is shown schematically in Figure 5.6.

Figure 5.6 shows an idealised relationship which in practice is not likely to be so linear and the crossover may not be at the centre of the dimension. Further, in many real-life tasks there is likely to be an interaction between the two dimensions and the condition, rather than an effect of only one of the dimensions without any effect of the other. However, single dimension interactions have been observed.

For the wholist-analytic dimension, this type of interaction was observed in the case of Douglas and Riding (1993) in a study on recall of the effect of the position of a prose passage title, and by Riding and Grimley who found that wholists learned better from computer presented information and analytics from more traditional methods.

In the case of the verbal-imagery dimension the interaction was found in the studies by Riding and Douglas (1993) on 'text-plus-text' versus 'text-plus-picture' presentation of learning material, and by Riding and Watts (1997) in the observed preference for verbal or pictorial formats of instructional material.

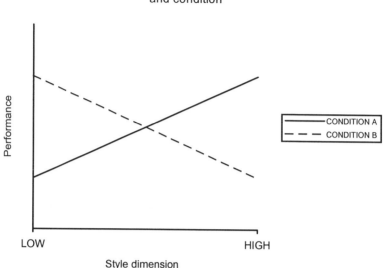

Figure 5.6 Schematic graph of performance and condition

Intelligence and tests of embedded shapes

The study by Riding and Pearson (1994) also found that a Test of Embedded Shapes[2] (TES) did not correlate significantly with wholist-analytic style (r = 0.04), but it did correlate with IQ (r = 0.47). The TES comprised a Worked Example Section, a Practice and a Response Section, containing four, four and thirty-two items, respectively. The test required that a simple shape be located within a complex shape. The items were presented in a booklet with four per page. The simple shape was located by the side of the complex shape, but with a different orientation to its position within the complex shape. The subjects were required to indicate the embedded simple shape by drawing around it with a pencil. The simple and complex shapes were derived from overlapping arrangements of three or four circles, sometimes with the addition of straight lines. For the Response Section, the subjects were allowed 12 minutes, and their score was the number of embedded shapes correctly located.

This was an interesting finding, since the TES was of a type similar to, and administered in the same timed manner as, the Group Embedded Figure Test (GEFT) (Witkin *et al.* 1971) which has been used to assess field-dependence–independence. Both tests are scored in terms of the number of simple shapes that can be found in a series of more complex geometrical figures in a given time. It has been questioned whether this approach to assessing style is valid since it is usually found that field-independents are superior in performance to

2 Unpublished test. Frank Pearson, Assessment Research Unit, University of Birmingham, 1989.

field-dependents, and do better on tests of intelligence (see e.g. Goldstein and Blackman 1978: 185–6; Flexer and Roberge 1980). McKenna (1984) has argued that the Group Embedded Figures Test does not meet the criteria of a cognitive style, but correlates with ability tests.

This is not to question the validity of the construct of field-dependence–independence as such, but only the method commonly used for its assessment. The GEFT has tended to be used as a more convenient alternative to the original instrument, the Rod and Frame Test. However, the correlation between them is not very high, and according to Goldstein and Blackman (1978: 183–4) ranges from 0.30 to 0.65. An important implication of this is that the results of studies assessing field-dependence–independence by means of the GEFT need to be treated with caution.

By contrast, the Cognitive Styles Analysis positively assesses both the wholist and the analytic ends of the dimension, and consequently probably more accurately assesses this dimension of style. Certainly, studies have shown evidence of bipolarity with wholists often being superior to analytics in performance.

Personality and style

Personality dimensions
In attempting to compare cognitive style and personality it would be convenient if the personality dimensions and their underlying physiological mechanisms had been clearly identified, but this is not yet the case. As in other areas of research, there are difficulties in the identification of personality dimensions. Factor analysis, a frequently used tool in grouping descriptors in personality research, often yields different results depending upon the investigator (see Cattell 1995: 207).

In view of this, it is not surprising that there is still debate about how many factors the descriptors of personality should be resolved into (see e.g. Boyle *et al.* 1995: 431–3; Cattell 1995: 207). Bouchard (1995: 95–7), among others, saw the two major personality paradigms as Eysenck's 'Big Three' of Extraversion, Neuroticism and Psychoticism (Eysenck and Eysenck 1985), and the 'Big Five' of Extraversion, Neuroticism, Openness, Agreeableness and Conscientiousness (McCrae and John 1992; Deary and Matthews 1993: 299). There appears to be general agreement about Extraversion and Neuroticism. Psychoticism is seen either as a singe factor or as encompassing Agreeableness and Conscientiousness (see Bouchard 1995: 95).

Style and personality
With 12-year-old children, Riding and Dyer (1980) found a correlation of –0.67 for boys and –0.76 for girls between an earlier measure of verbal-imagery

style (the verbal-imagery Code Test) and introversion–extraversion. There are aspects of the verbal-imagery dimension that affect social behaviour, since this dimension influences the focus and type of an individual's activity, externally in the case of verbalisers, and internally for imagers.

However, with the Cognitive Styles Analysis, Riding and Wigley (1997) in a study of 340 College of Further Education students aged 17–18 years used a range of questionnaire measures of personality and attitude, for comparison with cognitive style, and these included, EPQ-R Short Scale (Eysenck and Eysenck 1991) Extraversion, Neuroticism and Psychoticism, IVE Questionnaire (Eysenck and Eysenck 1991) Impulsiveness, Venturesomeness and Empathy, and State and Trait Anxiety Inventory (Spielberger 1977). A Principal Components factor analysis with Oblique rotation gave four factors which were labelled Anxiety, Impulsiveness, Empathy and Style. No personality measure loaded beyond ±0.33 on Style.

They also considered the interactive effect of wholist-analytic style and verbal-imagery style on personality measures. They found significant effects such that with neuroticism, wholist-verbalisers and analytic-imagers were more anxious than analytic-verbalisers and wholist-imagers. With impulsiveness, wholist-verbalisers and analytic-imagers were more impulsive/decisive than analytic-verbalisers and wholist-imagers. They proposed a tentative model in which physiologically based personality sources are independent of cognitive style but are moderated by style in their effect on behaviour.

Further considerations

The results suggest that cognitive style and personality sources are not the same since the correlations between them approximate to zero. However, the finding of significant interactions between the style dimensions in their effects on neuroticism and impulsiveness, and of a non-linear relationship between wholist-analytic style and psychoticism, raises the question of how personality sources and style combine to affect behaviour.

It is possible that the physiological sources of personality act through a cognitive control level comprising the two styles. Behaviour is then a combination of the level of the personality source, plus or minus the component due to style, which may either add to or decrease the effect of the source. Taking neuroticism as an example, a given level of physiological anxiety source is amplified by being wholist-verbaliser or analytic-imager, and perhaps moderated by being analytic-verbaliser. It seems likely that the major contributor to observed personality related behaviour is the underlying physiological source, with a lesser, but nevertheless, practically significant effect of style. This will be discussed more fully in Chapter 6.

Gender differences and style

There do not appear to be overall gender differences with respect to cognitive style. Differences are usually small and non-significant on both dimensions (P > 0.05) (e.g. Riding *et al.* 1995).

Achievement

With respect to academic achievement, there is the generally observed pattern of females out-performing males in most subjects but less so in mathematics and science (see e.g. Skaalvik and Rankin 1994). However, the interpretation of such overall sex differences is fraught with difficulty, since there is a confounding of cultural and biological variables. A step forward may be to consider information processing and also style and gender interactions.

Information processing and gender

A number of studies have shown sex differences in the performance on information processing tasks. These could be interpreted as caused by fundamental differences in the ways in which females and males process information. Riding and Vincent (1980) studied speech rate and the way in which information was structured. They found that increasing speech rate reduced the recall of related prose passage details that were positioned distantly from one another more for 7–15-year-old girls than for boys, compared to closely positioned details. An interpretation of this is that the girls undertake a more complete search of related information in memory. Consequently when processing details they take longer, and at the faster speech rate they run out of time to complete the processing.

Riding and Smith (1981) found that 11-year-old boys were superior to girls on the recall of prose passage details after listening to a single spoken presentation. With two consecutive presentations of the passage at a slow speech rate, girls were slightly better than boys. This could also be interpreted in terms of males processing faster to a more superficial level than females. Riding and Egelstaff (1983: 165) studied the detection of changed words in prose passages. In a condition where the change would not alter the image that could be generated of a scene, they found that 11-year-old boys were inferior to girls when the meaning change was small, but superior when it was great. This suggested that the processing by the males was more in the nature of an overall scan.

In conclusion, these results could be interpreted as indicating that males process faster, but to a more superficial level, than females, who are more thorough. The next step is to consider how this may interact with style.

Personality, style and gender

Interaction has also been found between the personality dimension of intro-version-extraversion and task performance such that the performance of the females tends to be a mirror image of that of the males.

Riding and Cowley (1986) noted that the reading performance of 7–8-year-old boys increased with extraversion, while for the girls it decreased. Riding and Armstrong (1982) found that with 11-year-old boys, performance on a geometry-type of mathematics test decreased with extraversion, while it increased for girls. Riding and Pearson (1994) used the Cognitive Styles Analysis to assess learning style and found that overall examination performance on a range of school subjects by 12–13-year-olds was highest for bimodals for boys, and lowest for bimodals for girls (bimodals are those at the central section of the verbal-imagery dimension).

These results suggest that males do best when their cognitive style theoretically suits the task, while females do not, particularly in situations where processing time is limited. This may be because of their different approaches to processing described above.

This mirror image has been found in studies of style and behaviour, and style and learning, described in Chapters 6 and 7. As reported earlier in this chapter, there is a hint that the verbal-imagery style dimension interacts with gender in terms of the location of brain activity, and this may account for the mirror image, with the fast, more superficial, processing of the males and the more thorough approach of the females.

The cognitive control model

The consideration of intelligence, personality, and gender has suggested that they have effects that are independent of those of style, and that they are therefore different sources of influence. This section will explore this independence and interaction.

A possible model, which is an elaboration of those of Curry (1983), of Riding and Rayner (1995), Riding 1997 (42–4), and Riding and Wigley (1997), and which also bears some similarities to that of Furnham (1995: 398), will be sketched in outline, and this is shown schematically in Figure 5.7.

At the lowest, inmost level there are a number of underlying Primary Sources comprising the memory of individuals' past experiences and knowledge, their underlying personality sources, and their gender. In order to make the model more concrete, some of the personality sources have been given tentative names, although clear physiological mechanisms for them have yet to be fully identified.

Figure 5.7 Cognitive control model

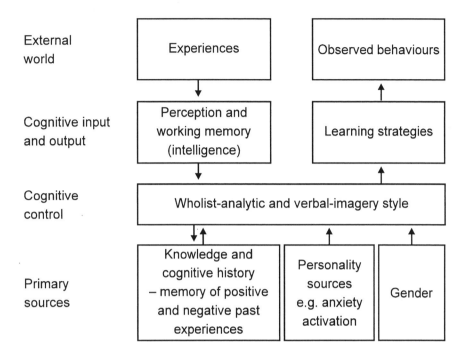

The next level is that of Cognitive Control. This comprises the two dimensions of style, the wholist-analytic and the verbal-imagery. It provides the organisational and representational interface between the internal state and the external world. It combines the internal state with the information from the external world and imposes on the response and view its own structure and form. The ways in which the wholist-analytic dimension and the verbal-imagery dimension may affect attitude and behaviour have been discussed by Riding (1991b, 1994).

At the input level will be the perceptual and working memory processing system which analyses the incoming information. The performance of this may be considered to be a major determiner of 'intelligence' as assessed by fluid intelligence tests since many test items seem to concentrate on this area.

At the output level there will be the learning strategies. These will have developed, by for instance, the individual sensing that certain modes are easier to use, and then recognising a learning preference, and then deciding to 'translate' new incoming information into that representation. At this level there will also be the cognitive response 'set' that influences social behaviour.

The perception of experiences will probably be moderated by the cognitive control level in interaction with the cognitive history and the primary personality sources within the individual. Taking anxiety as an example, and building on Spielberger (1966) and Eysenck (1991), external stimuli are assessed by the cognitive control level as to whether or not they are threatening. Those that are interpreted as being threatening trigger the anxiety source and the level of state anxiety increases and this in turn is reflected in behaviour. The interpretation of the threat will be affected by cognitive style and also the characteristics of the trait anxiety source.

Some tentative evidence for the model comes from observations of inter-actions between intelligence, style and gender in affecting academic achievement (Riding and Agrell 1997) and between style and personality sources in affecting social behaviour (Riding and Wigley 1997).

Concluding considerations

The available evidence indicates that the construct of style as assessed by the Cognitive Styles Analysis approach shows two clearly distinct dimensions, each of which has a physiological basis.

Since style is different from intelligence, common personality measures and gender, it represents a potentially important variable in explaining individual differences in behaviour. Chapter 6 will consider the relationship between style and a range of behaviours.

Cognitive style and behaviours

Chapter overview

This chapter will consider the two related areas of style and personal behaviour, and style and occupation.

Personal behaviour

- How does style affect decision making?
- In what ways does style influence social behaviour?
- How does style interact in affecting anxiety level?

Occupation and career development

- In what ways does style affect the ideal occupation for an individual?
- How can style understanding contribute to effective team building?

Since cognitive style affects the ways in which an individual thinks about and internally represents situations in the external world, it is reasonable to expect that it might also be related to aspects of a range of behaviours. This chapter will consider evidence for relationships between cognitive style and two areas of behaviour – personal behaviour and occupational performance.

Personal behaviour includes decision making, social behaviour, and anxiety. The making of decisions is important in everyday life both in the personal life of an individual and in their work. Social relationships form the basis of society and often have a great effect on the happiness of both the individual and the people with whom they live and work. Anxiety and the individual's response to stresses is a major contributor to personal happiness and health.

The consideration of occupation and career development will dwell on the implications of cognitive style for occupational suitability and team building. Both of these are relevant to the career development of the individual and to effectiveness in the workplace.

Personal behaviour

Decision making

An important aspect of behaviour is the ability to make up one's mind and be decisive. In practice, this will range from an individual being very impulsive and perhaps giving insufficient thought to decisions, to, at the other extreme, being too ponderous and spending so much time considering all the options, that the person is indecisive to the point of being inefficient. To facilitate a consideration of the interaction between the style dimensions and decision making, their possible effects in combination will be outlined first.

Style dimensions in combination

It has been observed (e.g. Riding and Sadler-Smith 1992: 336) that where a dimension of their style is not appropriate to the task, individuals often employ a strategy of using, where possible, the other dimension as an alternative. For instance, an analytic-imager, whose analytic style aspect would not provide an overview of a situation, could attempt to use the whole-view aspect of imagery to make good the deficiency. If another person were a wholist-verbaliser, then since the analytic facility is missing, that person might use the 'analytic' property of verbalisation as a substitute. It is possible to arrange the style groupings in order, in terms of the degree to which there is an 'analytic' facility present.

The 'analytic' to 'wholist' axis
In terms of analytic facility, individuals may be ranked in terms of 'analytic-ness', from the lowest in the wholist-imagers to the highest in the

Figure 6.1 The cognitive style dimensions

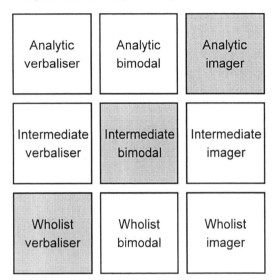

analytic-verbalisers. Neither of these extremes has the facility to use the other style dimension to supply the missing facility. On this basis, style may be ordered approximately from least analytic/most 'wholist' (1) to most 'analytic' (9) to as shown by the numbers in Figure 6.1.

From Figure 6.1 the continuum of 'extreme wholist' to 'extreme analytic' is then as shown in Figure 6.2.

Figure 6.2 Wholist–analytic continuum

extreme 'wholist'						extreme 'analytic'		
WI	WB	II	WV	IB	AI	IV	AB	AV

This continuum, and the shaded axis, will now be used in the consideration of style and decision making in the next section.

Style and decisiveness

Riding and Wigley (1997) assessed cognitive style using the Cognitive Styles Analysis and impulsiveness by means of the IVE Questionnaire (Eysenck and Eysenck 1991) in a sample of 340 16–18-year-old college of further education students. It may be noted that the dimension implied by the questionnaire items was really as follows:

very indecisive ----------- indecisive ----------- decisive ------------- impulsive
(min 0)   (max 19)

Those who are higher on the scale are more decisive, while those on the lower end tend to be indecisive. Here the relevant aspect of style would appear to be the wholist to analytic facility. The mean impulsiveness scores when ordered in this manner are shown in Figure 6.3 (adapted from Riding and Wigley 1997).

Inspection of Figure 6.3 indicates that those who are most 'analytic' (i.e. analytic-verbalisers) are relatively indecisive since they will be inclined to consider and weigh-up all the possibilities before making a decision. Those who are very 'wholist' (i.e. wholist-imagers) will be able to see a broad perspective and the relevance of all aspects of the situation in an overall balance, and they also will not be decisive. People who are more decisive will be those who lack the constraint of the high analytic on the one hand, and the overall very wholist or balanced perspective, on the other, and this will include those whose style lies on the wholist-verbaliser to analytic-imager axis which is shaded in Figure 6.1.

Further considerations

It is important to bear in mind, as already observed, that 'impulsive' in the context of the test items could also be interpreted as 'decisive' particularly bearing in mind the largest mean score of approximately 11.4 out of a maximum

Figure 6.3 Style and impulsiveness

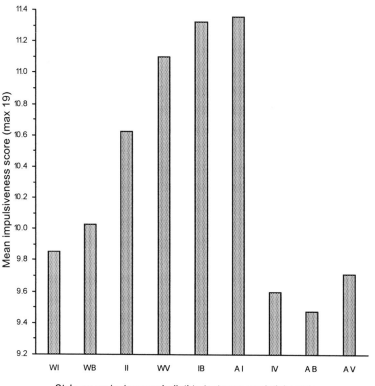

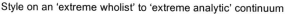
Style on an 'extreme wholist' to 'extreme analytic' continuum

of 19. There is a sense in which extreme analytics are so good at seeing all the possibilities that they cannot bring themselves to make a decision. Similarly, extreme wholists can be so mindful of the wider view, that they do not say 'yes' and they do not say 'no'. This area needs further examination within practical contexts to see what are the effects on learning performance and problem solving. It will also have implications for management.

Style and social behaviour

In Chapter 5 it was argued that, while the cognitive style dimensions affect behaviours similar to those associated with personality, they appear to be distinctly different. The available evidence, while not yet making the picture completely clear, will be examined, initially by taking each cognitive style dimension in turn.

Wholist-analytic style and social behaviour

The wholist-analytic style represents a family of styles which includes field-dependence–independence. Witkin *et al.* (1979) considered the effects of this dimension on aspects of personality related to the perception of self and non-self. They argued that self–non-self segregation increases with field-independence (see also Korchin 1986). Riding (1991b) has suggested that the wholist-analytic style will be reflected socially in such dimensions as being dependent–self-reliant, flexible–consistent, realistic–idealistic, vague–organised. Wholists will tend to the first mentioned extreme and analytics to the other.

Figure 6.4 Characteristic and wholist-analytic style

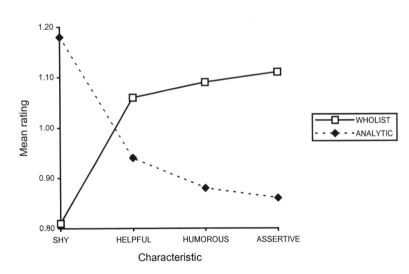

Some evidence for this suggestion comes from a study by Riding and Wright (1995) who asked 149 undergraduate students living in university flats with typically five per flat to rate their flatmates in terms of personal characteristics, and these are shown in Figure 6.4 (adapted from Riding and Wright 1995).

The graph in Figure 6.4 shows that the wholists were rated as more assertive, humorous and helpful, while the analytics were seen as more shy. It should be noted that there was a restricted choice of people to rate in the flats which might explain findings at variance with the results of Riding *et al.* (1995) below.

Verbal-imagery style and social behaviour

Riding *et al.* (1995) asked 380 12-year-old pupils to rate the children in their class in terms of seven characteristics: outgoing, lively, humorous, shy, quiet, serious, patient. They were asked to name the four highest in their class group on each of the seven attributes. These were then scored 4 for each highest, through to 1 for the fourth names and zero if not named. The ratings were then grouped as Active (outgoing, lively, humorous), Modest (shy, quiet) and Responsible (serious, patient). A significant interaction between verbal-imagery style and characteristic was found and this is shown in Figure 6.5 (adapted from Riding *et al.* 1995).

They found verbalisers scored highest on Active and decreased through Responsible and Modest. Bimodals increased in score from Active to Modest, while imagers were rated highest on Responsible.

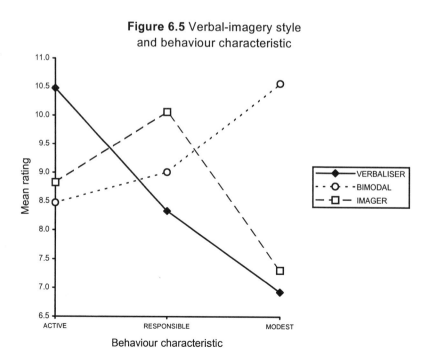

Figure 6.5 Verbal-imagery style and behaviour characteristic

As discussed in Chapter 5 in the section on Personality and Style, it is not simply that extraversion–introversion and verbaliser-imager are respectively the social and cognitive manifestations of the same underlying mechanism. Rather, there are aspects of the verbal-imagery dimension that affect social behaviour, since this dimension influences the focus and type of an individual's activity. This behaviour is externally focused and engaging in the case of verbalisers, and internally focused and more passive for imagers.

Style interactions with social behaviour

Just as the style dimensions can interact to affect decisiveness, they can also interact in affecting social behaviour, although the order of the combinations of style will be different.

Style and harmony among flatmates

Riding and Wright (1995) in the study described above also assessed the degree of unity in each flat by means of rating questions such as, 'Relations in my accommodation have been harmonious'. In terms of the majority style type in each flat, the order of reported unity from least to highest was: analytic-imager, wholist-imager, analytic-verbaliser, wholist-verbaliser. This order was as expected since analytics are likely to be more separate than wholists and imagers are likely to be more inward and detached than verbalisers.

Further considerations

There is evidence that the two style dimensions act separately, and also in interaction with one another, in affecting social behaviour, although further studies are needed to clarify the picture. The tendency seems to be that the wholist-analytic dimension alone affects an assertiveness–shyness dimension. For the verbal-imagery dimension there is an active–passive dimension, in the sense of being outwardly active versus inwardly focused in terms of thought, but not so in terms of action, that is, an externalisation leading to action versus an internalisation of thought focusing on an inner world. These two effects will then operate in interaction.

Style and anxiety

The ways in which the two style dimensions may act together will be considered first, although a different axis will be taken.

Complementary–unitary axis

As noted earlier in this chapter, the style dimensions may either complement or intensify one another, depending on the combination of the dimensions.

Figure 6.6 The cognitive style dimensions

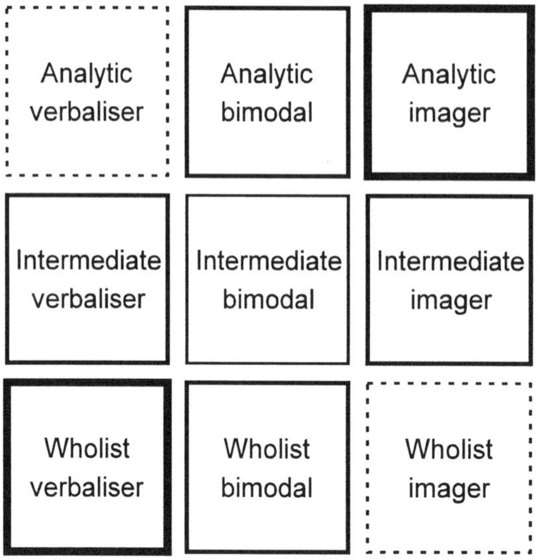

Previously, it was suggested that the style combinations could be ordered from extreme 'wholist' to extreme ' analytic' in terms of the facility that they offer. In this section it is proposed that an ordering may be obtained on the basis of a combination of styles offering complementary facilities, in contrast to those that offer similar facilities. Examples of complementary styles are, for instance, if someone were an analytic-imager. Since the analytic aspect of their style will not provide an overview of a situation, they could attempt to use the whole-view aspect of imagery to supply it. If another person were a wholist-verbaliser, then since the wholist facility does not support analysis, they might use the 'analytic' property of verbalisation as a substitute.

The ordering may be done by starting with the wholist-verbalisers, who have a complementary combination and progressing in step-wise manner to the wholist-imagers who have the most unitary combination. The order is given by the numbers in Figure 6.6, with the most complementary having a very bold border to their boxes, through to the most unitary having a light broken border. If these are then ordered from Complementary to Unitary they will be as shown in Figure 6.7.

Figure 6.7 Complementary to unitary continuum

Complementary								Unitary
WV	AI	IV	II	WB	AB	IB	AV	WI

Style and neuroticism

Riding and Wigley (1997) found a significant interaction between wholist-analytic and verbal-imagery dimensions such that neuroticism was highest for the wholist-verbalisers and the analytic imagers and lowest for the analytic-verbalisers and the wholist-imagers. In order to facilitate the interpretation of the findings for neuroticism, the styles were ordered from complementary to unitary, as described above, and this is shown in Figure 6.8 (adapted from Riding and Wigley 1997).

Inspection of the graph in Figure 6.8 shows that neuroticism is highest for the styles that are complementary (i.e. wholist-verbaliser and analytic-imager) and lowest for those that are not. A possible reason for this is that wholists who lack any analytic facility will be able to see all aspects of a situation in balance and will not focus just on some negative aspects. In reality, nothing is totally bad, only some parts, and this style evens out the bad with the good. Similarly, those who have only an analytic facility will have everything ordered and under control and will perceive less stress. Those who seem most susceptible to neuroticism are those with the facility to switch between the two modes.

Further considerations

As Riding and Wigley (1995) noted (as discussed in Chapter 5), it is likely that the observed level of neuroticism is a combination of the level of the physiological source of anxiety, which is then moderated by cognitive style in such a way that for the complementary styles it is increased and for the unitary ones it is decreased.

Figure 6.8 Style and neuroticism

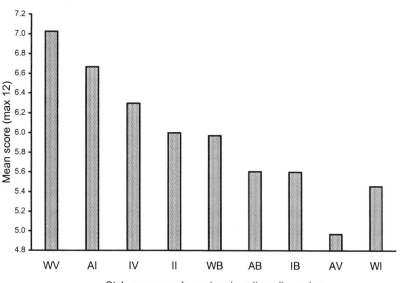

Style on a complementary to unitary dimension

It is possible that the physiological sources of personality act through a cognitive control level comprising the two styles. Behaviour is then a combination of the level of the personality source, plus or minus the component due to style, which may either add to or decrease the effect of the source. Taking neuroticism as an example, a given level of physiological anxiety source is amplified in individuals who are wholist-verbalisers or analytic-imagers, and perhaps moderated in analytic-verbalisers. It seems likely that the major contributor to observed personality related behaviour is the underlying physiological source, with a lesser but nevertheless practically significant effect of style.

The notion of the style dimensions acting in combination is related to the possible development of coping strategies in a social context. This development has a parallel with the acquisition of learning strategies described in Chapter 4.

Optimism versus pessimism

People may be described in terms of whether they tend to optimism or pessimism. There has been interest in the notion of optimism since it may be related to psychological and physical well-being (see e.g. Scheier and Carver 1992). Whether optimism-pessimism is a separate dimension or related to stability – neuroticism is not clear (see Wiebe and Smith 1997: 903–5). In the present context, optimism is used to describe an inclination to interpret situations positively rather than negatively.

Inclination to be sensitive to stress

In a study of optimism,[1] 40 Methodist Church members were asked to rate on a scale from 1 to 5 the Threat or Comfort they felt when they read each of 25 verses taken from the Bible. Examples of the verses were: comfort, 'The Lord is my shepherd, I shall not want' (Psalm 23:1); threat, 'The wages of sin is death' (Romans 6:23). Figure 6.9 shows the tendency to perceive verses as threatening rather than comforting. Note that the data have been inverted to make fear high and comfort low.

The male imagers and the female verbalisers were more inclined to see the negative aspects of verses and could be seen as more pessimistic than the male verbalisers and the female imagers. While the reason for this is not clear, it will be seen below that a similar pattern has been found with respect to perceived stress.

---

1 Data collected by the Revd Phyl Fanning, Assessment Research Unit, University of Birmingham 1997.

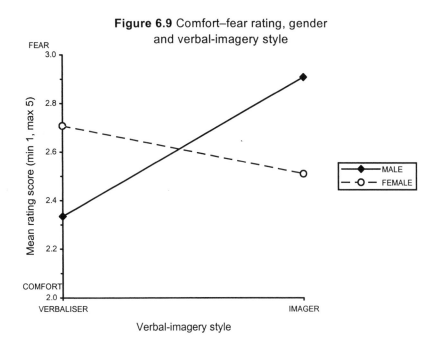

Figure 6.9 Comfort–fear rating, gender and verbal-imagery style

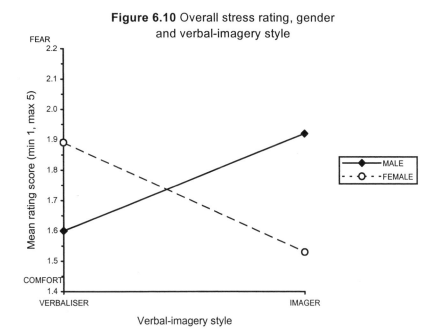

Figure 6.10 Overall stress rating, gender and verbal-imagery style

Perceived level of stress

Borg and Riding (1993) gave a sample 212 Maltese secondary school teachers a 30 item stress questionnaire where the items were rated on a Likert-type scale labelled from 'no stress' to 'extreme stress' and scored from zero to four. Four sub-scales were derived from the inventory: 'pupil misbehaviour', 'poor working conditions', 'poor staff relationships' and 'time pressures'. They found that the male imagers and the female verbalisers reported the greater overall stress, as shown in Figure 6.10 (adapted from Borg and Riding 1993).

Inspection of the graph in Figure 6.10 shows a similarity with that obtained in the study of the reaction to Bible verses giving comfort or threat. It may be that those who report the greater stress are those who are more pessimistic.

Further considerations

The findings are examples of a gender by style interaction where the males are a mirror image of the females, as described in Chapter 5. Further, it may be noted that optimism represents an interaction between style and gender, while neuroticism is affected by style alone, suggesting a distinction between optimism-pessimism and stability-neuroticism.

Practical applications

Cognitive styles have considerable potential implications for personal development.

How can learning styles aid personal development?

In one sense people know themselves very well, and in another they do not, because they can see themselves only from the inside, and not as others see them. Furthermore, their only experience of thinking is of their own, and it is easy for them to assume that everyone else sees things and thinks in a similar way.

In reality, all people are different, not only in the obvious respect of looking different, but also in the ways in which they think and view things. While the former is readily seen, it is more difficult to observe the second, because it is not possible to look inside people to see how they think.

An important requirement for personal development is that people should see themselves as others see them and have some understanding of their make-up. They will then be more able to work with others effectively, since they will be able to use their strengths and to moderate their weaknesses. They will also be able to understand others better and to appreciate their strengths. A useful tool for personal development is the Personal Style Awareness (PSA) booklet (Riding 1994) for use with the Cognitive Styles Analysis. This helps an individual to interpret their learning style result and to see how it influences their behaviour. The PSA can be used to facilitate the steps in personal development set out below.

Personal development and style awareness

Style awareness and its application to the way people think and behave needs to progress through several stages.

- Before having their style assessed, people are largely unaware of it, and, while it is there, it is *hidden* from view by the fact that they have no experience of being any different.
- The first stage in personal development is *awareness* of style and its implications for the way a person's method of thinking affects their behaviour.
- The next stage is the *application* of this awareness to the range of situations that make up the individual's life (Figure 6.11). This will lead to an increasing self-actualisation and consequently make the person more effective.

Figure 6.11 Application of awareness

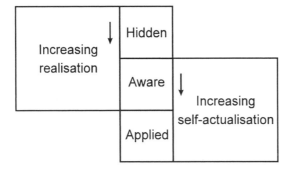

What practical steps can be used?

Personal development involves the following stages of self-actualisation.

Raising self-awareness

It is important that individuals find out more about the ways other people are likely to see them. This can be a bit like the experience of someone who hears a recording of their voice for the first time, and exclaims, 'Do I really sound like that?' Until people have clear self-perceptions they cannot begin personal development.

Riding (1991b) outlined the probable effects on social attributes of the wholist-analytic and the verbal-imagery dimensions, and these are shown in

Tables 6.1 and 6.2 (adapted from Riding 1991b). Materials of this type could be used to help raise the self-awareness of individuals to their positive and negative attributes.

Table 6.1 Probable wholist-analytic style social attributes

Social attribute				
Social activity	Wholists		Analytics	
	Positive	Negative	Positive	Negative
Social approach	Social	Dependent	Self-reliant	Isolationist
	Open	Pushing	Sharing	Scheming
	Aware	Jealous	Dependent	Resentful
Relating to others	Realistic	Changeable	Idealistic	Inactive
	Not extreme	Vague	Organised	Rigid
	Flexible	Inconsistent	Consistent	Inflexible
Response to others	Spontaneous	Shallow	Attributes cause	Inactive
	Generous	Rash	(blames others)	Detached
	Caring	Superficial	Accountable	Sentimental
			Pitying	

Table 6.2 Probable verbal-imagery style social attributes

Social attribute				
Social activity	Verbalisers		Imagers	
	Positive	Negative	Positive	Negative
Social approach	Outgoing	Overwhelming	Polite	Withdrawn
Social activity	Lively	Overactive	Restrained	Inhibited

People can become more self-aware, and this will change the way they view themselves and others. Self-awareness has two benefits:

- individuals recognise their strengths
- they are more sensitive to their limitations.

In addition to knowing oneself more fully, it is helpful to know more about other people so that one can be aware of their styles, both in appreciating their positive qualities and being more tolerant of the more negative aspects.

Application: developing enabling strategies
In a variety of situations, it is useful for people to pause and ask themselves if they could think or behave differently from how they would perform naturally, particularly to avoid the more limiting aspects of their style.

As has been noted above, it is helpful to distinguish between a *style* which is relatively fixed and not liable to substantial change, and a *strategy* which may be developed to deal and cope with situations for which the style is not ideally suited. People develop strategies, or ways, to make the most of their positive points, and to enable them to utilise their style to do tasks that they would normally find difficult. They also develop strategies to reduce the effects of their limitations, and to constrain the adverse effects of the areas where they are less strong.

Individuals can also learn to increase their effectiveness by linking, in their work, with people of complementary learning styles so that they can benefit by

- recognising their own strengths
- actively acknowledging the areas in which they are less strong
- positively recognising the strengths of others
- working collaboratively with others, listening to what they have to say, and paying attention to their views.

Style and occupational suitability

Since style is related to social behaviour and decision making, it is likely to be related to the suitability of an individual for a particular occupation.

Stress and type of occupation

Borg and Riding (1993) found an interaction between the source of stress and wholist-analytic style of the teachers, and this is shown in Figure 6.12 (adapted from Borg and Riding 1993).

Inspection of Figure 6.12 suggests that the amount of stress reported was in line with the expectation of wholists being more open and people orientated, and analytics being more structured and organised. The wholists reported more stress from time pressures and staff relations, while the analytics found pupil misbehaviour and working conditions more stressful.

Stress in nurses
Riding and Wheeler (1995), in a study of 204 nurses, found evidence that the type of nursing that most suited individual nurses was related to their style. A questionnaire was used to assess their reported level of stress and of general satisfaction with their job. Two aspects will be considered here: style by gender interaction and style and job suitability.

Figure 6.12 Teacher stress and wholist-analytic style

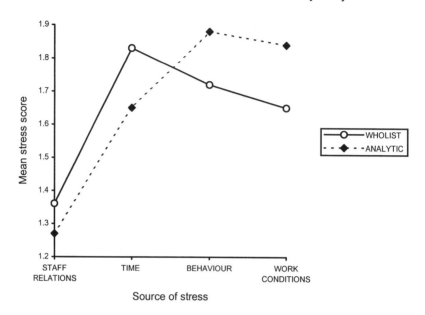

- Style by gender interaction. In this study the interaction between gender and verbal-imagery style in their effect on overall stress was not significant. The sample was unbalanced with respect to gender with 80 per cent of the nurses being female. However, the pattern of the means was similar to that for the Borg and Riding study – that is, with the male imagers and the female verbalisers reporting higher levels of stress than the male verbalisers and the female imagers.
- Job suitability. A Suitability Index was obtained from (Satisfaction minus Stress), and this was compared with their style and type of nursing. The styles with the highest and lowest indices on three types of nursing are shown in Table 6.3.

Table 6.3 Style and suitability for type of nursing

Suitability level	Type of nursing and style		
	General	Orthopaedic	Psychiatric
Highest	Analytic-verbaliser	Intermediate-bimodals	Wholist-imagers
Lowest	Wholist-imager	Analytic-imager	Intermediate-verbaliser

It could be argued that general nursing is dynamic, requiring conscientious activity; orthopaedic nursing is slower, needing patience; and psychiatric nursing is demanding, benefiting from tolerance.

This approach could usefully be applied to other occupations.

Style and occupational type

The findings reported in the previous section that certain styles appear more suited to particular types of employment suggests that some occupations may be more appropriate for some styles than for others. While a large-scale formal study still has to be undertaken, data from a range of sources suggest that this may be so. Figure 6.13 shows the most frequently represented style groups for occupations for which data are available.

The groupings used are those given by the Cognitive Styles Analysis (Version 1.0), which was based on a standardisation sample of 1,147, and divides each style dimension into three equally sized groups in term of numbers of individuals. This gives nine style groups. The divisions, with the ratio ranges, were: for the wholist-analytic dimension, wholist up to 1.02, intermediate 1.03–1.35, analytic 1.36 and above, and for the verbal-imagery dimension, verbalisers up to 0.98, bimodals 0.99–1.09, imagers 1.10 and above.

For any occupation where there was an equal spread of individuals across the style groups, with nine groups there would be 11.1 per cent in each. In order to show the frequency for certain styles for particular occupations, where these were between 16 and 21 per cent in a style grouping, Figure 6.13 sets the name of the occupation in lower case letters; for 22–7 per cent, upper case letters are used; and for 28 per cent and above, bold upper case letters are used.

Inspection of Figure 6.13 suggests that a number of major occupations are represented by distinct style types in a predominant manner as indicated by their entry in bold type. For example, architects need to have a whole view of the buildings they are designing. With computers, the user is limited to what is displayed on the screen at any particular time, so the facility for forming an overall view of data or a document will be useful in the case of the computer operators. Roadworks supervisors, who oversee the digging and back filling of holes in roads for inspecting or laying pipes, will find it an advantage to be able to have a spatial facility for their work.

The absence of occupations in some style groups is probably a reflection of those occupations considered so far. Wholist-verbalisers are likely to include, for instance, marketing personnel.

Team development

Since most people work with others, and in one way or another are part of a team, the development of interpersonal relations will improve team performance. Team development can be further facilitated by helping people to identify their team roles and to appreciate one another's attributes, so that they can consider how they can work more effectively together.

Figure 6.13 Occupations for style groupings

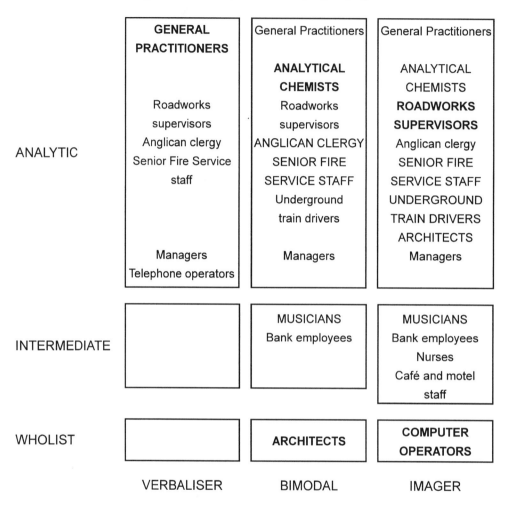

	VERBALISER	BIMODAL	IMAGER
ANALYTIC	**GENERAL PRACTITIONERS** Roadworks supervisors Anglican clergy Senior Fire Service staff Managers Telephone operators	General Practitioners **ANALYTICAL CHEMISTS** Roadworks supervisors ANGLICAN CLERGY SENIOR FIRE SERVICE STAFF Underground train drivers Managers	General Practitioners ANALYTICAL CHEMISTS **ROADWORKS SUPERVISORS** Anglican clergy SENIOR FIRE SERVICE STAFF UNDERGROUND TRAIN DRIVERS ARCHITECTS Managers
INTERMEDIATE		MUSICIANS Bank employees	MUSICIANS Bank employees Nurses Café and motel staff
WHOLIST		**ARCHITECTS**	**COMPUTER OPERATORS**

Style and team types and team development

Obviously, the intended functions of teams within organisations will vary from one team to another, depending on the purpose for which they were set up, and the tasks they are required to undertake. However, there are two main functions of teams. The first of these, *initiation*, will be the generation of ideas of how tasks can be undertaken, problems solved, and new initiatives originated. The second, *application*, will have to do with the implementation of those ideas. Some teams will have either one function or the other, and occasionally will have both.

A model of teams is proposed on the basis of the theory of style in which the cognitive style groups differ both in role, and effectiveness, in these two team functions. For each it is suggested that there is a dominant axis along which the main activity will take place, with those on the other axis having a supporting role. The two main proposed activity axes are shown in Figures 6.14 and 6.15 below by shading. For each activity there are five roles, three central to the activity and two supporting.

Style and initiating teams

Initiating team function

An important function of a team is to initiate new ideas and ways of achieving their goals. This activity involves the creative axis of the cognitive style map, which is shaded.

The main players in creative activity are the analytic-imagers and the wholist-verbalisers, and it is their interaction which will be most productive in generating possibilities and ideas. The role of the intermediate-bimodals will be to provide information and also to act as assessors of the ideas.

In supporting roles, the analytic-verbalisers will perform a useful contribution in terms of the feasibility of ideas in terms of the availability of resources, as will wholist-imagers with respect to being a restraining influence where ideas are not socially acceptable or otherwise harmful to the organisation.

For a team to be successful in initiation then it must have members of at least the three key map positions, and ideally the two supportive roles as well (see Figure 6.14).

Figure 6.14 Initiation of plans in teams

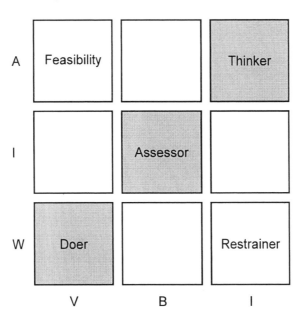

Characteristics of the style types and roles

- *Thinker.* This style will be creative and have a lot of ideas. However, these are not necessarily always sensible or feasible. Further, the type may be limited by their knowledge, which may be restricted. Nevertheless, the person often has a fluent torrent of ideas, or can see things in a new way, or can see how things might be done. Also this style will have an enthusiasm for ideas and of how to solve problems.
- *Assessor/informer.* This person is not particularly creative, but is good at learning facts and information. The person is able to convey this to the team, particularly for the benefit of the Thinker, who may lack all the necessary information to combine for creative thought.
- *Doer.* This individual has energy and drive and motivation, and this in turn leads to ideas and ways of accomplishing goals. This is particularly effective in interaction with the Thinker and Informer. The practical outgoing view of the Doer, linked to the reflective, creative generation of the Thinker could be very productive of worthwhile plans and strategies.
- *Restrainer.* The person is good at taking a balanced view of plans and of offering cautionary advice when they are unlikely to be unsuccessful. The person is often able to refine a plan by making small, but significant, changes to guide the plan in the best direction for its workability. This person will be politically sensitive to implications and be able to see what is best.
- *Feasibility.* This individual is good at assessing whether the necessary resources are going to be available to enable a plan to be carried out. This person will be able to determine whether it is feasible.

Team structure and problem-solving

A demonstration study undertaken during a workshop showed the effect of the ways in which individuals are grouped with respect to style on the team's problem-solving performance.[2] Ten managers from a company who were attending a workshop on team building were assessed for style by means of the Cognitive Styles Analysis, and were then allocated to one of two teams with five per team, on the basis of their style: a Mixed-Style Team comprised two analytic-verbalisers and three wholist-imagers, while a Similar-Styles Team consisted of five people of fairly similar style (two analytic-bimodals and three analytic-imagers).

The two teams were placed in separate rooms and were given tasks to complete which required an element of problem-solving and which encompassed both

---

2 Unpublished study, R. J. Riding, Assessment Research Unit, University of Birmingham, 1992.

verbal and spatial skills but were unrelated to their work (two crossword puzzles and three map-reading tasks). The instruction was that each team was to work on the tasks until they were all completed, and that they would be timed. The Mixed-Style Team completed both tasks (a total of 28 minutes) much more quickly than the Similar-Style Team (50 minutes). The faster time of the Mixed-Style team was attributed to the availability of a range of style strengths which facilitated the problem-solving.

Delegation
Although delegation is not strictly a team topic, it does have implications for team-working. It may be that imagers are more 'hands on' in their approach, while verbalisers tend to be more ready to delegate tasks to others. This area needs further study.

Style and application teams
In the implementation of team plans and initiatives, the application axis of the cognitive style grid is dominant (Figure 6.15). Those who are good at generating ideas and strategies will not be the best at implementing them. Here a different axis is required, and will be the analytic-verbaliser as Implementer, and the wholist-imager as Activator, mediating through the intermediate-bimodal as Informer. In this case the supporting roles will be performed by wholist-verbalisers who will be Facilitators, and analytic-imagers who will be Correctors who keep the plan on course.

Figure 6.15 Application of plans in teams

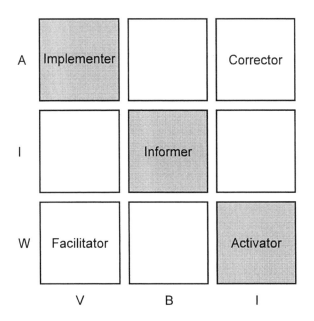

Team balance and effectiveness

It is important that the outcomes of a team be clearly specified in operational terms. Thought will also need to be given to how the outcomes of the teams fit into the overall objectives of the organisation. An effective team will be one which has the necessary members to fulfil its functions. Obviously, the members of the team must have the necessary knowledge and skills as well as the appropriate styles.

A team that is set up only to address problems and to make suggestions for their possible solution could be reasonably effective with only members on the initiation axis. Similarly, a team which only had an application function might be moderately efficient with only individuals from the application axis, as long as no new problems emerged. To fulfil the two basic functions, this will require people who approximate to the five role types, so that both initiation and application can be undertaken efficiently.

Practical applications

Team development

From the point of view of styles, a team will often benefit from considering the styles of the members of the team and of their roles, within the context of the purpose of the team. The use of the Cognitive Styles Analysis in conjunction with the Personal Styles Awareness package may facilitate this.

Team construction

Where new teams are being formed then, bearing in mind the main function of the team, style can be used to ensure that the construction of the team has the necessary styles represented within it.

CHAPTER 7

Cognitive style and learning

Chapter overview

This chapter will consider three groups of questions related to cognitive style and learning.

Style and learning performance

- How does the structure of the material to be learned interact with style?
- Does the mode of presentation of the material affect learning?
- What effect does the type of content have on style and learning?

Style and learning and representational preferences

- Do individuals of different styles differ in their learning preferences?
- What about style and preferred mode of presentation?

Subject preferences and attainment

- How are subject preferences affected by style?
- How does style affect educational achievement?

Since the two fundamental cognitive style dimensions are likely to affect the structure of an individual's thinking and the forms in which information can be represented by a person, style has potential implications for learning performance. This chapter will review the research on style and learning performance, learning preferences, and educational attainment.

Style and learning performance

The learning performance of an individual is likely to be affected by an interaction between cognitive style, and

- the way the instructional material is structured
- its mode of presentation
- its type of content.

Structure of the material

The material to be learned may be considered to have structure both in terms of its external format, and also its internal conceptual form and content.

Several studies have found that an individual's position on the wholist-analytic dimension in particular interacts with both the external and internal structures of the learning material to affect performance. Structure can include the *format* structure in terms of its layout:

- position of title
- presence of headings
- size of viewing 'window'

and the *conceptual* structure and order of the information:

- the processing decision process
- the addition of overviews and their position
- large step versus small steps.

Format structure

Format structure refers to the external appearance and physical arrangement of the presentation of the information. Included within format structure are such features as the position of titles, how the text is divided into paragraphs, sub-headings, and also the size of the display, or 'viewing window' – large spread versus small which affects how much can be seen at a glance.

Position of title

When presented with a prose passage for recall, Douglas and Riding (1993) found that with 77 11-year-old pupils, wholists did best when the title of the passage was given before the passage was presented, rather than at the end, although this had little effect for intermediates and analytics as shown in Figure 7.1 (adapted from Douglas and Riding 1993).

The result was interpreted as due to the wholists, who were less able to impose their own structure on material, being helped by a title at the beginning to give some organisation to the material. It has been argued that wholists tend to organise information into loosely clustered wholes, while analytics are inclined to organise information into clear-cut conceptual groupings. In the present context, wholists actively attempted to form an overall integrated model of the information. However, the information was complex in nature and provided few integrating cues in the title-after condition. As a result, a poor mental model was formed and this was reflected in subsequent recall. In the title-before condition, the title provided the necessary cue which allowed a greater understanding of the whole.

Analytics actively attempt to divide the information into its parts. The position of the title made little difference to this task as the links between the parts were not actively sought. As a result, the recall performance of the analytic individuals in the two presentation orders did not differ a great deal.

Figure 7.1 Recall and position of title

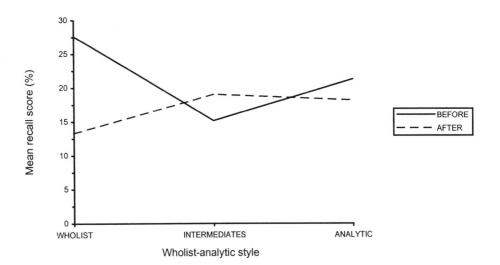

Wholist-analytic style

Figure 7.2 Structure, gender and wholist-analytic style

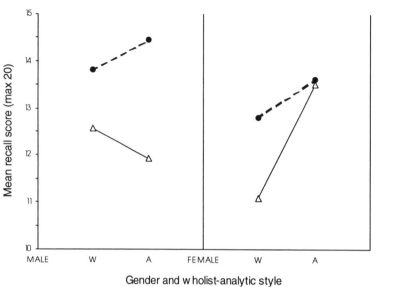

Gender and wholist-analytic style

Presence of headings

Riding and Al-Sanabani (1998) with a sample of 200 10–15-year-old pupils attending a Yemeni school in the UK, studied the effect on reading comprehension (as indicated by recall performance) of dividing a one-page textual narrative describing the visit of an old friend into three paragraphs, each with a sub-heading. They found that this improved recall performance and that the degree of the facilitating effect was affected by the wholist-analytic style and gender of the student and this is shown in Figure 7.2.

For wholists there was a similar improvement with the addition of format structure by both males and females, while for the analytics the males improved much more than the females. Gender interactions with style were discussed in Chapters 4 and 5. It may be that female analytics prefer to impose their own structure and find externally imposed structure less helpful than do males. Certainly the analytic females did well without the external structure.

Size of viewing window

Riding and Grimley (1999) with a sample of 80 11-year-old pupils compared learning from computer-presented CD-ROM multimedia instructional materials on science topics with performance from traditional methods as indicated by the results of Standard Assessment Tasks (SATs) in science. The measure of performance in traditional work was taken as the total raw score

Figure 7.3 Wholist-analytic style and type of learning

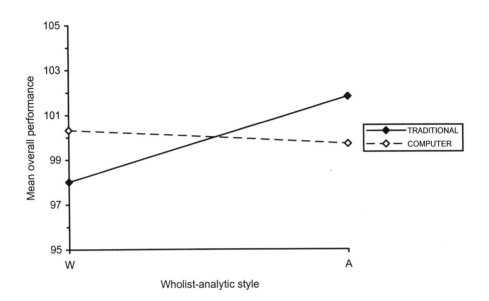

SATs for science, since this content appeared to be similar to that of the multimedia material. The overall multimedia performance was taken as the mean of the performance on 57 questions based on the information presented. Since the two measures were on different scales, in order to compare performance on traditional work with the computer-presented multimedia material, the two measures were standardised with a mean of 100 and a standard deviation of 15. There was a significant interaction between wholist-analytic style and mode of presentation in their effect on recall. The scores for the traditional and computer methods of learning are given in Figure 7.3.

When compared to the traditional work attainment for the analytics, the lower multimedia performance may in part reflect the fact that the computer has a limited window of viewing and this reduces the performance of the analytics who find it more difficult to obtain a whole view, but does not adversely affect wholists. casual observation suggests that wholists frequently enjoy working with computers, and in Chapter 6 it was noted that there was evidence that computer operators were most frequently wholist-imagers.

Analytics tend to see material in parts and the restricted 'viewing window' which computer presentation affords can exacerbate this tendency. When using a computer to produce large word-processed documents, they may prefer to produce hard copies of it so that they can scan the pages to obtain a feel for the overall structure. Wholists are less likely to need to do this, since they naturally appreciate the whole.

Conceptual structure

All information has a potential for being structured. This may be in terms of a logical sequence of the ideas or concepts it contains, or a serial, temporal order of the events it describes. However, there are often different ways in which the material can be arranged for the same topic. In the present section this will be considered in terms of the effect of structure and style on the decision process.

Another aspect of structure is whether there is the use of an *organiser* before the main presentation of the material to provide the student with a structural framework on which to hang the material. This would also supply a context for the interpretation of the information. In addition to, or instead of this, there could be a summary at the end to provide an overview of the whole.

There is also the question of whether the information is presented in large chunks or in smaller steps. With the latter the student is guided through the information more closely than in the former.

Structure and the decision process

A study of 84 12-year-old pupils considered the effect of context generated by direct and indirect antecedents on the response time taken to judge statements.[1] An example of both is shown in Figure 7.4. In practice, either a direct or an indirect antecedent would be presented and not both at the same time as shown. For each condition the sentences were computer-presented, one at a time. When the pupil had understood a sentence a key was pressed. In the case of the last sentence, the pupil indicated whether it was true or false by pressing one of two marked keys.

Figure 7.4 Examples of direct and indirect antecedents

DIRECT ANTECEDENT

INDIRECT ANTECEDENT

(1) June was happy
    lying in the hot sun.

(1) June joined the other
    bathers on the beach.

(2) As a result she got
    mildly sunburnt.
(3) The sun can burn people.

They found that in the case of the indirect and direct antecedents, the verbalisers were faster than the imagers. The reason for this was probably that imagers take longer than verbalisers because their habitual mode of processing is to generate

1 Data collected by Derek Adams, Assessment Research Unit, University of Birmingham, 1997.

Figure 7.5 Style and judgement of direct/indirect statements

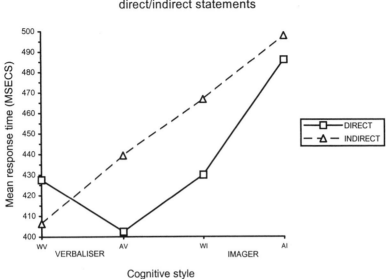

Cognitive style

mental pictures and these do not help in judging the final statement, while for the verbalisers the semantic area related to the statement is likely to be activated, facilitating a quick response, and this is shown in Figure 7.5.

For the imagers, the analytics took longer than the wholists perhaps because their processing is more exhaustive and considered a wider range of options. However, for the verbalisers, the analytics in the direct condition were faster than the wholists, probably because they would have been able to use the context to guide them quickly to the properties of the objects mentioned and they would have been able more quickly to make the logical inferences, since they were more focused. In a sense they could more efficiently disembed the main idea suggested by the context. By contrast, in the more diffuse indirect contexts the analytics could have generated too many possibilities and hence were slower than the wholists who probably just waited for the question.

These results suggest that even with fairly simple information, structural differences can affect processing by the style groups.

Addition of an overview

Riding and Al-Sanabani (a) in the study referred to above also investigated the effect on reading comprehension as indicated by recall performance of adding structure to prose passages in the form of a short summary, placed either before or after a main prose passage. They found that both of these methods improved recall performance to a similar extent and position did not interact with style. However, they found that, as with the addition of headings described earlier in this chapter, the degree of the facilitating effect of the structure was affected by the wholist-analytic style and gender of the student. For wholists there was a similar improvement with the addition of structure by both males and females, while for the analytics the males improved much more than the females.

Large step versus small step and overview

Riding and Sadler-Smith (1992) compared performance on three differently structured versions of computer-presented instructional material on central heating systems with 129 14–19-year-old students. The three versions presented that same information about five topics.

- *Version L* had large steps and consisted of relatively large chunks of verbal information with simple line diagrams.
- *Version O* comprised small steps of verbal information interspersed with pictorial or diagrammatic content, plus overviews at the start, before and after each topic and at the end.
- *Version S* was as Version O with small steps but minus the overviews.

There was a total of 17 recall test questions and the time taken to work through the material ranged from 16.5 minutes to 47.2 minutes, with a mean of 27.18 minutes. The recall efficiency in terms of the percentage correct recall per hour was used as an index of learning performance and this is given in Figure 7.6 (adapted from Riding and Sadler-Smith 1992). The four styles are grouped as Complementary (wholist-verbalisers and analytic-imager) and Unitary (wholist-imager and analytic-verbaliser).[2]

Inspection of Figure 7.6 indicates that for the two Complementary style groups, different ways of structuring the material had quite a large effect on performance, with the small-step format being most effective. For the Unitary groups, the structure had relatively little effect, with the groups performing in an 'average' manner irrespective of the format.

The wholist-verbalisers and the analytic-imagers did least well on the large-step format, but improved greatly with the overview-plus-small-step format. With the small-step version minus the overview they did even better. This was probably because the small-step format enabled them to analyse the information into its structure and to build up a whole view of it for themselves. The additional material in the form of summaries was therefore redundant and depressed performance, such that when it was not present, as in the case of just the small-step format, performance was considerably further improved.

By contrast, the analytic-verbalisers, who were good at analysing but not at having a whole view, and the wholist-imagers, who were the reverse, did

---

2 This method of grouping styles was introduced in Chapter 6.

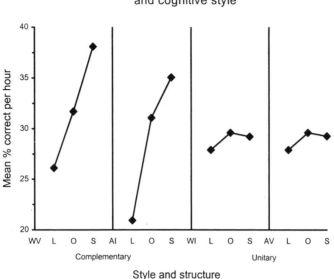

Figure 7.6 Learning efficiency, structure and cognitive style

better than the Complementary groups on the large-step format, probably for different reasons: the former being very able to undertake their own analysis, the latter obtaining a whole view of the material without additional help. Consequently, neither the overviews nor the small steps improved performance very much, perhaps because they were constrained by their rather restricted methods of representing and structuring. Further work is necessary to find effective methods of helping these groups.

Further considerations

There is evidence that the structure of the material to be learned interacts particularly with the wholist-analytic style dimension. Basically, the findings appear to be as follows:

- Analytics need a large 'viewing window' compared to wholists, when dealing with information.
- Individuals of complementary style (wholist-verbalisers and analytic-imagers) are affected by the step size of the learning material and improve from large to small steps, while those of unitary style are not affected.
- There is an interaction between gender and wholist-analytic style in the facilitating effect of structure in the form of both headings and overviews, such that these most help male analytics and female wholists.

Having established that style interacts with structure in its effects on learning performance, further work needs to be done to investigate other aspects of conceptual structure that may have a bearing on practical learning effectiveness.

For example, learning can proceed from the parts to the whole or from the whole to the parts. If one were teaching about how a telescope works, the *parts to whole* method would begin with the refraction, or bending, of light which passes through materials such as glass and plastic, on to lenses and magnification, and then to lenses combined together in a tube to make a telescope. The *whole to parts* method would be the reverse of this, and would start with the telescope and its practical use, and then would question how it works by taking it apart and examining the lenses and their arrangement, and then examining the action of light through the lenses, and so on to refraction.

Mode of presentation

There is a range of verbal, pictorial and auditory modes available for the presentation of information. It can be spoken, read, obtained from illustrations, or from a combination of these. Since different styles have preferences for particular types of representation, they are likely to find particular media easier to learn from than others.

Text versus picture

Riding and Ashmore (1980) compared two modes of presentation (the textual and the pictorial) in a study with 74 11-year-old pupils. These presented groups of verbalisers and imagers (as assessed by the earlier Verbal-Imagery Code Test) with either a textual or a pictorial version of the same information. They found that verbalisers were superior with the verbal version and imagers when learning in the pictorial mode. Within the instructional context, while purely verbal presentation is often possible, an alternative entirely pictorial version without any text is rarely an option, as some words will also be necessary. However, it will usually be feasible to present information in both modes to some extent.

Text-plus-text versus text-plus-picture

Riding and Douglas (1993), with 59 15–16-year-old students, found that the computer-presentation of material on motor car braking systems in a text-plus-picture format facilitated the learning by imagers, compared to the same content in a text-plus-text version as shown in Figure 7.7 (adapted from Riding and Douglas 1993).

Further, the extent of the improvement was substantial for the imagers, approaching a doubling of their score. With the verbalisers, both modes resulted in similar learning.

Figure 7.7 Recall and mode of presentation

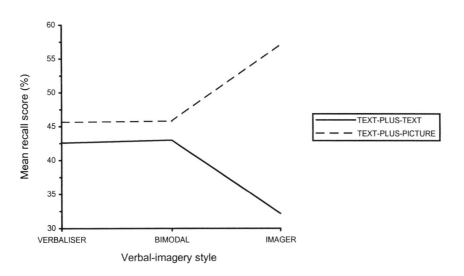

Multimedia presentations

Riding and Grimley with a sample of 80 11-year-old pupils, considered learning from CD-ROM multimedia instructional materials on science topics. Three CD-ROMs were used with content on Gravity and Motion, the Geography of New Zealand, and the Natural History on Reptiles. A pool of 57 recall test questions (16 about Gravity and Motion, 18 about New Zealand, and 23 about Reptiles) was constructed to reflect the types of presentation and content of the instructional material. They were analysed in terms of the mode of presentation of the information on which they were based into picture-plus-sound (PS), picture-plus-text (PT) and picture-plus-text-plus-sound (PTS). There was a significant interaction between wholist-analytic style, verbal-imagery style, gender and mode of presentation, and this is shown in Figure 7.8 for the Complementary and Unitary style groups.

Inspection of Figure 7.8 indicates that, overall, PTS is superior to PS and PT. The most likely reason for this is that with PTS the wider range of methods of presentation means that there are more options for the individual learner to choose from; consequently this meets the needs of a wider variety of styles, and results in better learning by more pupils.

There are gender differences for both PTS, and for PS and PT. With PTS the non-complementary groups do best in the males (analytic-verbalisers and wholist-imagers), and in the females the analytics (verbalisers and imagers).

In the PS and PT case, there is a *reversal* with gender which is related to whether the styles are complementary (as with wholist-verbalisers and analytic-

Figure 7.8 Recall, mode of presentation and style

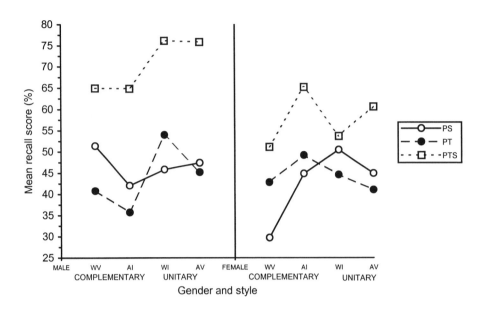

imagers), or unitary (as with analytic-verbalisers and wholist-imagers). PS involves two senses, 'look and listen' (two channels), while PT is 'look' only (a single channel). For the wholist-verbalisers and analytic-imagers (the complementary groups), males did better on PS than on PT, while this is reversed for females. For the unitary groups, the wholist-imagers and analytic-verbalisers, the tendency is the other way round with the male wholist-imagers better on PT, and the females on PS.

Basically with males, complementary groups are best on a separation of the channels of pictures and words, while the females are best on the single channel of pictures and words. With the unitary groups, the males are best on a single channel, while the females are superior on separate channels. This hints at a fundamental gender difference in information processing which also involves style (as discussed in Chapter 5).

Further considerations

Generally, imagers learn better from pictorial presentations than verbalisers, while verbalisers learn better from verbal presentations than imagers. It is also likely that lecturers and teachers will reflect their own style in the ways in which they present information, such that, for instance, verbalisers will use a highly verbal content, while imagers will use pictures and diagrams to illustrate their words. This is worthy of further study.

As with the wholist-analytic dimension, there was a gender interaction with the verbal-imagery dimension. The precise reasons for these are not clear and gender differences in information processing deserve considerably more research than they have received.

Type of verbal content

This section will consider the effect on performance of the type of verbal content of material to be learned. The section will begin with reading performance, which is verbal in nature. It is also possible to discriminate between types of verbal material in terms of whether the content lends itself to the generation of images or is more abstract.

Reading performance

Initial reading performance, which is obviously a highly verbal task, has been found to be superior in verbalisers. Riding and Anstey (1982), with 40 7-year-old children, assessed reading accuracy and comprehension and found that both declined from verbaliser to imager, as assessed by the Verbal-Imagery Code Test. Riding and Mathias (1991), with 80 11-year-olds, observed that for reading accuracy this effect was still very pronounced for wholists, where wholist-verbalisers showed much greater proficiency at reading compared to wholist-imagers.

Concrete versus abstract content

In the case of the type of content of learning material, studies of 7-, 11- and 12-year-old pupils indicated that imagers recall concrete, highly visually descriptive text better than more abstract, acoustically complex and unfamiliar text, while the reverse holds for verbalisers (Riding and Taylor 1976; Riding and Dyer 1980; Riding and Calvey 1981).

Riding and Calvey asked 40 11-year-old children to listen to tape recordings of four prose passages and after each passage to complete a recall test. The prose passages were selected to range on a continuum from highly visually descriptive and capable of being imagined, through to a high level of acoustic and semantic complexity with unfamiliar names and few visual details. Position of the verbal-imagery dimension was assessed by means of the Verbal-Imagery Code Test. Recall for the two extreme passages is shown in Figure 7.9 (adapted from Riding and Calvey 1981).

Inspection of Figure 7.9 shows that recall performance of the semantically complex content decreases from verbaliser to imager and for the visually descriptive material it increases.

Figure 7.9 Recall of content type and verbal-imagery style

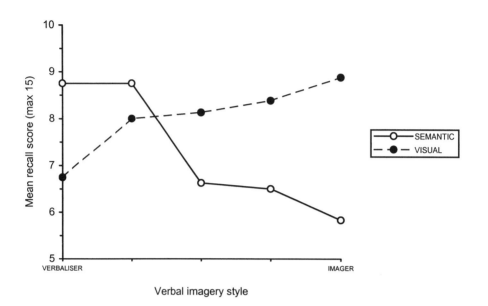

Further considerations

In terms of content type, individuals appear to learn best when information can be readily translated into their preferred verbal-imagery mode of representation. It is of interest to note that not only the mode of presentation, but also the content itself, affects learning performance to an extent that is of practical significance.

Style and learning and representational preferences

This section will consider, learning preferences and representational preferences. The section is important partly since preferences, as will be seen later in the chapter, are an important part of strategy development. Further, if people's preferences are in accordance with actual performance differences reported in the previous section, then it shows a consistency and persuasiveness about style.

Learning preferences

Two methods of assessing learning preferences have been used: self-report measures and observed behaviour choices.

Self-report measures: English and science preferences

In an investigation by Riding and Read (1996), 78 12-year-old pupils were individually questioned about their preferences in the subjects of English language and science with respect to mode of working and social context. With respect to mode of working, in the case of the higher ability pupils, imagers – particularly wholists – reported that they used less writing and more pictures than verbalisers, especially where the subject allowed, as in science. The tendency by imagers to report the use of pictures, and verbalisers writing, increased with ability. There was evidence that lower ability pupils were more constrained by the usual format of the subject than were those of higher ability.

The preferences for group, pair and individual working were that all pupils reported that they preferred group or pair work to individual work, and group work was especially liked by wholists, and by lower ability wholist-imagers in particular. Individual work was least disliked by analytics, particularly in the case of higher ability verbalisers.

Self-report measures: business studies preferences

Sadler-Smith and Riding (b), used a questionnaire approach to study instructional preferences in 245 university business studies students. In terms of locus of control the analytics preferred to have control themselves rather than to be controlled, while the wholists had no preference.

The self-report approach suffers from some significant limitations such as the subject's possible inability to report behaviour accurately and objectively, unwillingness to make the necessary effort to respond accurately, and bias due to the pressure of social desirability in making responses (see e.g. Kline 1995: 512). However, the importance of self-reporting here is to see whether individuals can show an awareness in line with actual performance, and there is evidence that they can.

Observed behaviour choices: format preferences

While questionnaire approaches have some uses, where possible observation of real behaviour is likely to be more relevant. In a study by Riding and Watts (1997), 90 female 16-year-old pupils were told within their class groups that three versions of a sheet giving information on study skills had been prepared for them, and that each sheet contained the same information but that the formats were different. They were then invited to come one at a time to the front of the class and to take one of the versions from the teacher's desk. Their choices were noted by the teacher. The versions were unstructured-verbal (paragraphs, without headings), structured-verbal (paragraphs, each with a clear heading), and structured-pictorial (paragraphs, each with a clear heading, plus a pictorial icon depicting the activity placed in the left margin). No pupils

Figure 7.10 Verbal-imagery style
and percentage choosing version

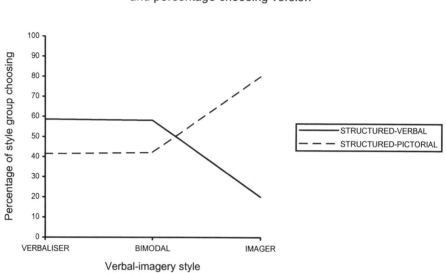

chose the unstructured-verbal version. With the two structured versions, there was a significant interaction with verbal-imagery style, with the majority of the verbalisers selecting the 'verbal' version and most of the imagers the 'pictorial' as shown in Figure 7.10 (adapted from Riding and Watts 1997).

There was a lesser, but still significant effect on the wholist-analytic dimension the pictorial version was more attractive to the wholists, perhaps because it looked more 'lively', while with the analytics there was a slight preference for the more 'neat and tidy' verbal format. The results suggested that pupils are attracted to, and prefer to select, materials that appear to suit their own style.

Representational control and representation preferences

Voluntary and involuntary control

Riding and Dyer (1980: 278–9) distinguished between two levels of control of verbal and imagery performance: voluntary and involuntary. They suggested that in the former the individual makes a deliberate and conscious decision to generate an image or verbal response, while in the latter the image or verbal representation occurs spontaneously without conscious effort. In the present context it may be argued that verbalisers do not use images greatly during involuntary information processing, although they can generate them successfully by conscious effort.

By contrast, imagers habitually use involuntary imagery as a means of representing information. Further, for imagers, mental pictures are likely to be less stable than those produced by verbalisers since they will be liable to interference and displacement by further involuntary intrusive images. It may follow that the converse applies to verbalisers and imagers with respect to verbal associations, and that verbalisers find that verbal associations tend to be less stable for them than they would be when consciously evoked by imagers.

Style and drawing from sight and memory

Douglas and Riding (1994) with 71 11-year-old pupils studied drawing performance. The pupils were asked to draw two pictures, one from memory and one from a picture. Judges rated the drawings of the verbalisers as significantly better than those of the imagers. It may be that the fluid mental pictures of the imagers interfered with the external representations.

Representational preferences

Riding and Douglas (1993), with 59 15–16-year-old students, studied the computer-presentation of material on motor car braking systems. A text-plus-picture format facilitated the learning by imagers, compared to the same content in a text-plus-text version. They found that at recall in the text-plus-picture condition, 50 per cent of the imagers used illustrations as part of their answers compared to only 12 per cent of the verbalisers. In other words, there are differences between the styles in the preferred mode of representing information.

It may well follow from this that in the case of individuals of the same ability and similar on the wholist-analytic dimension, the verbalisers are superior in speech, which benefits from involuntary verbal fluency, and relatively inferior in writing, where the lack of verbal control due to spontaneous involuntary verbal associations may be a hindrance. By contrast, imagers may be superior in written mode but inferior in the spoken mode.

Extending this notion to include the wholist-analytic dimension, it may be that the style groups will have most preferred and least preferred modes of expression. Common modes of expression are writing, drawing diagrams, drawing pictures, and speaking, and the possible preferences are shown in Figure 7.11, by means of the numbers in brackets after each to denote first, second and third preferences.

Figure 7.11 shows that each of the four style groups have possible different basic preference for expression, and the further a group is away from the one that has the first preference, the lower their preference for that mode. Each group also has a least preferred mode. This arrangement is the probable one, and a systematic investigation of preferences is required.

Figure 7.11 Possible preferred modes of expression

	ANALYTIC VERBALISER	ANALYTIC IMAGER	
Text (1) Speech (2) Diagrams (2) Picture (3)	ANALYTIC VERBALISER	ANALYTIC IMAGER	Diagrams (1) Picture (2) Text (2) Speech (3)
Speech (1) Text (2) Picture (2) Diagrams (3)	WHOLIST VERBALISER	WHOLIST IMAGER	Picture (1) Diagrams (2) Speech (2) Text (3)

Subject preferences and attainment

Difficulties in assessing subject preferences

Students' reactions to particular subjects are likely to be affected by a number of variables. For instance, there is the style and commitment of the teacher, the range and attractiveness of instructional materials available, the perceived degree of relevance and coherence of the curriculum approach to the topic, the particular content that is being considered at the time when the preference is being assessed, even the time of day when the topic is studied (late on Friday afternoon may colour preference because of fatigue), which other students do the subject (the absence of particular friends in the group, or the presence of more hostile students, could carry over to overall perception of the topic), and even the venue – a cold, depressing room versus pleasant accommodation could influence response to a subject.

All of these are likely to add 'noise' to any stated preference and reduce observed effect due to style.

Business studies preferences

Riding and Staley (1998) gave a questionnaire to 204 university business studies students which assessed their preferences about the content and presentation of their courses. For analysis the courses were grouped as Information Technology, Accounting (accountancy and quantitative methods, since both of these involved largely numerical concepts and computation), and Management (organisational behaviour and business workshop, both of which were concerned with the running of organisations). On the wholist-analytic dimension, intermediates were least happy with Accounting and Information Technology and most happy with Management. For Accountancy and Information Technology, in terms of being positive about the courses, having a clear overview of the courses, least needing content overviews, finding the presentation order logical, and liking the tutor's style, wholists were highest in their ratings, followed by the analytics, with the intermediates having the lowest ratings. Accounting and Information Technology require both a capacity for an overall view of the processes and their purposes, and the methodological following of rules. Wholists fit the first requirement and analytics the latter. Intermediates tend to *alternate* between both, which is useful for a more creative approach, but does not *consistently* give either.

With Management, it was intermediates who were most positive, who generally found the presentation order logical, and who most liked the tutor's style. Wholists in particular rated these less highly. Management requires a more creative approach, involving more problem solving activities, which suits the intermediates more than the wholists.

With respect to the wholist-analytic dimension, when performance was considered it was noted that individuals underestimated their performance on the subjects that did not suit their style and overestimated it on those that did.

Difficulties in considering educational achievement

As with subject preference, the study of educational achievement and style poses problems. These derive from the nature of the subject, the ways in which it has been taught, and the methods of assessment. A subject usually varies considerably within itself in terms of the type of content, the modes in which it is represented, and the range of processing required. Further, the method of instruction will vary from teacher to teacher, and probably be a reflection of their styles. In addition, the form of assessment can be varying proportions of course work and unseen examination, and can also vary in mode (verbal/pictorial).

Large-scale formal studies of style, attainment and age have not yet been undertaken. An approximate picture may be obtained using data collected as part of other studies, and this will be reported below.

Attainment in pupils aged 11–14 years

In the 11–14-year age range, data were available from the following sources.

- Data collected as part of the Riding and Grimley study considered attainment as assessed by the SATs in 72 11-year-olds in English, mathematics and science.
- Data collected by Burton on school achievement from 136 12-year-olds as part of the Riding et al. (1995) study.
- Riding and Pearson (1994) looked at the course work performance of 120 12–13-year-old pupils in mathematics, English, French, science, geography and history.
- Riding and Agrell (1997) compared Grade 9 performance of 205 14–16-year-old anglophone Canadian students with style in mathematics, English, French, science and geography.

Four style groups have been used in all cases to allow comparison between the samples. Where the original article used more than two divisions on either style dimension, the data from the studies were reworked using the same cut-off points as the Riding and Agrell (1997) study to produce four style groups. For each set of data the performance of the four style groups was arranged in order in the core subjects of English, mathematics and science, and these are shown in Table 7.1.

This approach is crude but does point to some trends in performance. Inspection of Table 7.1 indicates that for all three core subjects, the analytic-verbalisers and the wholist-imagers (unitary style) are among the best two groups, while the wholist-verbalisers and the analytic-imagers (complementary style) are the worst. In mathematics, it is noteworthy that the wholist-verbalisers are the lowest in all four cases.

In a study of the performance of 182 Kuwaiti students in the public grade examination at 14 years in the subjects mathematics, chemistry, biology, English and Arabic, using the Arabic version of the Cognitive Styles Analysis and similar divisions as in the studies above, an overall significant effect of style was found with the order of the style groups from best to worst: wholist-imager, analytic-verbaliser, analytic-imager, wholist-verbaliser.[3]

Bearing in mind that the data were from different schools, ages, indices of performance, and even countries, this justifies further consideration and investigation. In addition, it shows that style needs to be taken into account if school performance is going to improve and meet the needs of all students.

---

3 Data collected by Ahmad Al-Loughani, Assessment Research Unit, University of Birmingham, 1997.

Table 7.1 Style and attainment at 11–14 years

	11 years SATs (Riding and Grimley)	12 years School Achievement (Burton data)	13 years School Achievement (Riding and Pearson 1994)	14 years Grade 9 (Riding and Agrell 1997)	Overall order
	Style groups in order from best to worst for age of pupils				
English	AI	WV	WI	WV	AV
	AV	AV	AV	AV	WV
	WI	WI	AI	WI	WI=AI
	WV	AI	WV	AI	
Maths	AV	WI	WI	AV	WI
	WI	AI	AV	WI	AV
	AI	AV	AI	AI	AI
	WV	WV	WV	WV	WV
Science	AV	AI	WI	WI	WI
	WI	WI	AV	WV	AV
	AI	AV	WV	AV	AI
	WV	WV	AI	AI	WV

Attainment at GCSE in pupils aged 16 years

Three sources of data are relevant to performance in the General Certificate of Secondary Education (GCSE) (the British public examination at 16 years).

- GCSE performance of 149 16-year-olds as part of the Riding *et al.* (1994) study.
- Newton *et al.* (1995) considered GCSE performance in English, mathematics and science with 150 16-year-olds.
- Riding and Caine (1993) looked at the performance of 182 16-year-old pupils in the GCSE in mathematics, English, and French.

The findings of the above studies are summarised in Table 7.2 in a form similar to that used in Table 7.1.

Overall, the poorest performance is by the wholist-imagers, who were the lowest in both English and mathematics. The most likely reason for this is that the verbal emphasis and analytical qualities of the subjects is least suitable for the wholist-imagers. It may be questioned whether this does them justice.

Table 7.2 Style and GCSE performance at 16 years

GCSE performance of style groups in order from best to worst

	Riding *et al.* (1994)	Newton *et al.* (1995)	Riding and Caine (1993)	Overall order
English	W V	W V	AV	W V
	AV	AI	W V	AV
	AI	AV	AI	AI
	W I	W I	W I	W I
Maths	W V	W V	W V	W V
	AV	AV	AI	AV
	AI	AI	AV	AI
	W I	W I	W I	W I
Science	AI	W V	–	AI
	W I	AI		W V
	W V	AV		W I
	AV	W I		AV

There appears to be an age shift with the wholist-imagers doing well up to 14 years in mathematics and science, but doing much worst by 16 years in the GCSE. Conversely, the wholist-verbalisers, who do not perform well up to 14 years in mathematics, are much better placed at 16 years.

This needs further investigation, since it is possible that either the content of the subjects changes in the final year or two preceding 16 years, or the nature of the GCSE examination is such that it does not favour some style groups.

Further considerations

With respect to subject preferences, as has been noted, there are many possible variables, although the one study reported does suggest that subject preference may be influenced by style. In terms of actual performance, the available evidence suggests that in English from 11 years through to 16 years, the verbalisers (wholist and analytic) do consistently well, as would be expected for a verbally based subject in both content and expression. In mathematics, there is an interesting age interaction with the wholist-imagers doing best between 11 and 14 years and the wholist-verbalisers at GCSE at 16 years, which requires further investigation. In science, the wholist-imagers do well when younger and if anything, the analytic-imagers best at 16 years.

A large-scale study of subject attainment, style and age is required. However, the basic finding is that style is implicated in attainment performance.

Conclusion

Cognitive style appears to be a comparatively major influence on learning performance both at the specific level of interacting with material structure or presentation mode, through to the level of overall attainment at public examinations.

Since style is unrelated to intelligence, it represents an under-researched area in connection with learning and instruction. Further work is required to clarify the following four areas.

Gender-style interactions

The occurrence of gender interactions needs careful study since these suggest a possible fundamental difference in information processing between males and females and if these were better understood then both sexes might be helped to learn more effectively.

Style accommodation

One way of improving learning performance is to adapt the mode of presentation to suit the individual student. This is particularly so for students of lower ability for whom style presentation-matching is likely to be more crucial because of their limited processing capacity. Research is needed to find the most efficient ways of doing this.

Strategy development

Work is required on the identification of strategies for particular styles and specific types of learning tasks. Further research is then necessary to see how students can be helped to develop strategies that will enable them to deal with learning materials that they would naturally find difficult.

Style-based pedagogy

Research is needed to consider the practical application of individual differences in style to the type of teaching and instructional presentation a student receives. A pedagogy which incorporates style-led differentiation will achieve authentic accommodation of individual differences in the classroom. Further studies are necessary to facilitate such approaches in teaching and training.

CHAPTER 8

Cognitive style and problem behaviour

Chapter overview

The relationship between style, emotional and behavioural difficulties (EBD) and success or failure in the learning context are considered in this chapter. A number of key questions are raised.

Problem behaviour and learning performance

- What are the causes of problem behaviour?
- What are the implications of style for problem behaviour and learning performance?

Style and problem behaviour

- What is the relationship between style and psychoticism?
- How does style affect pupil behaviour in school?
- What are the style characteristics of pupils in EBD special schools?
- Which styles of pupils are likely to refuse school?

Personal style and effective pedagogy

- How can style be taken into account to improve learning in EBD schools?
- How can style be used to develop a more effective pedagogy?

There is a relationship between learning and behaviour, such that learning affects behaviour and behaviour affects learning. Furthermore, the nature of curriculum content and its method of delivery will strongly influence student behaviour. It is not the least surprising, therefore, that this relationship should be a constant and continuing consideration for the practising trainer or teacher.

Teachers will always be interested in the effective management of classroom behaviour. If the class behaves badly or individual students experience emotional or behavioural difficulties (EBD), instruction, learning and understanding are all adversely affected. Conversely, if a student is finding difficulty with the learning task, is uncertain about what to do, or how to do it, failure and problem behaviour can result.

What seems obvious, then, is the importance of either individual or group behaviour, for the success or failure of learning. It is this importance which has led to the viewpoint expressed by Her Majesty's Inspectorate:

> Good behaviour is a necessary condition for effective teaching and learning to take place, and an important outcome of education which society rightly expects.

> (HMI 1987: viii)

A second, and equally important point, is the realisation that effective approaches with students experiencing EBD have a relevance for working with all students. Such approaches reflect principles and methods of instruction which are aimed at meeting the individual needs of the learner. Weber (1982) and Cooper (1993) have argued that this required an approach which recognised and embraced the importance of individuality within the classroom. An appropriate response to individual needs, identified as the 'corner-stone' of school effectiveness, is also seen as a key factor in school improvement (Cooper 1993: 26).

Thinking about how emotional and behavioural difficulties affect the learning process, or how an effective educational response to problem behaviour requires successful teaching, leads to a growing realisation that managing problem behaviour in the learning context is synonymous with effective teaching and learning enhancement. If meeting individual needs is seen as a key aspect of this approach, then it must involve a consideration of individual differences in the learning context.

Problem behaviour and learning performance

This chapter considers the relationship between problem behaviour, learning, and cognitive style. It is clear that EBD adversely affects learning behaviour and performance, and a successful response to such problem behaviour will result in learning enhancement. It is also argued that while the causes of EBD are several, the influence and effect of school and teacher is extremely important. As part of this influence, it is proposed that the development of a style-centred pedagogy should be attempted, aimed at meeting individual needs and having a positive effect upon learning difficulty and problem behaviour.

Causes of problem behaviour

Jones and Charlton (1996), among others, emphasised the 'multiplicity of factors' associated with learning and behaviour difficulties. They advocated an eclectic approach to meeting the individual needs presented by students experiencing failure. They pointed to several types of factors causing or sustaining EBD. These included the following:

- learner characteristics within the individual
- learner characteristics located within the wider community or social context
- learning process within the learning environment (including the classroom, the school, pedagogy, ethos)
- learning process within the curriculum.

Learner characteristics within the individual

Factors associated with problem behaviour and learning failure have for a long time been identified as personal and unique to the individual. Such factors might include genetic causes (learning disabilities which relate to heredity, for example, cerebral palsy, dysgraphia or dyslexia) or traumatic causes, such as physical, emotional and intellectual barriers to learning caused by traumatic experience, for example congenital disorders or birth complications affecting the central or peripheral nervous systems, or injuries sustained through a crash leaving partial paralysis, elliptical speech and haphazard memory.

Other biological factors include a range of medical disorders and conditions which may cause problem behaviour. Most of these are complex and far from understood, producing disagreement and debate among experts about their actual influence upon individual behaviour and readiness to learn. More well-known examples include asthma, epilepsy and, perhaps less often linked to severe EBD, eczema. Eczema is also linked to hyperactivity, often in association with a diagnosis of allergic reaction. A sensitivity to a range of environmental triggers is often suggested as an explanation for EBD, and can involve a wide range of factors, including sunlight, food intake, exposure to chemicals, or simply contact with a particular material, such as fur or plastic.

Lastly, problem behaviour may be attributed to personality traits or characteristics which are inherited as well as learnt. This explanation is probably one most often expressed in day-to-day conversation. A student presenting EBD will be perceived to have personal problems. The deficit or failing is regarded as belonging to the student, and attributed to heredity or parenting. In this instance, rehabilitation and reforming character are bound up with a belief that EBD is primarily caused by defects within the individual.

Learner characteristics within the social context

Cultural or environmental causes of EBD are frequently associated with the home or community. One such set of factors are value or belief systems to which the school or institution does not subscribe. The result can be a culture clash and may pose considerable difficulty for an individual student. One example of this kind of trigger is when parents are identified as the source of anti-social attitudes and problem behaviour in the student. Similarly, factors associated with adverse living conditions, poverty, or conditions of inadequacy may result in long-term or severe EBD.

More specific 'family factors' generally relate to child-rearing practice and its developmental effect. Bowlby (1946), for example, has provided a full account of the effect of separation at infancy as a cause for EBD. A similar concern for the effect of disruption to 'bonding' between the child and a significant carer (parent) is also identified as a long-standing cause of EBD (Rutter 1972).

Other explanations of EBD connected to family background or the local community reflect the importance of a secure and loving relationship. They include a range of deprivation or neglect found within family life. They may also involve physical or emotional abuse and can often be described as part of a family pathology. The influence of peer relationships may also play a similar role in causing problem behaviour, and is more particularly associated with adolescence.

The same analogy of family pathology or breakdown is used to describe the effects of divorce. Charlton and George (1993: 33) reported that for every two marriages in 1990 in the UK, there was one divorce, very often involving young children. The effect of divorce on children is hotly debated. There is evidence that many are deeply distressed and present long term problem behaviour as a result of their experience. It is also true, however, that not all children with divorced parents experience EBD. What must be acknowledged, nevertheless, is the considerable influence home, family and community play in the development of problem behaviour.

Learning process within the learning environment

A number of writers during the previous decade have reported that school-based experiences contribute to EBD. Poor staff–student relations, peer-related problems including bullying, truanting or delinquency, and an inappropriate curriculum have been cited as examples of such causes (Rutter *et al.* 1979; Lawrence *et al.* 1984; Steed 1985; Galloway and Goodwin 1987). Rutter's study marked a turning point in educational research into school effectiveness, with its findings pointing to 'within school' factors determining contrasting levels of EBD in schools from the same socio-economic area.

Further studies reported by Reynolds and Cuttance (1992) and Mortimore *et al.* (1988) emphasised the benefits of good schooling on pupils experiencing personal problems. The latter, at the end of a large study of junior schools in London, stated that 'the school makes a far larger contribution to the explanation of progress than is made by pupil background characteristics, sex and age' (Mortimore *et al.* 1988: 204). More recent studies examining the relationship between school effectiveness, school improvement and learning outcomes have focused upon the classroom. School effectiveness is seen to be, in larger measure, a direct result of the learning and teaching taking place in the classroom (Reynolds 1991). The success or failure of the teacher-student relationship has been identified as a critical factor in setting standards of learning performance, as well as greatly influencing positive or negative individual behaviour.

Learning process within the curriculum

Clearly work presented by the teacher or trainer which is too difficult or irrelevant may create learning difficulties and problem behaviour. The Mortimore study found that pedagogy and curriculum process played an important role in generating or preventing EBD. They identified several markers associated with effective schools that included

- consistency among teachers
- structured, well-planned lessons
- intellectually challenging teaching
- a work-centred focus within lessons
- maximum dialogue between teachers and pupils
- good record keeping (personal/social/academic)
- a positive climate.

The ethos of a classroom and a school, the quality of staff–student relationships, a structured and purposeful learning situation with adaptive flexibility, within which individual contribution is encouraged and acknowledged are arguably prime factors in the successful classroom. Their absence will make for difficulties, troublesome behaviour and learning failure. Such conditions may also produce EBD, or at the very least, reinforce such behaviour and result in learning failure.

Problem behaviour, learning performance and style

Weber (1978, 1982) presented a thought-provoking account of teaching students with EBD. He drew upon this experience to develop a curriculum-based approach in response to their learning difficulty. Weber argued that 'EBD students' were often stigmatised by learning difficulty and a lack of success. They would typically respond to the learning task by either 'shrinking' from a fear of failure, or 'assaulting' authority and defying the teacher who represented a threat, in the shape of more learning failure. A reaction to personal stress, frequently described as the typical response of 'fight or flight', is clearly reflected in these examples of student behaviour, which Weber deliberately labelled a 'learning problem' rather than a 'learner problem'.

Weber (1982) argued that

> Of all of the things that are supposedly 'wrong' with adolescents who have learning difficulties, the one factor that seems to be common to all of them – a truth that is depressingly obvious to classroom teachers – is that these students do not think efficiently or effectively . . . they need . . . to be taught, first, that there are strategies and, secondly, that they must *use* them.
>
> (Weber 1982: 97–8)

Weber suggested that a learning-centred approach was essential to working successfully with students experiencing learning failure or EBD.

Students experiencing difficulty in the learning context are quite clearly going to experience anxiety, insecurity and perhaps distress. In terms of behaviour, individual need, and the learning context, Weber described three basic needs which often underlie learning problems as

- success
- security
- hope and a perception that things can get better.

He argued that the 'teacher was the key' to meeting these needs within the learning situation. The role of the teacher was viewed as one of 'mediation', that is, acting as a go-between, linking a demand made of the individual student to a coping response and success in learning. This notion of the teacher as a key to successful learning is not unlike Feuerstein's more generalised concept of mediator in learning to think, as described in 'instrumental enrichment' (Sharron 1987). The term is also used by Smith and Laslett (1993), who develop the role of teacher as 'mediator' in their description of effective classroom management.

Weber (1982) suggested that successful 'mediation' carried out by the teacher within the learning context involved

- support in developing strategies for thinking and learning
- intrinsic rather than imposed 'momentum'
- learning style
- clear direction.

In curriculum terms, meeting these individual needs was achieved through structure, momentum and direction. At the heart of the curriculum was a priority target – the teaching of strategies for thinking and learning. Linked to this was the suggestion that concern for a student's learning style should be reflected in the teaching programme. Weber's response to learning difficulty was individual. The idea that the student was literally the central focus of the teaching activity permeated his approach to teaching 'process-skills' and emphasising the importance of teaching learners 'how to learn'.

Stott (1983) similarly criticised 'deficit-bound' or 'within the individual' explanations of learning failure or EBD. He argued a case for perceiving difficulty as a result of the non-use or limited use of learning capacity. He suggested that 'effectiveness-motivation' and 'learning style' combined to determine a pupil's approach to the learning task (Stott 1983: 21–4). This concept, led in turn, to an individualised view of learning. Stott argued that this kind of approach should involve the need for an analysis of learning skills and behaviour, as part of a response to learning failure.

Stott (1983: 150–1) presented an assessment-based programme for learning difficulty which involved a 'study of the child's learning and coping styles', a 'focus on reshaping the child's learning style', and a reinforcement of a child's 'learning strategies' by an 'enhancement of their feelings of effectiveness'. Working through the medium of the curriculum, Stott argued that profiling learning style offered a unique opportunity for building 'intrinsic rather than imposed momentum' and enabling 'support in developing strategies for thinking and learning'.

Stott and Weber both presented interesting arguments supporting an approach to learning performance and problem behaviour. Each emphasised a pedagogy taking account of individual differences in the learner. In this respect, both writers argued that 'learning style' or 'strategies' offered not only a way to reach the hard to teach, but also an approach which would generate appropriate learning behaviour.

Such an approach is developmental, positive, success orientated and builds upon an acknowledgement of the importance of individual differences in the learning context. It is also an approach which reflects the writers' view that cognitive style and learning strategies are important considerations in a teaching response to learning failure and problem behaviour. It is this issue which is more closely considered next, in a discussion of style and problem behaviour.

Style and problem behaviour

Given the emerging consensus among educationists, that learner characteristics and the learning process are important factors in any explanation for EBD, it is not long before the question of style is raised. While there are, of course, several causal factors frequently attributed to EBD, we have argued that school-related factors are equally important, and significantly, are perhaps more easily 'accessible' to the teacher or trainer. It is also suggested that learner characteristics, individuality and the degree to which these are included as an integral feature in pedagogical practice are equally relevant. It is therefore not surprising to reach the conclusion that style offers the opportunity for further developing an effective approach and response to EBD!

Conceptually, it is reasonable to expect that style will be related to some extent to problem behaviour. The wholist-analytic dimension of style has to do with structure and control, while the verbal-imagery dimension may affect aspects of affect, such as inwardness and fantasy. Empirically, it is also reasonable to ask what evidence can be provided to explore the relationship between style and problem behaviour. Several studies have reported on this relationship, involving a consideration of cognitive style and various aspects of problem behaviour or personality.

Wholist-analytic style and psychoticism

Riding and Wigley (1977) in a study of 17–18-year-old college of further education students, found that wholists (mean 3.27, sd 2.18) were significantly more psychotic than the analytics (mean 3.03, sd 1.81), who in turn were more than the intermediates (mean 2.57, sd 1.81), although since the maximum possible psychoticism score was 12, all scores were modest. Cook (1993: 87) observed that the psychoticism scale probably measures a tendency to social deviance.

Style and pupil behaviour in school

Riding and Burton (1998) with a sample of 341 pupils (149 boys and 192 girls) from two urban secondary schools. From School A there were 158 Year 10 (14–15-year-old pupils: 69 males and 89 females) and from School B 183 Year 11 (15–16-year-old pupils: 80 males and 103 females). The pupils comprised the whole of one school year from each school. The form/tutor-group teachers of the pupils in each school, who had generally known the pupils over several years,

Figure 8.1 Behaviour ratings for gender and wholist-analyst style groups

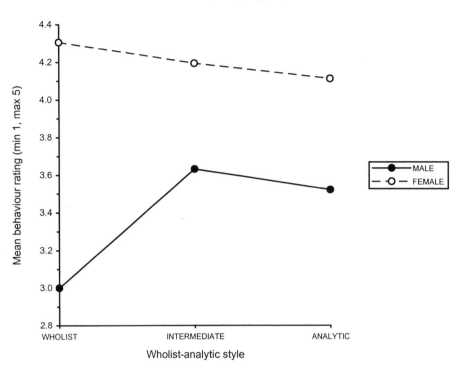

were asked to rate the classroom behaviour of each child on a five-point scale from 1 to 5 where 1 was the worst behaviour and 5 the best. The pupils had been with the same form/tutor-group teachers over several years. The intention was to obtain an overall global impression of conduct behaviour. The teachers were likely to be influenced in their rating by outward active manifestations of misbehaviour such as verbal interruption, distracting other pupils, inappropriate moving about, physical aggression to other pupils or the teacher. Passive misbehaviour, such as inattention, was not likely to be counted since it was not disruptive. There was a significant relationship between Wholist-Analytic style and behaviour and this is shown in Figure 8.1 (adapted from Riding and Burton 1998).

Inspection of Figure 8.1 indicates that the males had worse behaviour than the females and that of these the wholists had the worst behaviour.

Style and referral of pupils to special schools

Riding and Craig (1997) assessed the style of 83 10–18-year-old pupils in two residential special schools to which the pupils had been referred because of behaviour problems. In addition the personal files of the 14 most wholist (ratio range 0.44–0.63) and 14 most analytic (ratio range 1.32–2.01) subjects; plus the 14 most extreme verbalisers (ratio range 0.59–0.93), and 14 most extreme imagers (ratio range 1.22–3.30) were examined. These files contained personal information, including the Statement of Special Educational Need and current school reports, supplying pertinent details of the pupil's domestic, health, social, academic and psychological status. The data were considered in terms of the cognitive style distribution of the special school pupils, and the behaviour characteristics of the cognitive style sub-groups.

Cognitive style distribution of the special school pupils

The style of the sample of the 83 special school pupils was compared to the distribution on the two style dimensions of a secondary school comparison group which comprised a total of 413 male 12–16-year-old secondary school students from the whole ability range, but excluding pupils with learning difficulties, in ten mainstream secondary schools. Their cognitive style data were obtained from that collected for the following studies: Riding and Pearson (1994), Riding et al. (1995), Riding and Read (1996), Riding and Adams,[1] and Rayner and Riding (1996). The group was sufficiently large and from enough schools to be considered representative of secondary school students. The comparison sample was considered likely to represent a wide ability range and to reflect the distribution of style within the male school population as a whole.

In order to contrast the distribution for the special school pupils on each style dimension with that of the comparison group, the two dimensions were divided on the basis of the style ratios of the comparison group into three divisions with equal numbers of comparison group students (i.e., 33.3 per cent) in each.

On the basis of the comparison group divisions, a loglinear analysis of school [2] by wholist-analytic style [3] by verbal-imagery style [3] was performed on the distribution of the special school pupils and the application of Backward Elimination indicated that there was a significant effect of wholist-analytic style ($P < 0.016$) and of verbal-imagery style ($P = 0.048$), and there was no significant interaction between the style dimensions or with school. In other words the style effects apply to the pupils from both schools, and independently for each dimension. The percentages of special school pupils in the divisions on the style dimensions are shown in Figures 8.2 and 8.3 (adapted from Riding and Craig 1997).

Inspection of Figures 8.2 and 8.3 indicates that the proportion of wholists and of verbalisers was greater in the special school sample than the comparison sample, which had equal proportions in each division (i.e. 33.3 per cent).

---

1 Data collected by Derek Adams, Assessment Research Unit, University of Birmingham, 1997.

Figure 8.2 Wholist-analytic style of special pupils in terms of comparison group

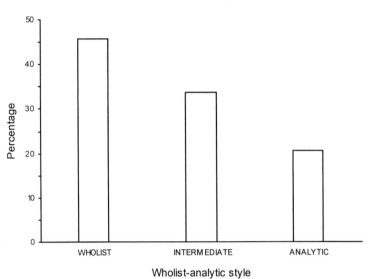

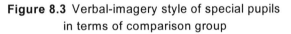

Figure 8.3 Verbal-imagery style of special pupils in terms of comparison group

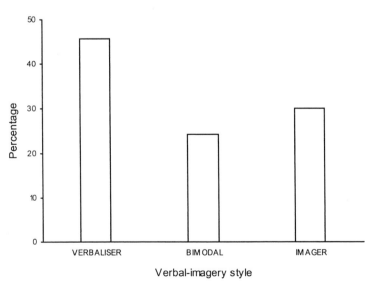

Behaviour characteristics of the cognitive style sub-groups

In order to investigate behaviours associated with particular styles, the record files of the 14 most wholist and the 14 most analytic, and the 14 most verbaliser and the 14 most imager pupils were examined. The comments made about them were grouped into three categories: those referring to sociability, those dealing with problem behaviours, and those describing ability. Where the percentage exhibiting a behaviour was less than 30 per cent at both ends of a dimension, the item will be omitted since it did not represent a major behaviour, nor could it show a difference between the styles. The main effects were observed for the wholist-analytic dimension and only this will be considered here.

Sociability

Comments describing social behaviour, including external versus internal focus of activity, were ordered from high to low difference between the wholists and analytics. The order of the behaviours and the percentage reported as having the observed behaviours is shown in Table 8.1.

Table 8.1 Behaviours associated with sociability

| Behaviour | Percentage displaying behaviour | | Difference |
	Wholist	Analytic	W–A
Sociable	71.4	0	71.4
Pleasant/likeable	57.1	0	57.1
Immaturity	64.3	50.0	14.3
Indulge in fantasies	14.3	42.9	−28.6
Subject to mood swings	7.1	50.0	−42.9
Solitary	7.1	71.4	−64.3
Tendency to blame others	0	71.4	−71.4
Unsociable	0	92.9	−92.9
Lacking in empathy	0	100.0	−100.0

Inspection of Table 8.1 indicates that wholists tend to be sociable and outward, while analytics are described as more unsociable and detached.

Problem behaviours

The reported problem behaviours were again arranged in a descending order of difference between wholists and analytics. The percentage reported as having the observed behaviours is shown in Table 8.2.

Inspection of Table 8.2 suggests that the wholists are inclined to be disruptive, often in a verbal manner, whereas the analytics display more anger and physical aggression.

Table 8.2 Behaviour problems

| Behaviour | Percentage displaying behaviour | | Difference |
	Wholist	Analytic	W–A
Disruptive	100.0	0	100.0
Verbally aggressive	78.6	0	78.6
Abscond	35.7	14.3	21.4
Out of parental control	35.7	28.6	7.1
Bully	35.7	50.0	−14.3
Exhibit frustration	50.0	78.6	−28.6
Display extreme sibling rivalry	0	35.7	−35.7
Physically aggressive	57.1	92.9	−35.8
Cruelty	7.1	57.1	−50.0
Display anger/temper	28.6	100.0	−71.4

Style and truancy

Rayner and Riding (1996) studied 17 15–17-year-old pupils attending a truancy unit because of their previous failure to attend school. Again comparison with a control sample showed a significant difference on the wholist-analytic dimension as shown in Figure 8.4 (adapted from Rayner and

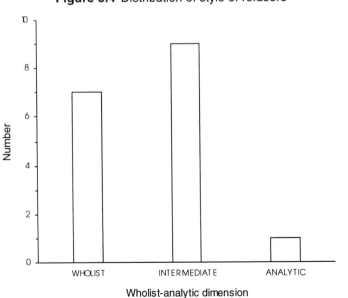

Figure 8.4 Distribution of style of refusers

Inspection of Figure 8.4 shows that the greater number of children attending the truancy unit were either wholists or intermediates.

Personal style and effective pedagogy

Providing for individual difference in the learning process is a key issue for any pedagogical practice. A sensible way of managing this issue must surely involve consideration of cognitive style.

Cognitive style, EBD and effective pedagogy

Research (described in the previous section) revealed interesting relationships between cognitive style and EBD presented by students in the special school context. It is perhaps useful, at this juncture, to interpret these studies further and consider their implications for an effective pedagogy.

Style and truancy
One study focused on the cognitive style of students who were attending a unit for school refusers. Rayner and Riding (1996) reported that this special group, when compared to a large sample of secondary pupils in mainstream schools, reflected one dimension of cognitive style. The school refusers group was significantly skewed to the wholist end of the wholistic-analytic dimension of cognitive style. This reflected a tendency for school refusers as a group to process information wholistically. The high proportion of wholists with problem behaviour might possibly be related to a lack of strong internal control on the part of Wholists if they are then in a situation where there is insufficient structure and parental discipline within their home environment.

Cognitive style in an EBD school
A second study (Riding and Craig 1997) reported that a significant relationship existed between the cognitive style dimensions of learners and problem behaviour in a residential school for pupils with EBD. The aim of the study was to investigate whether the style of pupils with behaviour problems was different to that of children with no reported problems. When the cognitive style of the pupils in two EBD school were compared with a sample from mainstream school, the special school group had a significantly higher proportion of pupils with a wholist or verbaliser cognitive style. The study also revealed that social and problem behaviour displayed by the pupils consistently varied with style.

Educational implications

This research suggests several implications for building an effective pedagogy and appropriate response to problem behaviour. These include developing a 'regime'

- to 'suit' particular cognitive styles thereby alleviating learning difficulties and problem behaviour
- for wholist learners which would provide a clear structure for behaviour and support the direct instruction of strategies for internalising ways of structuring their learning
- for analytic learners which would provide a set of strategies aimed at changing how they internally structure their learning.

The logical conclusion to this thinking is that an assessment-based approach to individual differences is a requirement in the enhancement of learning and the building of an effective pedagogy. If learning and behaviour are basic ingredients in learning performance, it naturally follows that learning enhancement must involve addressing individual differences, as part of the management of a learning and teaching relationship.

Style, pedagogy and learning performance

There appear to be three useful ways of moving forward in thinking about learning performance, style and pedagogy. These would reflect an approach involving a direct consideration of learning styles to enable the development of learning strategies and instructional method (see Chapter 4), a consideration of what constitutes 'learning behaviour' (see the next section) and an integration of one and two in an assessment-based approach to learning.

Part of this approach leads to a reconsideration of contemporary models of learning style, with a view to identifying and then reinforcing the development of an emerging construct of style – personal learning style (see Chapter 3). The latter, rather than forming what might be regarded as yet another style concept, is intended to represent a synthesis of previous style theory. It therefore should help to rationalise theory for the practitioner in a meaningful way rather than add to the confusion of a disparate and disconnected literature. The construct would help to distinguish between cognitive 'hard-wiring' and learning 'soft-wiring' in an individual's personal learning style, made up of cognitive style and learning strategies. It would give real opportunity for a full development of the student's personal learning style.

Building better learning behaviour: pedagogy and practice

If learning behaviour is adopted as a basis for developing pedagogy, it is possible to begin working towards a model of individual performance. Further development of a profiling assessment and supporting curriculum development would at this stage, attempt to integrate affective, cognitive and behavioural aspects of the student's personal learning style. The former would address the features associated with style and strategy development, the latter, more properly, would address behaviour as part of a profiling of strategy enhancement and learning behaviour.

At a first level, the profiling of individual pupils would offer one method of assessment which could record individual performances in each of the aspects previously described. Tracking performance in terms of on-task behaviour or motivation could be used diagnostically, to support both a continuous process of strategy development as well as providing information in the construction of learning tasks for the individual learner.

At a second level, the use of such a profile could also be built into classroom management to encourage student self-monitoring of learning performance and the exploitation of a benchmark in reinforcing appropriate learning behaviour. A simple example would be the targeting of on-task behaviour in a certain learning activity, repeated over a period of time. This kind of pedagogy will encourage active learning, levels of independent and interactive learning, and a 'dialogue' between teacher and student, mirroring the dynamic of teaching and learning.

The identification of aspects of learning behaviour enable the teacher or trainer in the process of targeting activity aimed at supporting and reinforcing appropriate learning behaviour. Clearly, such an approach is process rather than subject-domain bound. It would require a commitment to teaching process as well as content. It does not, however, mean that the subject-content of a programme of study is of secondary importance. The effective management of teaching and learning, and successful support of learning performance, is ultimately an inseparable combination of process and content.

Summary: a way forward

The need for an educational emphasis in a response to learning failure has been discussed in this chapter. An argument has been made for a renewed focus upon individual differences in the learner. It is undoubtedly true that effective management of teaching and learning, and the successful support of learning performance, is ultimately an inseparable combination of process and content. It is, however, necessary to focus on the question of how to facilitate individual learning in order to enhance the learning performance. This means making far greater use of differential psychology and the construct of learning style.

A key issue underlying much concern for school effectiveness, is that too much teaching and learning remains an intuitive, hit-and-miss management of the relationship between learning and behaviour. This is also true of the management of pedagogy, the integration of curriculum process and content, and more particularly, the individual learning style of students in the learning context. A major implication of the work being carried out in the field of individual differences, is to flag up the challenge of achieving authentic differentiation in the curriculum. This is perhaps succinctly and poignantly illustrated in the idea that the construct of learning style may very well offer a way forward in teaching the hard to reach and reaching the hard to teach!

CHAPTER 9

Conclusion, implications and future developments

Chapter overview

This chapter will draw together the conclusions of the research and theory on cognitive style, indicate existing practical implications of style, and suggest areas where further research would be useful.

The validity of cognitive style

The chapter will argue that there is an impressive range of evidence for validity of the construct of style, that style is fundamental in nature, and it has an influence on a wide spectrum of feelings, behaviour and cognition.

Practical implications

Cognitive style has a number of applications and examples of these will be taken from education and training, such as school development, and designing integrated learning systems, and from facilitating personal development.

Further research

In view of the evidence for style and its practical import, further research is justified to clarify, its fundamental nature, and the ways in which it interacts with other variables in affecting behaviour.

The validity of cognitive style

In order to pursue research, and particularly to develop a psychological model and evaluate a construct, the researcher needs to have sufficient evidence that the construct may exist in order to maintain the energy to undertake the research. It is also necessary to have a degree of scepticism in order to retain the openness required to evaluate the findings objectively. The psychological study of any construct poses difficulties. Even a generally accepted notion, such as intelligence, has been questioned. Does it really exist as a valid construct (see e.g. Howe 1990)? Howe warns, 'It is particularly important not to fall into the trap of believing that by describing someone's performance we are also providing the reasons for it' (Howe 1990: 493).

A common pitfall for test producers is to focus only on a narrow range of psychometric properties of a test, and if these appear satisfactory to assume that the test measures what they claim it measures. Often the emphasis is on the test's reliability and whether a factor analysis of it produces clear factors. There is the tendency then to assume that this apparent psychometric robustness justifies the test's widespread use. In reality, until a test's *construct validity* has been demonstrated by showing that it relates to, and can predict, other objectively assessed behaviours, and further that it is distinctly different from other assessments, its use cannot be justified.

This section will summarise the evidence for the validity of the construct of style based on the Cognitive Styles Analysis approach, consider the position of style with respect to other constructs, and reflect on the range of behaviours that style affects.

Range of evidence for validity

Evidence for the validity of the construct of cognitive style, as assessed by the Cognitive Styles Analysis approach, comes from a range of research in a variety of contexts. These may be summarised as follows, with cognitive style having the following important characteristics.

- *Independence from other variables.* Studies indicate that the style dimensions are independent of one another. They are also separate from intelligence, common personality measures and gender.
- *A relationship to a wide range of behaviours.* The style dimensions are related to observed behaviours, such as learning performance, learning preferences, subject preferences, social behaviour, decisiveness, personal feelings such as anxiety and optimism, and occupational suitability.

- *Evidence of a physiological basis.* There is also an indication of a relationship between both style dimensions and physiological measures, as assessed by EEG brain activity.
- *Conformity to the requirements for a style.* In addition cognitive style fulfils the requirement for the distinction between style and ability.

Such a range of evidence supports the view that the construct validly exists, and leads naturally to further questions concerning how fundamental a variable style is.

The fundamental nature of style

The problem of identifying fundamental constructs

If one takes the construct of self-esteem as an example, is this a fundamental source of behaviour or is it derived from other more primary sources? This type of question is not easy to answer since such measures of the construct will correlate with other constructs such as anxiety or neuroticism, and determining which is the more fundamental is often problematic. The same sort of problem is associated with the search for fundamental personality variables and this is reflected in the controversy as to whether there are three or five basic personality sources (see e.g. Boyle *et al. 1995:* 431–3).

Style as a fundamental behaviour source

Since the two basic style dimensions do not correlate with intelligence, personality or gender, on the one hand, and since style is related to a wide range of behaviours on the other, it is likely that style is a fundamental source of behaviour.

   The level that style occupies in not clear. In Chapter 5 a model was proposed which placed style at a cognitive control level such that it had a moderating effect on the primary physiological personality sources and gender. It is possible, of course, that style itself is a primary source and is at the same level as the sources of personality. Further physiological investigations may clarify the model.

Extent of the influence of style

The observed relationships between the style dimensions and behaviour are consistent with the view that the wholist-analytic dimension is concerned with organisation, and the verbal-imagery dimension with representation.

Style seems to be all pervasive in its effect and not limited to just affecting learning performance or some other narrow aspect of behaviour. It may be noted that often the two style dimensions interact with one another in affecting behaviour. In fact it is likely that interaction is the norm rather than simple main effects of a single dimension. It may be this interactive effect that has caused style to be difficult to detect in the past.

It may also be stressed that the style dimensions are continuously distributed and group labels have only been used as convenient descriptors of sections of a dimension.

Cognitive style has emerged as affecting a wide range of human activity from cognition, through affect to behaviour. Since it is independent of and unrelated to common measures of intelligence and personality, it represents a missing variable in the hunt for an explanation of individual variation. This would suggest that it is centrally placed within the human system.

This leads to the question of the ways in which style acts. Any variable that influences behaviour either does so because it is the source and motivating effect for the action, or because it acts at a moderating level and influences and modifies other sources. It is possible that it is the latter effect in the case of style.

Practical implications

Cognitive style has a range of applications. Instances will be taken from two areas: education and training, and personal development.

Education and training

With education and instruction two examples will be taken to illustrate the applications of style.

School development

Riding and Rayner (1995) have developed the Learning Enhancement Package which is aimed at increasing school effectiveness. It is designed to do this by means of an 'improvement cycle' as follows.

- It begins by providing a way for teachers to become more aware of their own cognitive style which in turn will have affected their teaching style.
- In addition the package will make teachers more sensitive to the range of cognitive style of their pupils and of the need, within their teaching, to

broaden their teaching style to suit the range of style within the pupils they teach.

- This in turn has the potential to result in improved teaching, since the teaching methods adopted will appeal to a wider range of pupils.
- The effect of this should then be increased pupil performance, which should lead to improved attainment, an enhancement of motivation, and a consequent improvement in behaviour.
- This then feeds back to the teacher who can put the energy, that was previously used to control bored, frustrated and disaffected pupils, into teaching. The cycle is then repeated with a further enhancement in outcomes.

Such an approach on a whole school basis over a period of time has the possibility of substantially improving school effectiveness, teacher job satisfaction, and pupil attainment.

Design of integrated learning systems

Developments such as the information superhighway and advances in technology-based learning allow the design of integrated learning systems which can have the capability of acting as intelligent tutors and controlling the presentation and assessment of learning and instruction (see e.g. Rayner and Riding 1996). The effectiveness of such systems is likely to be greatly enhanced by the incorporation into their control systems of the means of assessing cognitive style and of the capability of the system to adapt instruction to suit the style of the individual student (see Riding 1996).

To be feasible and practically useful, an integrated learning system will require a framework for making decisions about the requirements of an individual student. The section that follows attempts to set out in concrete terms such a framework. This would permit software to control the integrated learning system to be produced. An executive control within the system would undertake the following types of decisions taking into account the student's cognitive style (see e.g. Riding 1996).

These will include:

- the initial assessment of student knowledge necessary to give understanding to the new topic
- the controlling of aspects of presentation to facilitate ease of learning and to reduce information load by taking account of the student's learning style and intelligence, in terms of
  - conceptual structure (the needs for an organiser or an overview)
  - type of content, (verbal or visual)
  - layout of information (e.g. tables, tree diagrams, etc.)
  - choice of mode of presentation (words or pictures)

- the determination of the locus of control and other motivational aspects with respect to
  - stimulation level preferences (lively and outgoing or less dynamic)
  - 'open' or 'closed' in terms of whether the trainer or the student is in control
  - choice of learning activities (e.g. convergent or reflective).

This outline indicates the feasibility of such a system. It is argued that to omit style from any system that claims to be an integrated learning system is a serious defect that will greatly limit the effectiveness of such a system.

Personal development

Self-awareness is both liberating and empowering. Liberating in that if one is aware of why certain things are found to be difficult, then one feels more relaxed about not being able to do them easily. Empowering since one is more aware of one's strengths and can also develop strategies for dealing with the areas that are less strong.

Since style appears to be very pervasive into a wide range of feelings, behaviours and information processing situations, an understanding of style and its effects is a positive way of increasing self-understanding. The Cognitive Styles Analysis can be used in conjunction with the Personal Style Awareness package (Riding 1994) which provides style group descriptions, an explanation of how style operates, and ways of applying style.[1] The package has been used to facilitate management development and has potential for continuing professional development, career guidance and work on effective team building.

Further research

While there is evidence to support the notion of style, a number of questions remain and further research is needed to clarify these. Possible research areas include the fundamental nature of style, and the interaction between style and other behaviour influences.

---

1 The PSA package is available in two formats, as a booklet for individual or group use, and as a computer-presented feedback facility.

The fundamental nature of style

What are the sources of style?

An obvious question concerns the origins of style. Style is either inbuilt or develops with experience. It could be that an individual is born with a predisposition to use one mode of representation in preference to another. If style is inbuilt what is the mechanism of transmission? Are there style genes?

On the other hand there is the possibility that a style emerges from a difference between two complementary abilities. In order to illustrate this, if one deliberately oversimplifies how the brain works, one can imagine that there is one processor for verbal information and another for pictorial information within the brain. Suppose that, in an individual, these two processors have unequal speed and processing capacity, then the individual will tend to use the one in preference to the other whenever possible, and this will lead to the establishment of a style, or habitual preference for one over the other.

Whatever the mechanism, style appears to be present at a relatively early age. Riding and Taylor (1976) found that the verbal-imagery style dimension was strongly in evidence in 7-year-olds. Methods of assessing style in young children and infants need to be developed. Studies of style distributions at various ages need to be undertaken, bearing in mind that the whole population range will need to be represented at each age.

Are there other fundamental style dimensions?

Do the wholist-analytic and the verbal-imagery dimensions encompass all style descriptors or are there possibly other dimensions? If there are, they must fulfil the condition that for a style dimension to exist; the two sources must represent opposites in some sense. In the case of the verbal-imagery dimension, while words are not the opposite of pictures, they can be used as alternative ways of representing the same information. For the wholist-analytic style dimension, it is possible to see a progression from the whole to the parts. The whole is, in this sense, the opposite of the parts; the wood comprises the individual trees.

Studies are required to compare other existing measures of style and strategy, provided they have also been shown to possess a reasonable degree of construct validity, with the wholist-analytic and verbal-imagery dimensions, to see whether they come within either of those families or represent other independent dimensions.

A further question arises in considering whether pairing the wholist-analytic and verbal-imagery dimensions which have been called 'style' dimensions is helpful or limiting and whether they should be thought of as different from, but analogous to, some of the personality dimensions. Of course, they are different in the sense that they fulfil the requirements for a style, although it might be considered that some of the personality dimensions also qualify in that both ends of some dimensions have both positive and negative aspects. Take extraversion for example. Which is it best to be, extravert or introvert? Both have advantages and disadvantages. This is in contrast to a dimension like intelligence where all the advantage seems to lie in being high on intelligence.

Additional research could usefully undertake a further study of personality measures and style, both in terms of possible relationships between them and with their interactive effects on observed behaviour. Riding and Wigley (1997), in their consideration of personality variables and style, did not include three of those listed by McCrae and John (1992), namely, openness to experience, agreeableness-antagonism, and conscientiousness-undirectedness. The fundamentalness of the personality dimensions needs to be questioned since it may be that some of the 'Big Five' are actually the result of style interactions.

What is the relationship between physiological measures and style?

The identification of the underlying physiological mechanisms as evidenced by EEG activity associated with style was important. However, EEG methods are limited to brain-surface activity and do not necessarily indicate the locus of the style activity within the brain. Further studies using more sophisticated brain-scanning techniques to compare neural activity during a range of tasks would be useful. This might then indicate more clearly what style does and how it operates.

Are there cultural differences in style?

Most of the studies using the Cognitive Styles Analysis approach have been undertaken in the United Kingdom. The possible effect of culture on style is of interest. If similar style patterns were to be demonstrated in a wide range of cultures then this would contribute to the understanding of the nature of style. There are English language versions of the Cognitive Styles Analysis for use in the contexts of the UK, North America and Australia. In addition French, German, Spanish, Dutch, Malay and Arabic versions have been developed. Data from studies showing style effects consistent with those in the UK have already been obtained in the USA, Australia, Canada, the Netherlands, Belgium, Malta, and Kuwait.

Style in context

Research possibilities with respect to style and other sources of behaviour and a range of behaviours will be outlined.

What is the interaction between other sources and style?

Range of variables affecting behaviour

In considering the impact of styles on a behaviour, such as learning performance, it is necessary to bear in mind the whole range of variables that might affect learning performance by an individual.

For a particular task these will usually include the individual's

- level of ability/intelligence
- present relevant knowledge which is necessary to give meaning to the new information
- degree of motivation, including the perceived relevance of the task
- gender
- cognitive style.

Clearly style will be only one of a number of individual influences. The relative effect of these variables will depend upon the relative ease of task for the individual. Studies are required which use a range of materials, modes of presentation and include measures of all the variables.

Style effects relative to other variables

Style is not likely to be critical when the task is simple, since there will be insufficient load on the information processing system for there to be an effect. It is likely to be important, however, where the learner is under pressure because, relative to their ability, etc., the task is difficult. The investigation of the conditions in which style is most critical is required.

Further, style will show a reduced effect if there is a lot of variance unaccounted for, occurring because other relevant variables are not measured and included in the analysis.

With intelligence measures it may be noted that these are likely to include more than just processing speed and capacity, since the items commonly used in intelligence tests often also assess learned knowledge, developed strategies and the application of acquired skills. They will often tend to have an element of crystallised intelligence and therefore include within the measure the ability to learn and perform, and hence explain more of the variance than style, because they are not pure measures of fluid intelligence. Studies are needed in which the amount of variance style accounts for, compared to other variables which include strategy development in the form of crystallised intelligence, is controlled for.

Adaptation of variables other than style

Studies are also required on how other variables, besides style, that affect learning performance can be adjusted to improve performance. Taking as an example fluid intelligence, if this is low it may be accommodated by reducing presentation rate, information display density, and conceptual complexity (examples of complex physical concepts are density, force, energy, and these may need unpacking).

What is the interaction between prior experiences and style?

It has been suggested that style is stable over time and likely to show little change. It has also been argued that there are sources of behaviour such as intelligence, personality and gender. Another important source is past experience. The effect of previous experiences on style reactions is of interest. For example, does the experience of stressful events make analytics more analytic and cautious and wholists more impulsive?

What are the mechanisms for strategy development?

Given that a person of a particular style finds certain tasks more difficult, how can the development of effective strategies be fostered in an individual? This is an important practical area particularly for individuals in situations that they find difficult whether this is with respect to feelings, behaving or learning. There are at least three ways of studying strategy development and these will be considered within the context of learning and instruction.

Observation

Observation of the strategies that individuals of a particular style develop as means of coping with situations which they naturally find difficult would be useful in cataloguing possible strategies.

Task performance

The progression of strategy development could be studied by investigating the progression from awareness of ease or difficulty in doing a task, through preferences, awareness of limitations, to the development and refinement of strategies to cope with stylistically inappropriate modes or situations.

Facilitating strategy development

Various approaches can be tried, for example pairing people of dissimilar style so that they learn from one another's approaches as they work together, deliberately presenting materials in mismatched mode to encourage the production of methods of recoding, or making people aware of the potential of the complementary nature of style dimensions where they exist, as in the case of analytic-imagers who could use their imaging facility to give an overall, 'whole' view which they lack as analytics.

As has been noted, coping strategies are relevant for the individual with respect to controlling feelings, enhancing behaviour and improving learning and information processing. This will also apply at the level of organisations with respect to making the best use of available staff and building effective teams. Riding (1994) suggested practical workplace applications of style for personal development, team roles, management style and interpersonal relationships. Systematic investigation of the types of application would clarify the practical use of style in work situations.

What is the range of influences of style?

Given the pervasive nature of style which has been shown to affect learning, feeling, decision making and social behaviour, what other areas are related to, or influenced by, cognitive style? Further areas that could be investigated are mental health, medical conditions and motor skills.

It is also possible that some mood changes result from a shift in emphasis from one style dimension to another. It may be that at any moment one style is dominant and has the primary influence. For instance, for an analytic-imager, if the analytic dimension were dominant then there might be a more serious intense approach than if the imager were dominant with its more overall emphasis.

Conclusion

It appears very likely that cognitive style is a missing piece in the jigsaw of understanding the self. Given its pervasive nature and range of effects it has considerable importance. It is a key element in a Personal Style Profile. Such a profile could include cognitive style, intelligence, personality, gender and prior knowledge. Cognitive style justifies a more prominent place in textbooks on psychology than it has previously occupied.

Much of the work on style to date has been exploratory in nature – mapping the ground. The next stage is now required to systematically investigate the aspects, nature, role, relationship to other constructs and practical applications of style. This should significantly advance the understanding of individual differences and indicate the extent of the practical importance of style.

References

Allard, M. and Carlson, E. R. (1963) 'The generality of cognitive complexity', *Journal of Social Psychology* **59**, 73–5.

Allinson, J. and Hayes, C. (1988) 'The Learning Style Questionnaire: an alternative to Kolb's Inventory?', *British Journal of Management* **25**, 269–81.

Allinson, J. and Hayes, C. (1990) 'Validity of the Learning Styles Questionnaire', *Psychological Reports* **67**, 859–66.

Allinson, J. and Hayes, C. (1994) 'Cognitive style and its relevance for management practice' *British Journal of Management* **5**, 53–71.

Allinson, J. and Hayes, C. (1996) 'The Cognitive Style Index: a measure of intuition-analysis for organizational research', *Journal of Management Studies* **33**, 119–35.

Allport, G. G. (1937) *Personality: A Psychological Interpretation*. New York: Holt.

Ashman, A. F. and Conway, N. F. (1989) *Cognitive Strategies for Special Education*. London: Routledge.

Atkinson, G. (1988) 'Reliability of the Learning Style Inventory', *Psychological Reports* **62**, 755–68.

Austin, M. (1971) 'Dream recall and the bias of intellectual ability', *Nature* **231**, 59.

Ausubel, D. P. and Robinson, F. G. (1966) *School Learning: An Introduction to Educational Psychology*. New York: Holt, Rinehart and Winston.

Baddeley, A. D. (1996) 'The concept of working memory', in Gathercole, S. E. (ed.) *Models of Short-term Memory*. Hove: Psychology Press.

Banta, T. J. (1970) 'Tests for the evaluation of early childhood education: The Cincinnati Autonomy Test Battery (CATB)', in Hellmuth, J. (ed.) *Cognitive Studies*, 1. New York: Brunner-Mazel.

Barker-Lunn, J. C. (1970) *Streaming in the Primary School*. Slough: National Foundation for Educational Research.

Baron, J. (1978) 'Intelligence and general strategies', in Underwood, G. (ed.) *Strategies in Information-processing*, 403–50). London: Academic Press.

Bartlett, F. C. (1932) *Remembering: A Study in Experimental and Social Psychology*. Cambridge: Cambridge University Press.

Bauer, E. (1987) 'Learning style and the learning disabled: experimentation with ninth graders', *The Clearing House* **60**(5), 206–8.

Benfari, R. (1966) 'The scanning control principle and its relationship to affect manipulation', *Perceptual and Motor Skills* **22**, 203–16.

Bergum, B. O. (1977) 'Undergraduate self-perceptions of creativity and independence', *Perceptual and Motor Skills* **44**, 187–90.

Bertini, M. (1986) 'Some implications of field-dependence for education', in Bertini, M., Pizzamiglio, L., Wapner, S. (eds) *Field-Dependence in Psychological Theory, Research and Application. Two Symposia in Memory of H. A. Witkin.* Hillsdale, NJ: Lawrence Erlbaum.

Betts, G. H. (1909) *The Distributions and Functions of Mental Imagery.* New York: The Teacher's College.

Bieri, J. (1966) 'Cognitive complexity and personality development', Harvey, O. (ed.) *Experience, Structure and Adaptability*, 13–37. New York: Springer.

Biggs, J. B. (1978) 'Individual and group differences in study processes', *British Journal of Educational Psychology* **48**, 266–79.

Biggs, J. B. (1979) 'Individual differences in study processes and the quality of learning outcomes', *Higher Education* **8**, 381–94.

Biggs, J. B. (1985) 'The role of metalearning in study processes', *British Journal of Educational Psychology* **55**, 185–212.

Biggs, J. B. (1987) *Student Approaches to Learning and Studying.* Hawthorn, Victoria: Australian Council for Educational Research.

Biggs, J. B. (1988) 'The role of meta-cognition in enhancing learning', *Australian Journal of Education* **32**, 127–38.

Biggs, J. B. and Moore, P. J. (1993) *The Process of Learning*, 3rd edn. Englewood Cliffs, NJ: Prentice Hall.

Bisiach, E. and Berti A. (1990) 'Waking images and neural activity', in Kunzendorf, R. G. and Sheikh, A. A. (eds) *The Psychophysiology of Mental Imagery: Theory, Research and Application.* Amityville, NY: Baywood.

Blagg, N. (1991) *Can We Teach Intelligence?* Hillsdale, NJ: Lawrence Erlbaum.

Bloom, B. (1976) *Human Characteristics and Learning.* New York: McGraw-Hill.

Bloomberg, M. (1971) 'Creativity as related to field-independence and mobility', *Journal of Genetic Psychology* **118**, 3–12.

Borg, M. G. and Riding, R. J. (1993) 'Teacher stress and cognitive style', *British Journal of Educational Psychology* **63**, 2.

Boring, E. G. (1923) 'Intelligence as the tests test it', *New Republic* **35**, 35–7.

Bouchard, T. J. (1995) 'Longitudinal studies of personality and intelligence: a behaviour genetic and evolutionary psychology perspective', in Saklofske, D. H. and Zeidner, M. (eds) *International Handbook of Personality and Intelligence* 81–106. New York: Plenum Press.

Bowlby, J. (1946) *Forty-four Juvenile Thieves: Their Characters and Home Lives.* London: Balliere, Tindall and Cox.

Boyle, G. J., Stankov, L., Cattell, R. B. (1995) 'Measurement and statistical models in the study of personality and intelligence', in Saklofske D. H. and Zeidner, M. (eds) *International Handbook of Personality and Intelligence*, 417–46. New York: Plenum Press.

Brennan, P. (1984) 'An analysis of the relationships among hemispheric preference and analytic/global cognitive style, two elements of learning style, method of instruction, gender, and mathematics achievement of tenth grade geometry students', doctoral dissertation, St John's University, Jamaica. *Dissertation Abstracts International* 45/11, 3271A.

Brumby, M. N. (1982) 'Consistent differences in cognitive styles shown for qualitative biological problem-solving', *British Journal of Educational Psychology* **52**, 244–57.

Bruner, J. S. and Tajfel, H. (1961) 'Cognitive risks and environmental change', *Journal of Abnormal Psychology* **62**, 231–41.

Brunner, C. E. and Majewski, W. S. (1990) 'Mildly handicapped students can succeed with learning styles', *Educational Leadership* October, 21–3.

Bruno, J. (1988) 'An experimental investigation of the relationships between and among hemispheric processing, learning style preferences, instructional strategies, academic achievement, and attitudes of developmental mathematics in students in an urban technical college', doctoral dissertation, St John's University, Jamaica. *Dissertation Abstracts International* 49, 1066A.

Campbell, S. B. and Douglas, V. I. (1972) 'Cognitive styles and responses to the threat of frustration', *Canadian Journal of Behavioural Science* **4**, 30–42.

Canadian Test Centre (1992a) *Canadian Test of Cognitive Skills: Level 4*. Markham, Ontario: Canadian Test Centre.

Canadian Test Centre (1992b) *Canadian Test of Cognitive Skills: Examiner's Manual*. Markham, Ontario: Canadian Test Centre.

Carroll, J. B. (1993) *Human Cognitive Abilities: A Survey of Factor-Analytic Studies*. Cambridge: Cambridge University Press.

Cattell, R. B. (1936) *A Guide to Mental Testing*. London: University of London Press.

Cattell, R. B. (1995) 'The fallacy of five factors in the personality sphere', *The Psychologist* **8**, 207–14.

Cattell, R. B. and Warburton, F. W. (1967) *Objective Personality and Motivational Tests*. Urbana, IL: University of Illinois Press.

Charlton, T. and George, J. (1993) 'The development of behaviour problems', in Charlton, T. and David, K. (eds) *Managing Misbehaviour in Schools*, 17–52. London: Routledge.

Christensen, C. A., Massey, D. R., Isaacs, P. J. (1991) 'Cognitive strategies and study habits: an analysis of the measurement of tertiary students' learning', *British Journal of Educational Psychology* **61**, 290–9.

Clapp, R. G. (1993) 'The stability of cognitive style in adults: a longitudinal study of the KAI', *Psychological Reports* **73**, 1235–45.

Clark-Thayer, S. (1987) 'The relationship of the knowledge of student-perceived learning style preferences, and study habits and attitudes to achievement of college freshmen in a small urban university', doctoral dissertation, Boston University. *Annotated Bibliography, 1991*. New York: The Learning Styles Network.

Claxton, C. S and Ralston, Y. (1978) 'Learning styles: their impact on teaching and administration', *Higher Education Report* 10. Washington, DC: American

Association for Higher Education.

Coan, R. (1974) *The Optimal Personality: An Empirical and Theoretical Analysis.* New York: Columbia University Press.

Cohen, B. H. and Saslona, M. (1990) 'The advantage of being an habitual visualiser', *Journal of Mental Imagery* **14**, 101–12.

Cohen, G. (1982) 'Theoretical interpretations of lateral asymmetries', Graham Beaumont, J. (ed.) *Divided Visual Field Studies of Cerebral Organisation*, 87–111. London: Academic Press.

Cohen, R. A. (1967) 'Primary group structure, conceptual styles and school achievement', unpublished doctoral dissertation, University of Pittsburgh.

Coles, M. J. and Robinson, W. D. (eds) (1989) *Teaching Thinking.* Bristol: The Bristol Press.

Cook, M. (1993) *Levels of Personality.* London: Cassell.

Cooper, P. (1993) *Effective Schools for Dis-affective Students.* London: Routledge.

Cornwell, J. M., Manfredo, P. A., Dunlap, W. P. (1991) 'Factor analysis of the 1985 revision of Kolb's Learning Style Inventory', *Educational and Psychological Measurement* **51**, 455–62.

Covington, M. Crutchfield, R. Davies, L. Olton, R. (1974) *The Productive Thinking Programme: A Course in Learning to Think.* Columbus: Merril.

Craik, F. I. M. and Lockhart, R. S. (1972) 'Levels of processing: a framework for memory research', *Journal of Verbal Learning and Verbal Behaviour* **11**, 671–84.

Cronbach, L. J. (1960) *Essentials of Psychological Testing,* 2nd edn. New York: Harper Brothers.

Crutchfield, R. S. (1965) 'Creativity thinking in children: its teaching and testing', in Brun, O. J., Crutchfield, R. S., Holzman W. H. (eds). *Intelligence Perspectives 1965: The Terman-Otis Memorial Lectures.* New York: Harcourt, Brace and World.

Curry, L. (1983) 'An organisation of learning styles theory and constructs', *ERIC Document 235 185.*

Curry, L. (1987) *Integrating Concepts of Cognitive or Learning Style: A Review with Attention to Psychometric Standards.* Ottawa, Ontario: Canadian College of Health Service Executives.

Curry, L. (1990) 'Learning styles in secondary schools: a review of instruments and implications for their use', paper prepared for the National Center on Effective Secondary Schools, University of Wisconsin.

Curry, L. (1991) 'Patterns of learning style across selected medical specialities', *Educational Psychology* **11**, 247–78.

Das, J. P. (1988a) 'Implications for school learning', in Schmeck, R. R. (ed.) *Strategies and Styles of Learning.* New York: Plenum Press.

Das, J. P. (1988b) 'Simultaneous-successive processing and planning', in Schmeck R. R. (ed.) *Strategies and Styles of Learning*, 101–30. New York: Plenum Press.

Deary, I. J. and Matthews, G. (1993) 'Personality traits are alive and well', *The Psychologist* **6**, 299–311.

DeBello, T. C. (1985a) 'A critical analysis of the effects on achievement and attitudes of administrative assignments to social studies instruction based on individual, eighth grade students' sociological preferences for learning alone, with peers, or with teachers', doctoral dissertation, St John's University, Jamaica. *Annotated Bibliography 1991*. New York: The Learning Styles Network.

DeBello, T. C. (1985b) 'Comparison of eleven major learning styles models: variables, appropriate populations, validity of instrumentation, and the research behind them', *Reading, Writing and Learning Disabilities* **6**, 203–22.

DeBello, T. C. (1990) 'Comparison of eleven major learning styles: variables, appropriate populations, validity of instrumentation, and the research behind them', *International Journal of Reading, Writing and Learning Disabilities* **6**, 203–22.

De Ciantis, S. M. and Kirton, M. J. (1996) 'A psychometric re-examination of Kolb's experiential learning style construct: a separation of level, style and process', *Educational and Psychological Measurement* **56**, 809–20.

Douglas, G. and Riding, R. J. (1993) 'The effect of pupil cognitive style and position of prose passage title on recall', *Educational Psychology* **13**, 385–93.

Douglas, G. and Riding, R. J. (1994) 'Cognitive style and gender differences in drawing from memory versus copying in 11-year-old children', *Educational Psychology* **14**, 493–6.

Doyle, W. (1990) 'Classroom knowledge as a foundation for teaching', *Teachers College Record* **91**, 347–60

Dunn, K. and Dunn, R. (1974) 'Learning style as a criterion for placement in alternative programs', *Phi Delta Kappa* **36**, 275–9.

Dunn, K. and Dunn, R. (1978) *Teaching Students through their Individual Learning Styles*. Englewood Cliffs, NJ: Prentice Hall.

Dunn, K. and Dunn, R. (1986) 'The look of learning styles', *Early Years – K8* March, 46–52.

Dunn, K. and Dunn, R. (1987) 'Dispelling outmoded beliefs about student learning', *Educational Leadership* **44**, 55–61.

Dunn, R. and Griggs, S. A. (1989) 'Learning styles: a quiet revolution in American secondary schools', *The Clearing House* **63**, 1.

Dunn, K., Dunn, R., Price, G. E. (1977) 'Diagnosing learning styles: a prescription for avoiding malpractice suits', *Phi Delta Kappa* January, 418–20.

Dunn, R., Dunn, K., Price, G. E. (1989) *Learning Styles Inventory*. Lawrence, KS: Price Systems.

Elliot, C. (1983) *The British Ability Scales*. Windsor, National Foundation for Educational Research.

Ennis, R. H. (1987) 'A taxonomy of thinking skills and dispositions and abilities, in Baron, J. B. and Sternberg, R. J. (eds) *Teaching Thinking Skills: Theory and Practice*, 9–26. New York: W. H. Freeman.

Entwistle, N. J. (1979) *Motivation, Styles of Learning and the Academic Environment*. ERIC Document Reproduction Service ED 190 636, University of Edinburgh: Edinburgh.

Entwistle, N. J. (1981) *Styles of Teaching and Learning: An Integrated Outline of Educational Psychology for Students, Teachers and Lecturers*. Chichester: Wiley.

Entwistle, N. J. (1988) 'Motivational factors in students' approaches to learning', in Schmeck, R. R. (ed.) *Learning Strategies and Learning Styles*, 21–52. New York: Plenum Press.

Entwistle, N. J. and Ramsden, P. (1983) *Understanding Student Learning*. London: Croom Helm.

Entwistle, N. J. and Tait, H. (1994) *The Revised Approaches to Studying Inventory*. Edinburgh Centre for Research into Learning and Instruction, University of Edinburgh.

Ernest, C. H. (1977) 'Imagery, ability and cognition: A critical review', *Journal of Mental Imagery* 2, 181–216.

Eysenck, H. J. (1960) *The Structure of Human Personality*. London: London University Press.

Eysenck, H. J. and Eysenck, M. W. (1985) *Personality and Individual Differences: A Natural Science Approach*. New York: Plenum.

Eysenck, H. J. and Eysenck, S. B. G. (1991) *Eysenck Personality Scales*. London: Hodder and Stoughton.

Eysenck, M. W. (1991) 'Trait anxiety and cognition', in Spielberger, C. D. and Sarason, I. G. (eds) *Stress and Emotion: Volume 14*, 77–84. Washington, DC: Hemisphere Publishing.

Fernandez, T., Harmony, T., Rodriguez, M., Bernal, J., Silva, J., Reyes, A., Marosi, E. (1995) 'EEG activation patterns during the performance of tasks involving different components of mental calculation', *Electroencephalography and Clinical Neurophysiology* 94, 175–82.

Ferrell, B. G. (1983) 'A factor-analytic comparison of four learning styles instruments', *Journal of Educational Psychology* 78, 33–9.

Flavell, J. H. and Wellman, H. M. (1977) 'Metamemory', in Kail, R. V. and Hagen, J. W. (eds) *Perspectives on the Development of Memory and Cognition*. Hillsdale, NJ: Lawrence Erlbaum.

Flexer, B. K. and Roberge, J. J. (1980) 'IQ, field-dependence-independence, and the development of formal operational thought', *Journal of General Psychology* 103, 191–201.

Fowler, W. (1980) 'Cognitive differentiation and developmental learning', in Rees H. and Lipsitt, L. (eds) *Advances in Child Development and Behaviour, Volume 15*, 163–206. New York: Academic Press.

Freedman, R. D. and Stumpf, S. A. (1980) 'Learning style theory: less than meets the eye', *Academy of Management Review* 5(3), 445–7.

Freedman, R. D. and Stumpf, S. A. (1981) 'Learning Style Inventory: still less then meets the eye. *Academy of Management Review* 6, 297–9.

Furnham, A. (1995) 'The relationship of personality and intelligence to cognitive style and achievement', in Saklofske, D. H. and Zeidner, M. (eds) *International Handbook of Personality and Intelligence*. New York: Plenum Press.

Galloway, D. and Goodwin, C. (1987) *The Education of Disturbing Children*. London: Longman.

Galton, F. (1883) *Inquiries into Human Faculty and its Development*. London: Macmillan.

Kagan, J. (1965) 'Individual differences in the resolution of response uncertainty', *Journal of Personality and Social Psychology* **2**, 154–60.

Kagan, J. (1966) 'Developmental studies in reflection and analysis', in Kidd, A. H. and Rivoire, J. L. (eds) *Perceptual Development in Children*. New York: International University Press.

Kagan, J., Rosman, B., Day, D., Albert, J., Philips, W. (1964) 'Information processing and the child: significance of analytic and reflective attitudes', *Psychological Monographs* **78**, 578.

Kagan, J., Pearson, J., Welch, L. (1966) 'Modifiability of an impulsive tempo', *Journal of Educational Psychology* **57**, 357–65.

Kaufmann, G. (1989) 'The Assimilator-Explorer Inventory', in Martinsen, O. 'Cognitive Style and Insight', PhD thesis, Faculty of Psychology, University of Bergen, Norway.

Keefe, J. W. (1987) *Learning Style: Theory and Practice*. Reston, VA: National Association of Secondary School Principals.

Keefe, J. W. (1989a) *Learning Style Profile Handbook: Volume I, Accommodating Perceptual Study and Instructional Preferences*. Reston, V. A: National Association of Secondary School Principals.

Keefe, J. W. (1989b) *Profiling and Utilising Learning Style*. Reston, VA: National Association of Secondary School Principals.

Keefe, J. W. (1990) *Learning Style Profile Handbook: Volume II, Developing Cognitive Skills*. Reston, VA: National Association of Secondary School Principals.

Keefe, J. W. and Monk, J. S. (1986) *Learning Styles Profile Examiner's Manual*. Reston, VA: National Association of Secondary School Principals.

Keogh, B. K. and Donlon, G. (1972) 'Field dependence, impulsivity and learning disabilities', *Journal of Learning Disabilities* **5**, 331–6.

Kirby, J. R. (ed.) (1984) *Cognitive Styles and Educational Performance*. New York: Academic Press.

Kirby, J. R. (1988) 'Style, strategy and skill in reading', in Schmeck, R. R. (ed.) *Learning Strategies and Learning Styles*, 229–74. New York: Plenum Press.

Kirby, J., Moore, P., Schofield, N. (1988) 'Verbal and visual learning styles', *Contemporary Educational Psychology* **13**, 169–84.

Kirton, J. W. (ed.) (1994) *Adaptors and Innovators*, 2nd Edn. London: Routledge.

Kirton, M. J. (1976) 'Adaptors and Innovators: a description and measure', *Journal of Applied Psychology* **61**, 622–9.

Kirton, M. J. (1987) *Kirton Adaption-Innovation Inventory (KAI) Manual*, 2nd edn. Hatfield, UK: Occupational Research Centre.

Klein, G. S. (1954) 'Need and Regulation', in Jones, M. P. (ed.) *Nebraska Symposium on Motivation*. Lincoln, NB: University of Nebraska Press.

Klein, G. and Schlesinger, H. (1951) 'Perceptual attitudes toward instability: 1. Prediction of apparent movement experiences from Rorschach responses', *Journal of Personality* **19**, 289–302.

Klein, G. S., Riley, W. G., Schlesinger, H. J. (1962) 'Tolerance for unrealistic experience: a study of the generality of cognitive control', *British Journal of Psychology* **54**, 41–55.

Kline, P. (1991) *Intelligence: The Psychometric View*. London: Routledge.

Kline, P. (1995) 'A critical review of the measurement of personality and intelligence', in Saklofske, D. H. and Zeidner, M. (eds) *International Handbook of Personality and Intelligence*, 505–24. New York: Plenum Press.

Kogan, N. and Morgan, F. T. (1969) 'Task and motivational influences on the assessment of creative and intellectual ability in children', *Genetic Psychology Monographs* 80, 92–127.

Kogan, N. and Wallach, M. A. (1964) *Risk-Taking: A Study in Cognition and Personality*. New York: Holt, Rinehart and Winston.

Kogan, N. and Wallach, M. A. (1967) 'Risk taking as a function of the situation, the person and the group', *New Directions in Psychology III*. New York: Holt, Rinehart and Winston.

Kolb, D. A. (1976) *Learning Style Inventory: Technical Manual*. Englewood Cliffs. NJ: Prentice Hall.

Kolb, D. A. (1977) *Learning Style Inventory: A Self-description of Preferred Learning Modes*. Boston, MA: McBer.

Kolb, D. A. (1984) *Experiential Learning: Experience as a Source of Learning and Development*. Englewood Cliffs, NJ: Prentice Hall.

Kolb, D. A. (1985) *Learning Style Inventory and Technical Manual*. Boston, MA: McBer.

Korchin, S. J. (1986) 'Field dependence, personality theory, and clinical research', in Bertini, M., Pizzamiglio, L. Wapner, S. (eds) *Field Dependence in Psychological Theory, Research, and Application*. Hillsdale, NJ: Lawrence Erlbaum.

Langhinrichsen, J. and Tucker, D. M. (1990) 'Neuropsychological concepts of mood, imagery, and performance', in Kunzendorf R. G. and Sheikh, A. A. (eds) *The Psychophysiology of Mental Imagery: Theory, Research and Application*. Amityville, NY: Baywood.

Lawrence, J., Steed, D., Young, P. (1984) *Disruptive Children: Disruptive Schools?* London: Croom Helm.

Letteri, C. A. (1980) 'Cognitive profile: basic determinant of academic achievement', *Journal of Educational Research* 73, 195–9.

Levy, J. (1990) 'Regulation and generation of perception in the asymmetric brain', in Trevarthen, C. (ed.) *Brain Circuits and Functions of the Mind*. New York: Cambridge University Press.

Lewis, B. N. (1976) 'Avoidance of aptitude-treatment trivialities', in Messick, S. (ed.) *Individuality in Learning*, 301–8. San Francisco, CA: Jossey-Bass.

Marks, D. F. (1973) 'Visual imagery differences in the recall of pictures', *British Journal of Psychology* 64, 17–24.

Marshall, J. C. and Merritt, S. L. (1985) 'Reliability and construct validity of alternate forms of the learning style inventory', *Educational and Psychological Measurement* 45, 931–7.

Martinsen, O. (1994) 'Cognitive style and insight', PhD thesis, Faculty of Psychology, University of Bergen, Norway.

Martinsen, O. and Kaufmann, G. (1991) 'Effect of imagery, strategy, and individual differences in solving insight problems', *Scandinavian Journal of*

Educational Research **35**, 69–77.

Marton, F. (1976) 'What does it take to learn? Some implications on an alternative view of learning', in Entwhistle, N. J. (ed.) *Strategies for Research and Development in Higher Education*, 200–22. Amsterdam: Swets and Zeitlenger.

Marton, F. (1988) 'Describing and improving learning', in Schmeck, R. R. (ed.) *Learning Strategies and Learning Styles*, 32–43. New York: Plenum Press.

Marton, F. and Saljo, R. (1976) 'On qualitative differences in learning. 1: Outcomes and process', *British Journal of Educational Psychology* **46**, 4–11.

Maslow, A. H. (1970) *Motivation and Personality*, 2nd edn. New York: Harper and Row.

Massari, D. J. (1975) 'The relation of reflective-impulsivity to field-dependence-independence and internal control in children', *Journal of Genetic Psychology* **126**, 61–7.

Massari, D. and Massari, J. A. (1973) 'Sex differences in the relationship of cognitive style and intellectual functioning in disadvantaged pre-school children', *Journal of Genetic Psychology* **122**, 175–81.

McCrae, R. R. and John, O. P. (1992) 'An introduction to the Five-Factor Model and its applications', *Journal of Personality* **60**, 175–215

McKenna, F. P. (1983) 'Field dependence and personality: a re-examination', *Social Behaviour and Personality* **11**, 51–5.

McKenna, F. P. (1984) 'Measures of field-dependence: cognitive style or cognitive ability?', *Journal of Sociology and Social Psychology* **47**, 593–603.

Mednick, S. A. and Mednick, M. T. (1967) *Examiners' Manual: Remote Associates Test*. Boston, MA: Houghton Miffin.

Messer, S. B. (1976) 'Reflectivity-impulsivity: a review', *Psychological Bulletin* **83**, 1026–53.

Messick, S. (1973) 'Multivariate models of cognition and personality: the need for both process and structure in psychological theory and measurement', in Royce J. R. (ed.) *Multivariate Analysis and Psychological Theory*. New York: Academic Press.

Messick, S. (ed.) (1976) *Individuality in Learning: Implications of Cognitive Styles and Creativity for Human Development*. San Francisco, CA: Jossey Bass.

Messick, S. (1984) 'The nature of cognitive styles: problems and promise in educational practice', *Educational Psychologist* **19**, 59–74.

Messick, S. (1996) 'Cognitive styles and learning', in De Corte, E. and Weinert, F. E. (eds), *International Encyclopedia of Developmental Psychology*, 638–41. London: Pergamon.

Messick, S. and Fritzky, F. J. (1963) 'Dimensions of analytic attitude in cognition and personality', *Journal of Personality* **31**, 346–70.

Messick, S. and Kogan, N. (1963) 'Differentiation and compartmentalisation in object-sorting measures of categorising style', *Perceptual and Motor Skills* **16**, 47–51.

Messick, S. and Kogan, N. (1965) 'Category width and quantitative aptitude', *Perpetual and Motor Skills* **20**, 493–7.

Messick, S. and Kogan, N. (1966) 'Personality consistencies in judgement:

dimensions of role constructs', *Multivariate Behavioural Research* **1**, 165–75.

Miller, A. (1987) 'Cognitive styles: an integrated model', *Educational Psychology* **7**, 251–68.

Miller, A. (1991) 'Personality types, learning styles and educational goals', *Educational Psychology* **11**, 217–38.

Moore, C. (1973) 'Styles of teacher behaviour under stimulated teaching conditions', doctoral dissertation, Stanford University. *Dissertation Abstracts International* 34, 3149A-3150A.

Morris, T. L. and Bergum, B. O. (1978) 'A note on the relationship between field-independence and creativity', *Perceptual and Motor Skills* **46**, 1,114.

Mortimore, P., Sammons, P., Stoll, L., Lewis, D., Ecob, R. (1988) *School Matter: The Junior Years.* Shepton Mallet: Open Books.

Murray-Harvey, R. (1994) 'Learning styles and approaches to learning: distinguishing between concepts and instruments', *British Journal of Educational Psychology* **64**, 373–88.

Myers, I. (1978) *Myers-Briggs Type Indicator.* Palo Alto, CA: Consulting Psychologists Press.

Myers, I. and Briggs, K. C. (1976) *Introduction to Type.* Gainesville, FL: Center for Application of Psychological Type.

Neimark, E. D. (1975) 'Individual differences and the role of cognitive style in cognitive development', *Genetic Psychology Monographs* **91**, 171–225.

Newstead, S. (1992) 'A study of two "quick and easy" methods of identifying student learning style', *British Journal of Educational Psychology* **62**, 299–312.

Newton, D., Tymms, P., Carrick, N. (1995) 'Is the GCSE fair? Examination success and cognitive style', *British Journal of Curriculum and Assessment* **6**, 21–5.

Nickerson, R. S. (1985) 'An introduction', in Nickerson, R. S. Perkins, D. N., Smith, E. E. (eds) , *The Teaching of Thinking*, 3–8. Hillsdale, NJ: Lawrence Erlbaum.

Nisbet, J. and Shucksmith, J. (1986) *Learning Strategies.* London: Routledge and Kegan Paul.

Noppe, L. D. and Gallagher, J. M. (1977) 'A cognitive style approach to creative thought', *Journal of Personality Assessment* **41**, 85–90.

Paivio, A. (1971) 'Styles and strategies of learning', *British Journal of Educational Psychology* **46**, 128–48.

Paivio, A. and Harshman, R. A. (1983) 'Factor analysis of a questionnaire on imagery and verbal habits and skills', *Canadian Journal of Psychology* **37**, 461–83.

Pask, G. (1972) 'A fresh look at cognition and the individual', *International Journal of Man-Machine Studies* **4**, 211–6.

Pask, G. (1976) 'Styles and strategies of learning', *British Journal of Educational Psychology* **46**, 128–48.

Pask, G. (1984) 'Review of conversational theory and a protologic (or protolanguage)', *Educational Communications and Technology Journal* **32**, 3–40.

Pask, G. (1988) 'Learning strategies, teaching strategies, and conceptual or learning style', in Schmeck, R. R. (ed.) *Learning Strategies and Learning Styles*, 83–100. New York: Plenum Press.

Pask, G. and Scott, B. C. E. (1972) 'Learning strategies and individual competence', *International Journal of Man-Machine Studies* **4**, 217–53.

Perkins, D. N. (1985) 'General cognitive skills: why not?', in Chipman, S. F., Segal, J. W. Glaser, R. (eds) *Thinking and Learning Skills*, 339–64. Hillsdale, NJ: Lawrence Erlbaum.

Pettigrew, P. F. (1958) 'The measurements and correlates of category width as a cognitive variable', *Journal of Personality* **26**, 532–44.

Presland, J. (1994) 'Learning styles and continuous professional development', *Educational Psychology in Practice* **10**(3), 179–84.

Price, C. E, Dunn, R., Dunn, K. (1976, 1977) *Learning Style Inventory Research Report*. Lawrence, KS: Price Systems.

Ramsden, P. (1979) 'Student learning and perceptions of the academic environment', *Higher Education* **8**, 411–27.

Ramsden, P. (1988) 'Context and strategy: situational influences on learning', in Schmeck, R. R. (ed.) *Learning Strategies and Learning Styles*, 159–84. New York: Plenum Press.

Rayner, S, and Riding R. J. (1996) Cognitive style and school refusal, *Educational Psychology*, **16**, 445–451.

Rayner, S. and Riding, R. (1997) 'Towards a categorisation of cognitive styles and learning styles', *Educational Psychology* **17**, 5–28.

Reinert, H. (1976) 'One picture is worth a thousand words? Not necessarily!', *The Modern Language Journal* **60**, 160–8.

Renninger, K. A. and Snyder, S. S. (1983) 'Effects of cognitive style on perceived satisfaction and performance among students and teachers', *Journal of Educational Psychology* **75**, 668–76.

Reynolds, D. (1991) 'Changing ineffective schools', in Ainscow, M. *Effective Schools for All*, 92–105. London: David Fulton Publishers.

Reynolds, D. and Cuttance, P. (1992) *School Effectiveness*. London: Cassell.

Richardson, A. (1977) 'Verbalizer-visualizer: a cognitive style dimension', *Journal of Mental Imagery* **1**, 109–25.

Richardson, A. (1994) *Individual Differences in Imaging: Their Measurement, Origins and Consequences*. Amityville, NY: Baywood.

Richardson, J. T. E. (1990) 'The reliability and replicability of the approaches to studying questionnair', *Studies in Higher Education* **15**, 155–68.

Riding, R. J. (1991a) *Cognitive Styles Analysis*. Birmingham: Learning and Training Technology.

Riding, R. J. (1991b) *Cognitive Styles Analysis User Manual*. Birmingham: Learning and Training Technology.

Riding, R. J. (1994) *Personal Style Awareness and Personal Development*. Birmingham: Learning and Training Technology.

Riding, R. J. (1996) *Learning Styles and Technology-based Training*. Sheffield: Department for Education and Science.

Riding, R. J. (1997) 'On the nature of cognitive style', *Educational Psychology* **17**, 29–50.

Riding, R. J. and Agrell, T. (1997) 'The effect of cognitive style and cognitive skills on school subject performance', *Educational Studies* 23, 311–23.

Riding, R. J. and Al-Sanabani, S. (1998) 'The effect of cognitive style, age, gender and structure on the recall of prose passages' *International Journal of Educational Research*, **29**, 173-185

Riding, R. J. and Anstey, L. (1982) 'Verbal-imagery learning style and reading attainment in eight-year-old children', *Journal of Research in Reading* 5, 57–66.

Riding, R. J. and Armstrong, J. M. (1982) 'Sex and personality differences in mathematics tests in 11-year-old children', *Educational Studies* 8, 217–25.

Riding R. J, and Ashmore, J. (1980) 'Verbaliser-imager learning style and children's recall of information presented in pictorial versus written form', *Educational Psychology* 6, 141–5.

Riding, R. J. and Buckle, C. F. (1990) *Learning Styles and Training Performance.* Sheffield: The Training Agency.

Riding, R. J., Buckle, C., Thompson, S., Hagger, E. (1989) 'The computer determination of learning styles as an aid to individualised computer-based training', *Educational and Training Technology International* 26, 393–8.

Riding, R. J. and Burton, D. (1998) 'Cognitive style, gender and conduct behaviour in secondary school pupils', *Research in Education.*

Riding, R. J., Burton, D., Rees, G., Sharratt, M. (1995) 'Cognitive style and personality in 12-year-old children', *British Journal of Educational Psychology* **65**, 113–24.

Riding, R. J. and Caine, T. (1993) 'Cognitive style and GCSE performance in mathematics, English language and French', *Educational Psychology* 13, 59–67.

Riding. R. J. and Calvey, I. (1981) 'The assessment of verbal-imagery learning styles and their effect on the recall of concrete and abstract prose passages by eleven year old children', *British Journal of Psychology* 72, 59–64.

Riding, R. J. and Cheema, I. (1991) 'Cognitive styles: an overview and integration', *Educational Psychology* 11, 193–215.

Riding, R. J. and Cowley, J. (1986) 'Extroversion and sex differences in reading performance in eight-year-old children', *British Journal of Educational Psychology* 56, 88–94.

Riding, R. J. and Craig, O. (1997) 'Cognitive style and problem behaviour in boys referred to residential special schools' (submitted for publication).

Riding, R. J. and Douglas, G. (1993) 'The effect of cognitive style and mode of presentation on learning performance', *British Journal of Educational Psychology* 63, 297–307.

Riding R. J. and Dyer, V. A. (1980) 'The relationship between extraversion and verbal-imagery learning style in twelve year old children', *Personality and Individual Differences* 1, 273–9.

Riding, R. J. and Egelstaff, D. W. (1983) 'Sex and personality differences in children's detection of changes in prose passages', *Educational Studies* 9, 159–68.

Riding, R. J., Glass, A., Douglas, G. (1993) 'Individual differences in thinking: cognitive and neurophysiological perspectives', *Educational Psychology* **13**, 267–79.

Riding, R. J., Glass, A., Butler, S. R., Pleydell-Pearce,. C. W. (1997) 'Cognitive style and individual differences in EEG alpha during information processing', *Educational Psychology* **17**, 219–34.

Riding, R. J. and Grimley, M. (1999) 'Cognitive style and learning from multi-media CD-ROMs in 11-year-old children' *British Journal of Educational Technology*, **30**, 43-56.

Riding, R. J. and Mathias, D. (1991) 'Cognitive styles and preferred learning mode, reading attainment and cognitive ability in 11-year-old children', *Educational Psychology* **11**, 383–93.

Riding, R. J. and Pearson, F. (1994) 'The relationship between cognitive style and intelligence', *Educational Psychology* **14**, 413–25.

Riding, R. J. and Rayner, S. (1995) *Personal Style and Effective Teaching.* Birmingham: Learning and Training Technology.

Riding, R. J. and Read, G. (1996) 'Cognitive style and pupil learning preferences', *Educational Psychology* **16**, 81–106.

Riding, R. J. and Smith, D. M. (1981) 'Sex differences in the effects of speech rate and repetition on the recall of prose in children', *Educational Psychology* **3**, 253–60.

Riding, R. J. and Sadler-Smith, E. (1992) 'Type of instructional material, cognitive style and learning performance', *Educational Studies* **18**, 323–40.

Riding, R. J. and Sadler-Smith, E. (1997) 'Cognitive style and learning strategies: some implications for training design', *International Journal of Training and Development* **1**, 199–208.

Riding, R. J. and Staley, A. (1998) 'Self-perception as learner, cognitive style and business studies students' course performance', *Assessment and Evaluation in Higher Education* **23**.

Riding, R. J. and Taylor, E. M. (1976) 'Imagery performance and prose comprehension in 7 year old children', *Educational Studies* **2**, 21–7.

Riding, R. J. and Vincent, D. J. T. (1980) 'Listening comprehension: the effects of sex, age, passage structure and speech rate', *Educational Review* **32**, 259–66.

Riding, R. J. and Watts, M. (1997) 'The effect of cognitive style on the preferred format of instructional material', *Educational Psychology* **17**, 179–83.

Riding, R. J. and Wheeler, H. (1995) 'Occupational stress and cognitive style in nurses: 2', *British Journal of Nursing* **4**, 160–8.

Riding, R. J. and Wigley, S. (1997) 'The relationship between cognitive style and personality in further education students', *Personality and Individual Differences* **23**, 379–89.

Riding, R. J. and Wright, M. (1995) 'Cognitive style, personal characteristics and harmony in student flats', *Educational Psychology* **15**, 337–49.

Riechmann, S. W. and Grasha, A. F. (1974) 'A rational approach to developing and assessing the validity of a student learning styles instrument', *Journal of Psychology* **87**, 213–23.

Rutter, M. (1972) *Maternal Deprivation Reassessed.* Harmondsworth: Penguin Books.

Rutter, M., Maughan, B., Mortimore, P., Ouston, J. (1979) *Fifteen Thousand Hours: Secondary Schools and their Effects on Children.* London: Open Books.

Sadler-Smith, E. (1996) 'Approaches to studying: age, gender and academic performance', *Educational Studies* 22, 367–79.

Sadler-Smith, E. (1997) unpublished study, University of Plymouth.

Sadler-Smith, E. and Riding, R. J. (a) 'A reinterpretation of the Learning Styles Questionnaire and its predictive validity' (submitted for publication).

Sadler-Smith, E. and Riding, R. J. (b) 'Cognitive style and instructional preferences' (submitted for publication).

Santostefano, S. and Paley, E. (1964) 'Development of cognitive controls in children', *Child Development* 35, 939–49.

Saracho, O. N. (1991) 'Students' preference for field-dependence–independence teacher characteristics', *Educational Psychology* 11, 323–32.

Saracho, O. N. and Dayton, C. M. (1980) 'The relationship of teachers' cognitive styles to pupils' academic achievement gain', *Journal of Educational Psychology* 72, 544–49.

Scheier, M. F. and Carver, C. S. (1992) 'Effects of optimism on psychological and physical well-being: theoretical overview and empirical update', *Cognitive Therapy and Research* 16, 201–28.

Schleifer, M. and Douglas, V. I. (1973) 'Moral judgements, behaviour and cognitive style in young children', *Canadian Journal of Behavioural Science* 5, 133–44.

Schmeck, R. R. (ed.) (1988a) *Learning Strategies and Learning Styles*. New York: Plenum Press.

Schmeck, R. R. (1988b) 'An introduction to strategies and styles of learning', in Schmeck, R. R. (ed.) *Learning Strategies and Learning Styles*, 3–20. New York: Plenum Press.

Schmeck, R. R., Ribich, F. D., Ramanaiah, H. (1977) 'Development of a self-report inventory for assessing individual differences in learning processes'; *Applied Psychological Measurement* 1, 413–31.

Schmeck, R. R., Geisler-Brenstein, E., Cercy, S. P. (1991) 'Self-concept and learning: the revised inventory of learning processes', *Educational Psychology* 11, 343–62.

Schonn, D. A. (1983) *The Reflective Practitioner*. New York: Basic Books.

Schroder, H. M., Driver, M. J., Streufert, S. (1967) *Human Information Processing*. New York: Holt, Rinehart and Winston.

Sharron, H. (1987) *Changing Children's Minds*. Bristol: Souvenir Press.

Sheehan, P. W. (1967) 'A shortened form of Bett's questionnaire upon mental imagery', *Journal of Clinical Psychology* 23, 386–9.

Signell, K. S. (1966) 'Cognitive complexity in person perception and nation perception: a developmental approach', *Journal of Personality* 34, 517–37.

Sims, R. R., Veres, J. G., Watson, P., Buckner, K. E. (1986) 'The reliability and classification stability of the Learning Style Inventory', *Educational and Psychological Measurement* 46, 753–60.

Skaalvik, E. M. and Rankin, R. J. (1994) 'Gender differences in mathematics and verbal achievement, self-perception and motivation', *British Journal of Educational Psychology* 64, 419–28.

Smith, C. J, and Laslett, R. (1993) *Effective Classroom Management.* London: Routledge.

Spielberger, C. D. (1966) 'Theory and research in anxiety', in Spielberger, C. D. (ed.) *Anxiety and Behavior*, 97–105. New York: Academic Press.

Spielberger C. D. (1977) *State and Trait Anxiety Inventory Form Y-1*. Palo Alto, CA: Consulting Psychologists Press.

Spielberger, C. D. and Vagg, P. R. (eds) (1995) *Test Anxiety: Theory, Assessment and Treatment.* Washington, DC: Taylor and Francis.

Spotts, J. V. and Mackler, B. (1967) 'Relationships of field-dependent and field-independent cognitive test performance', *Perceptual and Motor Skills* 24, 239–68.

Steed, D. (1985) 'Disruptive pupils, disruptive schools: which is the chicken? Which is the egg?', *Educational Research* 21, 3–9.

Sternberg, R. J. (1985) 'Instrumental and componential approaches to the nature and training of intelligence', in Chipman, S. F., Segal, J. W., Glaser. R. (eds) *Thinking and Learning Skills*, 215–44. Hillsdale, NJ: Lawrence Erlbaum.

Sternberg, R. J. (1987) 'Questions and answers about the nature and teaching of thinking skills', in Baron, J. B. and Sternberg, R. J. (eds) *Teaching Thinking Skills: Theory and Practice*, 251–61. New York: W. H. Freeman.

Stott, D. H. (1983) *Helping Children with Learning Difficulties.* London: Ward Lock Educational.

Street, R. F. (1931) *A Gestalt Completion Test.* New York: The Teacher's College.

Stroop, J. R. (1935) 'Studies of interference in serial verbal reactions', *Journal of Experimental Psychology* 18, 643–72.

Tannen, D. (1995) *Talking from 9 to 5.* London: Virago Press.

Taylor, J. (1994) 'The stability of school-children's cognitive style – a longitudinal study of the KAI Inventory', *Psychological Reports* 74, 1,008–10.

Tennant, M. (1988) *Psychology and Adult Learning.* London: Routledge.

Thurstone, L. L. (1944) *A Factorial Study of Perception.* Chicago: University of Chicago Press.

Thurstone, T. H. (1924) *The Nature of Intelligence.* London: Harcoat Brace.

Tiedemann, J. (1989) 'Measures of cognitive styles: a critical review', *Educational Psychology* 24, 261–75

Van der Molen, P. P. (1994) 'Adaption-innovation and changes in social structure on the anatomy of catastrophe', in Kirton, M. (ed.) *Adaptors and Innovators: Styles of Creativity and Problem-solving*, 2nd edn, 137–72. London: Routledge.

Veres, J. C., Sims, R. R., Locklear, T. S. (1991) 'Improving the reliability of Kolb's revised Learning Styles Inventory', *Educational and Psychological Measurement* 51, 143–50.

Vernon, M. D. (1963) *The Psychology of Perception.* Harmondsworth: Penguin Books.

Vernon, P. E. (1973) 'Multivariate approaches to the study of cognitive styles', in Royce, J. R. (ed.), *Multivariate Analysis and Psychological Theory*, 125–48. London: Academic Press.

Wallach, M. and Kogan, N. (1965) *Modes of Thinking in Young Children.* New York: Holt, Rinehart and Winston.

Watkins, C., Carnell, E., Lodge, C., Whalley, C. (1996) 'Effective learning', *SIN Research Matters*. London: Institute of Education, University of London.

Weber, K. (1978) *Yes They Can*. Milton Keynes: Open University Press.

Weber, K. (1982) *The Teacher is the Key*. Milton Keynes: Open University Press.

Wechsler, D. (1974) *Manual for the Wechsler Intelligence Scale for Children – Revised*. New York: The Psychological Corporation.

Weinstein, F. E. and Van Mater Stone, G. (1996) 'Learning strategies and learning to learn', in De Corte, E. and Weinert, F. E. (eds) *International Encyclopedia of Developmental Psychology*, 419–23. London: Pergamon.

Wiebe, D. J. and Smith, T. W. (1997) 'Personality and health: Progress and problems in psychosomatics', in Hogan, R., Johnson, J., Briggs, S. (eds) *Handbook of Personality Psychology*, 891–918. San Diego, CA: Academic Press.

Witkin, H. A. (1964) 'Origins of cognitive style', in Sheerer, C. (ed.) *Cognition: Theory, Research, Promise*. New York: Harper and Row.

Witkin, H. A. and Asch, S. E. (1948a) 'Studies in space orientation, III. Perception of the upright in the absence of visual field', *Journal of Experimental Psychology* 38, 603–14.

Witkin, H. A. and Asch, S. E. (1948b) 'Studies in space orientation, IV. Further experiments on perception of the upright with displaced visual field', *Journal of Experimental Psychology* 38, 762–82.

Witkin, H. A. and Goodenough, D. (1981) *Cognitive Styles: Essence and Origins: Field dependence and Field Independence*. New York: International Universities Press.

Witkin, H. A., Dyk, R. B., Faterson, H. F., Goodenough, D. R., Karp, S. A. (1962) *Psychological Differentiation*. New York: Wiley.

Witkin, H. A., Oltman, P., Raskin, E., Karp, S. (1971) *A Manual for Embedded Figures Test*. Palo Alto, CA: Consulting Psychologists Press.

Witkin, H. A., Moore, C., Goodenough, D., Cox, P. (1977). 'Field-dependent and field-independent cognitive styles and their educational implications', *Review of Educational Research* 47, 1–64.

Witkin, H. A., Goodenough, D. R., Oltman, P. K. (1979) 'Psychological differentiation: current status', *Journal of Personality and Social Psychology* 37, 1,127–45.

Zelniker, T. and Jeffrey, W. E. (1979) 'Attention and cognitive style in children', in Hale, G. A. and Lewis, M. (eds) *Attention and Cognitive Development*, 275–96. New York: Plenum Press.

Author index

9

Subject index